An Enduring Spirit

The Art of Georgia O'Keeffe

Katherine Hoffman

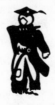

The Scarecrow Press, Inc.   Metuchen, N.J. & London 1984

Library of Congress Cataloging in Publication Data

Hoffman, Katherine, 1947–
  An enduring spirit.

  Bibliography: p.
  Includes index.
  1. O'Keeffe, Georgia, 1887–   . 2. Artists—
United States—Biography. I. O'Keeffe, Georgia,
1887–   . II. Title.
N6537.O39H63   1984   759.13   83-20312
ISBN 0-8108-1672-5

For Sean, Kristen, and Geoffrey
and a spirit yet unborn.

Acknowledgments

Rather than long lists of names I would like to thank in general the very helpful librarians and curators of the various libraries, museums, and archives that I visited, in particular, the Whitney Museum, the Museum of Modern Art, the Beinecke Rare Book and Manuscript Library, and the Archives of American Art. I am grateful to the time given me by individuals such as Lloyd Goodrich, Herbert Seligmann, Donald Gallup, Dr. Helen Boigon and John Gernand who were willing to share with me their knowledge of, and experience with O'Keeffe. I would also like to acknowledge the work of my student, Wesely Guiney, who assisted me on the bibliography and maintained a wonderful enthusiasm for the project. Further support was provided by assistance from a Bradford College Faculty Development award which allowed me to purchase some of the illustrations for the book.

Behind the scenes, a thank-you to my husband, Sean Gresh, for his continuing support and encouragement, and to my children Kristen and Geoffrey, for the time I stole from them to write, and for their own exemplary artistic spirits.

And finally, to Georgia O'Keeffe, an accolade, for the creation of a body of work that inspired this book, and continues to stand spirited and strong.

Katherine Hoffman
Bradford, Mass.
June 1983

Contents

For it is not yet the memories themselves. Not till they have turned to blood within us, to glance, and gesture, nameless and no longer to be distinguished from ourselves—not till then can it happen that in a most rare hour the first word of a verse arises in their midst and goes forth from them.

Rainer Maria Rilke

Like flame, like wine, across the still lagoon
The colors of the sunset stream.
Spectral in heaven as climbs the frail veiled moon,
So climbs my dream.

William Rose Benét

Preface

"The meaning of a word—to me—is not as exact as the meaning of a color. Colors and shapes make a more definite statement than words . . . where I was born and where and how I have lived is unimportant. It is what I have done with where I have been that should be of interest."[1] Since Georgia O'Keeffe's first show at Alfred Stieglitz's gallery 291 in 1916, O'Keeffe has grown to be an important figure in twentieth-century American painting. She has painted continuously and her work has been shown frequently at galleries and major museums throughout the century.

As Georgia O'Keeffe enters her ninety-sixth year, she appears to many as an enigma. Desert recluse myths have come to surround her and her work, particularly in terms of the sexual interpretations of some of her work. Enshrouded in the mysteries and rhythms of the desert, O'Keeffe has closed her doors to many critics and interviewers through the years. It is only in recent years that she has made herself more available to the public, particularly through her 1976 book that is an artwork itself, and the PBS documentary that was done about her life and work. But her private world remains a puzzle and she is often seen as a loner. Although basically alone in the New Mexican desert with her chow dogs, Georgia O'Keeffe continues to explore, to work much as she did as a young art student, hampered only somewhat by the changes that old age brings. Her spirit continues to endure and inspire. Her work is and has been her own "ism," an "ism" that has flowed from, concurrent to, and beyond the great "isms" of twentieth-century art.

Who is the woman, Georgia O'Keeffe, now considered a matriarch of the world of modern art? And with what is her work concerned? For O'Keeffe, her artwork has been like her offspring. It has been an integral part of her daily life since she was a child and set the perimeters for her very being. As she stated, "where I was born and where and how I have lived is unimportant. It is *what* I have *done*. . . ." The life, the work, and the times and places of the life and work must be considered simultaneously. For O'Keeffe, the work is most important. Thus, one must probe deeply into the work and its origins to better understand O'Keeffe and her world.

The following pages emphasize the art—why, how, where, when—rather than concentrate solely on biographical details as some of the other studies of O'Keeffe have. In this way some of the enigma surrounding O'Keeffe may be more easily dispelled. The early years of her career and the formative environment of the "new" New York, teeming with the intellectual and artistic ferment at the turn of the century in reaction to old nineteenth-century academic values, are particularly important in the development of O'Keeffe's work. This foundation period is thus given greater attention in order to better understand O'Keeffe's subsequent development.

The milieu, the critics, and the craftsmanship and spirit of O'Keeffe herself have reacted and interacted for almost a century. With this interrelationship O'Keeffe's vision has expanded and progressed through the years. As critic Robert Hughes has pointed out, "No other American artist, and few living painters, have fused their inner and outer worlds with such spare grace. The life and work are one."[2]

In the following pages, the doors will be opened to enter, confront, and understand this special world of Georgia O'Keeffe. It is hoped that this study will be provocative for artists, historians, critics, and the general public in order that the courage to follow one's deepest instincts, along with the practice of an immaculate craftsmanship, as exemplified by the enduring spirit of O'Keeffe and her work, will be continued.

Notes

[1]Georgia O'Keeffe, *Georgia O'Keeffe* (New York: Viking Press, 1976).

[2]Robert Hughes, "Loner in the Desert" *Time,* October 12, 1970, p. 68.

List of Illustrations

See Index for page references.

Note: In captions height precedes width in all measurements (which are in inches). Except where indicated, all illustrations are oil on canvas, and by O'Keeffe.

Prologue
The Land, the Light, and the Early Years

The sun gleamed brightly in the clear autumn air. It was November 15, 1887. In New York, the Roeblings' daring Brooklyn Bridge had recently opened. In Boston, McKim, Mead and White had begun construction of the lovely Boston Public Library. In Chicago, William Le Baron Jenney had just completed his Home Insurance Building, the first completely metal-framed building and monument for the development of the modern skyscraper. It was a world of growing industrialization, urbanization, and technology.

On this day in the small town of Sun Prairie, Wisconsin, a dark-haired child, Georgia Totto O'Keeffe was born in the farmhouse of Ida and Francis O'Keeffe. She was to become the second of seven children. The world of Sun Prairie belonged to the eighteenth and nineteenth centuries, caught in the patterns and rhythms of farm life and dependence on the land. This was America's heartland where O'Keeffe was born. The rhythm of this land was to have an important influence on the development of the young Georgia and her subsequent career as an artist.

Typical of many Americans of this time, Georgia's grandparents were immigrants of Irish and Hungarian descent, and hard working, having come to America during the first large wave of immigration to the United States. Georgia's grandmothers, Grandmother Totto and Grandmother O'Keeffe, as well as her mother, Ida, were reported to be strong, willful women, as O'Keeffe herself was to become. Ida O'Keeffe was greatly concerned about the education and schooling of her children and spent many hours reading aloud to them. The importance and tradition of the American land was passed on through these stories as well. Among the first stories O'Keeffe was reported to have heard were James Fenimore Cooper's *Leatherstocking Tales* of the rough and tumble life of cowboys and Indians in the expansive wilds of Texas and New Mexico.

As a young child, Georgia was a loner who enjoyed wandering about her father's 440-acre farm, which expanded as the years went by. The land and the light along with the changes in seasons attracted Georgia greatly. Her sensitivity to light and her surroundings is seen in her early recollections of the brightness of the light in her world—"My first memory is of the brightness of light—light all around. . . . This was all new to me—the brightness of light and pillows and a quilt out beyond."[1]

Enjoying her own company, Georgia spent much time playing with her dolls and

1

dollhouse, making wonderful dresses and a home for "her children." At one point she used an old shingle as a boat for her beloved dolls. The shingle motif was to appear years later in a powerful series of increasing abstractions of a shell and an old shingle. Her earliest memory of drawing "was a picture of a man lying on his back with his feet up in the air. . . . I wonder if I drew a man lying on his back, only bending his legs at his hips, because my dolls only bent their legs at the hips."[2]

As a young girl Georgia and her sisters were driven from their farm into the town of Sun Prairie to take painting lessons which were seen as proper accomplishments for a young lady of the time. Initially Georgia's sister Ida was seen as "the talented one" but Georgia progressed rapidly and by age twelve announced vehemently to a friend that she was going to be an artist when she grew up. O'Keeffe recalls a picture, "Maid of Athens," she saw in one of her mother's books that was very beautiful to her and started something moving inside her.

At age thirteen O'Keeffe was taken to a boarding school, a Dominican convent outside Madison, Wisconsin. There she was confronted with first attempts to mold her artistic spirit and abilities. One of her first assignments in drawing class was to draw a baby's hand from a white plaster cast model. O'Keeffe was severely criticized for drawing the hand too small and too black. Tears rolled down the young girl's cheeks, for she had worked very hard on the assignment. Consequently she worked in the style the nuns advocated the remainder of her stay at the convent. As a young girl, schooled in nineteenth-century mores, O'Keeffe did not dream of rebelling.

During the fall of 1902 as Georgia's family was moving to Williamsburg, Virginia in search of a milder climate and new land and business opportunities, Georgia was taken out of the convent and enrolled in Madison High School while she and her brother lived with their mother's youngest sister in Madison. Although she didn't like the art teacher there, O'Keeffe recalls the impact of being forced to examine the regal violets and varied shapes of a jack-in-the-pulpit—the princely flower that appeared nearly twenty-five years later in her memorable "jack-in-the-pulpit" series of six paintings.

Finishing her year at Madison High School in the spring of 1903, O'Keeffe headed for Virginia to join her family. The Wisconsin years were over but that rural midwestern background—the rhythms of the earth, the streaming light on the prairies, the hard working and egalitarian lifestyle of the Sun Prairie residents—were not to leave her. Indeed, images of those years, such as the sturdy red Wisconsin barns, were to appear later in her paintings.

During her first autumn in Virginia, O'Keeffe was sent to Chatham Episcopal Institute, a small, girls' boarding school, located about two hundred miles from her family. Having already been away from her family for two years, O'Keeffe was fast learning independence and individuality. Unlike the other girls at Chatham, she dressed very plainly and would not wear the customary ruffles and bows of the time. During her two years at Chatham, O'Keeffe had a supportive and encouraging art teacher, Elizabeth May Willis, who encouraged O'Keeffe to work at her own pace and in her own way. At this time, O'Keeffe also began to study music, which was to have a lasting impact on her artistic sensibilities. Some of her paintings came to have musical titles such as *Music—Pink & Blue I,* 1919. At one point in her career in 1922, she even proclaimed, "Singing has always seemed to me the most perfect means of expression. It is so spontaneous. And after singing, I think the violin. Since I cannot sing, I paint."[3] As a senior, O'Keeffe was awarded a special diploma in art as well as the art prize for one of her watercolors. The encouragement of Mrs. Willis was not forgotten by O'Keeffe and some thirty years later in New York, O'Keeffe attended a testimonial dinner for her teacher and principal.

Upon graduation from Chatham, Mrs. Willis helped convince Georgia's mother to send her to the Art Institute of Chicago, for in those days art school for a young lady was not considered altogether appropriate. (It was only since the turn of the century that women had been admitted to art schools. Indeed men and women were separated in life-drawing classes at that time.) Thus from 1905 to 1906 O'Keeffe attended the Art Institute and studied with John Vanderpoel, whose interest in line and the human form greatly impressed her. In his class her drawings were ranked first. However, O'Keeffe's art career was interrupted when she contracted typhoid fever and took nearly a year to recuperate.

The lights beckoned in New York City rather than Chicago, and in 1907 O'Keeffe boarded a train for New York to attend the Art Students League, where Elizabeth May Willis had studied. The sense of freedom felt by the young artists O'Keeffe encountered was inspiring to her. Renting a room near the League on West Fifty-seventh Street, O'Keeffe lived for the first time in her life without supervision. Known as Patsy at the League, O'Keeffe was considered a promising student. She served as model for Eugene Speicher, who won a prize for his portrait of her. Among those she studied with were William Merritt Chase, F. Luis Mora, and Kenyon Cox—all from an academic, neo-classical tradition, with set styles of teaching and painting. O'Keeffe has described Chase's class as most fun because of Chase's love of color and lively style. He would usually arrive in class with a top hat, a fancy brown suit, light colored spats and gloves, and a carnation in his lapel. In Chase's class O'Keeffe won a top still-life prize of $100 for an oil of a dead rabbit lying next to a shiny copper pot, done "à la Chase," and was then awarded a scholarship to attend the League summer school at Lake George, New York.

It was during her winter at the League that O'Keeffe first encountered Alfred Stieglitz when she and some fellow students went to see the Rodin drawings that Stieglitz was exhibiting at his gallery 291 on lower Fifth Avenue. O'Keeffe was intimidated by Stieg-litz and felt the free-flowing, organic drawings by Rodin were of little interest to her, since they were so different than the type of drawings she had been exposed to at the League. But something of the spirit of 291 had attracted her and she returned several months later to the gallery to see an exhibit of Matisse's new, abstract, and colorful forms.

When O'Keeffe returned to her family in Williamsburg in the summer of 1908, she found the family business beset with financial problems and her mother quite ill. Decid-ing she had to get a job, O'Keeffe gave up painting and went to Chicago where she found work drawing lace and embroidery for advertisements. After two years of what she considered meaningless work, and after coming down with the measles which weakened her eyes, O'Keeffe left Chicago.

In 1912 O'Keeffe's father moved the family to Charlottesville to open a creamery. And in the summer of 1912 the fire and light of O'Keeffe's artistic spirit was rekindled when she visited an art class at the University of Virginia given by Alon Bement, a teacher who had worked with Arthur Dow. Bement's classes had little to do with copying nature exactly or copying the old masters. Rather Bement encouraged his students to create interesting patterns of their own.

Bement later helped O'Keeffe get a teaching job as supervisor of art in the public schools in Amarillo, Texas. Although she had to fight the Texas legislature in not wanting to buy rigid copy books for the children, O'Keeffe kept her job for two years, while commuting back to Charlottesville to teach summer school from 1913 to 1916. O'Keeffe was excited by the infinitely expansive plains of Texas and felt pulled by the land, a land she had been attracted to so very young in her mother's storybooks. Through her association with Bement, O'Keeffe was indirectly introduced to new ideas in art filtering to Charlottesville from New York and Europe. Two books he recommended, Wassily Kandinsky's *On the Spiritual in Art,* (translated into English in 1914) and Jerome Eddy's *Cubists and Post Impressionist Art,* where she first saw some of Arthur Dow's work, were to become important in her development. Kandinsky's insistence on the expression of "an inner necessity" and his analogies of color and music were later to become seeds for O'Keeffe's growing innovations in color and form.

Bement also urged O'Keeffe to return to New York to study with Arthur Dow at Columbia Teachers College. At Columbia, O'Keeffe excelled in her art courses, but did not do well in academic subject areas and received a "D" in English. Although she did not receive a degree from the college, the instruction she received from Arthur Dow was to have a profound effect on her career. Many years later she stated in an interview, "I think it was Arthur Dow who affected my start, who helped me to find something of my own. . . . This man had one dominating idea: to fill space in a beautiful way—and that interested me. Afterall, everyone has to do just this—make choices in his daily life, even when only buying a cup and saucer. By this time I had a technique for handling oil and watercolor easily; Dow gave me something to do with it."[4]

Who, then, was this Arthur Dow who so influenced O'Keeffe? Thirty years older than O'Keeffe, Dow was a reserved New Englander from Ipswich, Massachusetts. He had studied with Gauguin and other Post-Impressionists in Brittany and in general had a good sense of European experiments in abstraction at the turn of the century. Further, Ernest Fenellosa, curator of the Japanese department at the Museum of Fine Arts in Boston, became Dow's mentor and schooled him in Japanese decorative and spacial principles. Following Fenellosa's resignation in 1897, Dow was appointed curator of Japanese art at the Boston Fine Arts Museum. Coming to Teachers College in 1903, Dow emphasized harmonious design and beauty as the expression of an evolving new social and religious order. His well-known text, *Composition,* contained a more decorative and abstract approach, more open to interpretation than the strict academic exercises O'Keeffe had encountered in her career training. Dow's approach emphasized structure rather than imitation. Like Fenellosa, Dow also felt that music was a key to the other arts and that the spacial arts might be called visual music. Dow's notion of filling space in a beautiful way greatly inspired O'Keeffe. In his writings, Dow once quoted Hegel in saying, "Wood, stone, metal, canvas, even words are in themselves dead stuff. What art creates upon this dead stuff belongs to the domain of the spirit and is living as the spirit is living."[5] Like Hegel, Dow professed this sense of beauty and devotion to a living spirit which greatly influenced O'Keeffe. Indeed some of her paintings bear a distinct resemblance to some of Dow's works such as his *Gay Head,* 1917 or *Deep Down,* 1913, in their open V-forms and curvilinear shapes.

The orientation of Dow and Fenellosa toward the Oriental arts and interest in music that so influenced O'Keeffe could be seen in other prominent artists' and critics' works of the time such as the poetry of Ezra Pound, the poetry of the imagists and symbolists, or the art criticism of Christian Brinton. O'Keeffe's continuing interest in Oriental art begun at this time, is evidenced in her letters to contemporaries such as Dorothy Brett, Mabel Dodge Luhan, and Sherwood Anderson, where she mentions various shows of Oriental art she particularly liked. To this day one of the few works of art hanging in O'Keeffe's long white studio in Abiquiu, New Mexico is an Oriental print by Hiroshige.

The stately Dow, in his turn, greatly respected O'Keeffe and her work. In a 1915 recommendation, Dow wrote of O'Keeffe, "She is one of the most talented people in art that we have ever had. She excels in drawing and painting. . . . Miss O'Keeffe is an exceptional person in many ways. She has qualities of character that enable her to work well with other people and to interest them."[6]

Soon, however, O'Keeffe felt the need to go beyond the harmonious exercises of Bement and Dow. Needing a job and wanting to explore some new visual ideas on her own, O'Keeffe took a teaching position at Columbia College in Columbia, South Carolina. Far from the stimulus of New York's intellectual and artistic circles, O'Keeffe found herself in a seemingly foreign world of southern femininity. Isolated and alone, she began to rethink her ideas concerning the very nature of art, and to freely experiment in her own work. Writing to Stieglitz, O'Keeffe commented, "Hibernating in South Carolina is an experience that I would not advise anyone to miss. The place is of so little consequence—except for the outdoors—that one has a chance to give one's mind, time and attention to anything one wishes."[7] It was in South Carolina that O'Keeffe decided to "start over" and to paint to please herself rather than one or another of her teachers. Seven years later O'Keeffe was to recall "I grew up pretty much as everybody else grows up and one day seven years ago found myself saying to myself—I can't live where I want to—I can't go where I want to—I can't do what I want to—I can't even say what I want to—school and things that painters have taught me even keep me from painting as I want to. I decided I was a very stupid fool not to at least paint as I wanted to. . . ."[8]

With her newfound sense of freedom, O'Keeffe began anew to do charcoal drawings, many of very beautiful budding and organic shapes. She sent some of these drawings to Anita Pollitzer, a friend from Columbia Teachers College, asking that Anita show them to no one. In these early days she confided to her friend Anita, "The thing seems to express in a way what I wanted it to but—it also seems rather effeminate—it is essentially a woman's feeling—it satisfies me in a way."[9] (A number of years later when critics referred extensively to a female sensibility in O'Keeffe's work, she was to strongly deny any such associations.)

Despite O'Keeffe's instructions, Anita Pollitzer, the plucky and brazen art student that she was, took the drawings to Alfred Stieglitz at 291, then the only gallery continuously showing new and modern art. Stieglitz's legendary statement, upon seeing the drawings, "Finally a woman on paper," marks the beginning of the recognition of O'Keeffe's art work in the avant-garde art world of New York at the time. Stieglitz kept the drawings and a few months later, exhibited them in a group show. Hearing Anita's confession, O'Keeffe was secretly pleased at Stieglitz's positive response.

Abruptly leaving Columbia in February 1916, O'Keeffe returned to New York to take Dow's teaching methods course in preparation for a new job she had been offered in Texas, to begin that fall. Hearing a fellow student at Teachers College refer to a show of "Virginia O'Keeffe" at 291, Georgia realized the show was hers and rushed to the gallery to ask Stieglitz to take the work down, annoyed that he had shown publicly her very private work without her permission. In his inimitable strong manner, Stieglitz refused to take down the work. He even extended the show and revelled in the controversial responses the work caused.

Buoyed with the enthusiasm of Stieglitz, O'Keeffe left New York that summer to teach summer school at the University of Virginia and then went on to the Texas plains that fall to become head of the art department at West Texas State Normal School in Canyon, Texas, where she was to teach for the next two years as well as continue her own experiments in drawing and painting. Here, too, she preferred to keep to herself and was labeled a bohemian by many of the townspeople. Companionship was provided though, by her seventeen-year-old sister Claudia, who came to Canyon after Ida O'Keeffe's death.

O'Keeffe inspired her students, using Dow's textbooks and urging her "hungry" students to read books such as Clive Bell's *Art* and Willard H. Wright's *The Creative Will*. She herself had recently read these. O'Keeffe also became very interested in Nietzsche at this time.

O'Keeffe loved to wander in the wide open spaces of the Texas plains and in particular explored the colors and contours of the nearby Palo Duro canyon. She began working in color again, producing a large number of bold and daring watercolors. She also corresponded with Stieglitz and from time to time sent him some of her work, for as she wrote, "because of what I had seen in his gallery, I was more interested in what Stieglitz thought about my work than in what anyone else would think."[10] Stieglitz in return encouraged and stimulated O'Keeffe. He also sent her issues of *Camera Work, The Seven Arts,* an avant-garde journal, and sent her one of his favorite books, Goethe's *Faust*.

Excited by O'Keeffe's work, Stieglitz opened the first solo exhibition of O'Keeffe's work in May of 1917. With this show came continued critical reviews concerning what was felt to be "the feminine experience" inherent in O'Keeffe's work. One such critic wrote in *The Christian Science Monitor* shortly after the show opened, that O'Keeffe

> *has found expression in the delicately veiled symbolism for 'what every woman knows,' but what women have heretofore kept to themselves . . . the loneliness and privation which her emotional nature must have suffered put their impress on everything she does. . . . Now perhaps for the first time in art's history, the style is the woman.*[11]

From this show, O'Keeffe sold her first painting for $400.

O'Keeffe, in her characteristic abrupt and spontaneous way, impulsively left for New York at the end of her spring semester classes to see her show, only to find it had closed, for war had come. The United States had declared war on Germany shortly after her show opened, and thereby entered World War I. Stieglitz, however, rehung the show for her. During that short visit to New York, Stieglitz also introduced O'Keeffe to several of the artists close to him, such as the painter John Marin and young photographer Paul Strand. Stieglitz also photographed O'Keeffe for the first time. Those photographs were the beginning of an intricate and moving composite portrait of O'Keeffe by Stieglitz that was made in hundreds of photographs over the next several decades.

O'Keeffe returned to Texas as planned to teach summer school. During a vacation, O'Keeffe and her sister Claudia toured the magnificent Colorado Rockies and detoured through New Mexico to avoid some washed-out bridges. The brilliant light and unusual terrain of New Mexico attracted O'Keeffe. "I loved it immediately," she has recalled. "From then on I was always on my way back."[12]

Georgia's pacifist and neutralist tendencies were not viewed kindly by the large number of war hawks in Canyon, and her strenuous teaching schedule began to take its toll on her health. In the early part of 1915 O'Keeffe became very ill and took a leave of absence from teaching to spend the spring in San Antonio, Texas, a more fertile area of Texas where flowers constantly bloomed.

O'Keeffe had written to Stieglitz of her plight. He in return offered her the opportunity to paint for herself in New York for a year and his niece Elizabeth offered O'Keeffe her studio on 114 East Fifty-ninth Street. Stieglitz sent Paul Strand to fetch her. Arriving in New York in early summer, O'Keeffe was quickly enthralled by the fervor of Stieglitz and of New York itself. By the end of the summer she had resigned her position at West Texas to stay in New York and paint. Thus the child of the Sun Prairie plains came to live in the bustling city of New York, alive with the fervor and ferment of social and artistic change.

To understand the impact of this new New York on O'Keeffe one must step back a few years to nearer the turn of the century to see the New York stage set along with the cast of characters that were to become an important part of O'Keeffe's ensuing development.

Notes

[1]Georgia O'Keeffe, *Georgia O'Keeffe* (New York: Viking Press, 1976), no p.

[2]*Ibid.*

[3]Georgia O'Keeffe, *N.Y. Sun,* December 5, 1922.

[4]Katherine Kuh, *The Artist's Voice* (New York: Harper & Row, 1962), pp. 89–90.

[5]Frederick C. Moffatt, *Arthur Dow* (Washington, D.C.: Smithsonian Press, 1977), p. 110.

[6]Arthur Dow, letter to Mr. C. J. Scott, Superintendent of Schools, Wilmington, Del., July 12, 1915.

[7]Georgia O'Keeffe, letter from O'Keeffe to Stieglitz, February 1, 1916, Museum of Modern Art, New York, press release.

[8]Georgia O'Keeffe, Exhibition Catalogue, Anderson Galleries, January–February, 1923, p. 1.

[9]Georgia O'Keeffe, letter from O'Keeffe to Pollitzer, January 4, 1916, Museum of Modern Art, New York, press release.

[10]Georgia O'Keeffe, *Georgia O'Keeffe.*

[11]Henry Tyrrell, *Christian Science Monitor,* "Esoteric Art at 291," May 4, 1917, no p.

[12]Sheila Tryk, "O'Keeffe," *New Mexico,* January–February, 1973.

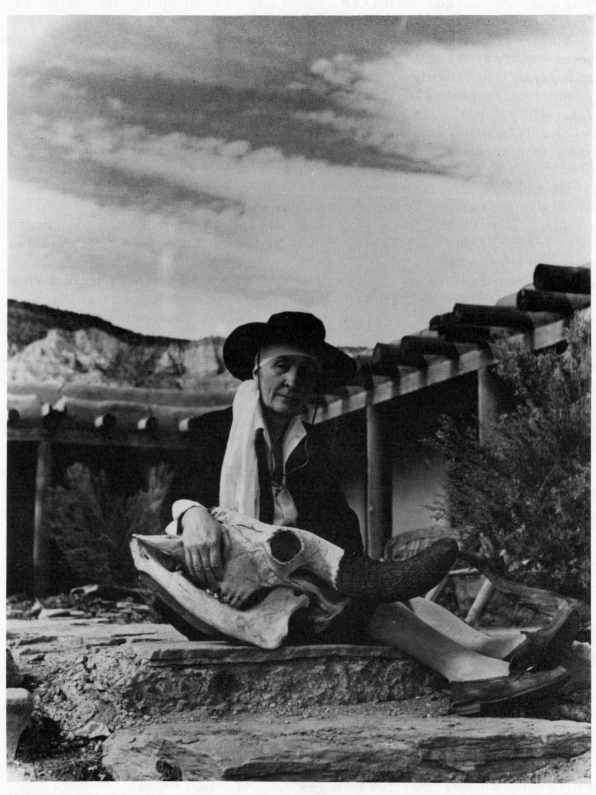

Georgia O'Keeffe, Abiquiu, New Mexico. 1948, photograph (11×13¼). Albright-Knox Art Gallery, Buffalo, New York. Gift of Seymour H. Knox, 1976.

I. THE MILIEU

No matter how banal the thought that the artist is a man of his time, the fact is that the history of art and literature is filled with statements, more or less eloquent, affirming the artist's sense of being shaped by the epoch in which he performs his art. In some cases, he is not so much shaped as prodded. In many statements there is a distinct impression of the artist's being drawn forcibly forward; to be reeled in by a future which cannot be evaded. The "time" of an artist makes itself felt, even if only as tyranny against which the artist reacts.[1]

Chapter One

The New New York, 1900–1917

The early twentieth century was a time of conflicting values and ideas for American culture. The turn of the century brought a small-scale rebellion against the Victorian and Puritan mores of the nineteenth century. Liberal and intellectual circles seemed to abound with talk of change, of modernism, of individuality. The early twentieth century was a fascinating period of cultural history and O'Keeffe, consciously and unconsciously, was part of the temper of that time.

In 1900 New York was becoming a modern city. The city was no longer marked only by genteel brownstones, gas-lit lamps, and horse-drawn carriages. Instead, sights such as the Brooklyn Bridge, growing skyscrapers, and the flashing lights of Broadway dominated the skyline. The Brown Decades were over. In 1907 motorbuses and cabs were introduced. There were electric lights and telephones. Hot running water was available on a widespread basis. Artist and writers were attracted to the new iconography that the city held out to them, first portraying New York in realistic and tonal styles, then turning to abstraction as the years progressed. In 1909 the art critic John C. Van Dyke published *The New New York*, detailing Manhattan's emerging modernity and emphasizing its newness.

By 1910 there was much talk in America (particularly in New York in intellectual circles) about rebellion against established Victorian and Puritan values that were dominant during the nineteenth century. The themes of modernism, involving a revolt against industrialism and the importance of freedom of the individual, instinct, and feeling, were often mentioned in the conversations of the educated and intellectual.

Since the turn of the century, with events such as the Wright brothers' successful flight at Kitty Hawk, North Carolina, in 1903, and the beginning of Henry Ford's manufacturing the Model T by assembly line in 1908, American was quickly growing up to a nation of urbanization, technology, and one of emphasis on material wealth. There was a feeling of optimism and faith in progress on the part of both conservatives and rebellious intellectuals. There was faith by the conservatives in the power of the United States' progressive democracy and faith by the rebellious in the themes of modernism. Primary representatives of the rebellion were artists, writers, and philosophers who were reacting to nineteenth-century values and materialism. Primary among art forms representing a new way of thinking and expression were poetry, photography, painting, and music.

For example, the works of the imagist poets, the dance performances of Isadora Duncan, or early music of Charles Ives, were new modes of expression considered appropriate for this new world. The search for new forms of expression reflected the change in the world around artists and writers, brought about by new technology and scientific research in areas such as psychology and physics. There was no longer one absolute reality to be represented by the old academic artistic forms.

At the turn of the century though, the academic tradition for most art forms still had a lot of power. Basically, academic referred to the value of inherited traditions, such as the studying and copying of the human figure in the visual arts, instead of the expression of nature or of the inner emotional world of the artist. And such had been the substance of most of O'Keeffe's training. There was also a growing sentimentality in the academic tradition due to the popularity of Romanticism in the mid-nineteenth century. Many involved with the ideas and forms of modernism found much of the academic art to be overly sentimental and dull.

Artists and writers were in general influenced by discoveries in other disciplines that affected how one looked at the world. Following discoveries such as the disintegration of the atom, Einstein's theory of relativity, Freud's theory of the unconscious (his book *Interpretation of Dreams* having been published in 1900), and quantum physics, the world could not be viewed through one's senses as a single concrete, unchanging reality. Instead there were multiple and varied modes through which to look at the changing world.

Prevalent philosophies that influenced American rebellious thinking of the time included the relativism and pragmatism of men such as William James and John Dewey, H. G. Wells' rejection of logic at the time, and Henri Bergson's concepts of time and perception. The tradition of pragmatism was not really new for America, but the work of Dewey and James emphasized the importance of direct experience as leading toward "the truth." Wells emphasized the importance of living and feeling thoughts, rather than analyzing them. For Bergson, who began to tamper with traditional notions of time, "before" and "after" were not important; rather time was a continuous duration, and there were no definite fixed objects in time. There were, according to him, ever-changing aspects of our life that made each moment very different. This concept of time came to be illustrated in artistic images of simultaneity and dynamism in cubist and futurist work and offshoots thereof. Further, Bergson felt that one could view the world in two ways—intellectually and intuitively. For Bergson the intellectual mode dealt with the rational, ordered, and external objects of one's life. Intuition dealt with the inner core of life, the spirit, the irrational. Through intuition one could transcend the facts and events of everyday life. For many young artists and intellectuals, Bergson, Wells, and Freud became fads, like the latest dances.

The emphasis on defense of the spirit and value of intuition was felt in the work of many of the writers of the time. D. H. Lawrence, one of the writers most admired by the artists at Stieglitz's gallery 291, was one of the most outspoken and strongest writers advocating the importance and power of the instinctual life. Not only were his works read by other artists and writers, but also articles of his appeared in avant-garde magazines such as *Seven Arts* and *Camera Work*. Lawrence spoke of "real touch" which was "not a contact of surfaces but a 'soft flow' coming from the middle of the human being. It issued from the blood not the calculating faculty, and was not amorous in any vulgar sense."[2]

Other writers such as Floyd Dell and Sherwood Anderson wrote of changing times in a variety of ways. Anderson wrote of an old, "grotesque" America of the nineties, in his *Winesburg, Ohio,* a collection of stories, and hinted at a new order. O'Keeffe eventually became close friends with Anderson, a gregarious but moody midwesterner who bought some of her work. The two corresponded over the years, and at one point O'Keeffe wrote to Anderson, "Making your unknown known is the important thing—and keeping the unknown always beyond you—catching—crystalizing [sic] your simpler clearer vision of life—only to see it turn stale compared to what you vaguely feel ahead—that you must always keep working to grasp."[3] O'Keeffe, as did the writers, came to search for a new vision, a new order, never wanting her vision to become static.

Among Floyd Dell's writings, was a feminist book, *Women as World Builders,* urging women to drop their conventional roles of being at home with children or in the kitchen. O'Keeffe was urged to read this by a friend, Arthur MacMahon, who taught goverment at Columbia University.

The poets rebelled in the cry for a new form, different from the traditional nineteenth-century narrative form. The beginning of such rebellion was seen in the work of the Imagists fostered by Amy Lowell and Harriet Monroe. Although the Imagist movement was short-lived, the beliefs in direct treatment of an object; clear, concise wording; freedom in the choice of subject matter; the importance of music; and rebellion against intellectual, didactic poetic forms of the nineteenth century, continued to live on in various forms in the works of other poets. Ezra Pound believed in the seeking of imagery from other traditions than the absolutist nineteenth-century Anglo-Saxon tradition, i.e., the modern French, the classics, the Chinese. At one point Pound was highly interested in the work of Ernest Fenellosa, the Oriental scholar who had influenced Arthur Dow so profoundly. Pound's long works such as the *Cantos* and the *Mauberley* sequence illustrated the new "poetic sequence" and use of "accretive imagery." Rather than a progression in time, the poems were like a circle, with various images contributing to the refinement of a central experience or figure. In some instances one has the sense of metamorphosis of a theme or person. Each of the parts of the long poem usually reflected the whole but was a unit unto itself. These methods were actually found earlier to some extent, in a work such as Walt Whitman's *Song of Myself,* and were to continue in various forms of the long poem in the work of other poets, contemporary to and following Pound. Whitman and later poets, such as William Carlos Williams, also advocated that the artist's expression be of his own time and place, that the portrayal of ordinary life revealed basic truths. O'Keeffe's painterly metamorphosis of an object such as a shell or a flower and her series of abstractions of a given object can easily be seen as visual parallels to these poetic concerns.

Some of these early poets' interest in music came from the French Symbolist theory of synaesthesia, where expression of one sense might evoke sensation of another (i.e., a color suggests a smell) and from having read Kandinsky's *Concerning the Spiritual in Art.* Kandinsky's famous adage of expressing an inner necessity and finding the important relationship between art and music influenced many artists at the time in Europe and the United States. For Kandinsky inner necessity originated from three elements: (1) "Every artist as a creator, has something in him which demands expression. . . (2) Every artist, as the child of his time, is impelled to express the spirit of his age. . . (3) Every artist, as a servant of art, has to help the cause of art. . ."[4] Further, Kandinsky wrote, "Color is the keyboard, the eyes are the hammers, the soul is the piano with many strings. . . .

Musical sound acts directly on the soul and finds an echo there since music is innate in man."[5] Both Stieglitz and O'Keeffe had read Kandinsky's work, and O'Keeffe in particular was interested in his ideas of color harmony. O'Keeffe and Arthur Dove, one of the Stieglitz's prodigies, titled a number of their paintings by musical references, as O'Keeffe's *Blue and Green Music,* 1919 or Dove's *Sentimental Music,* 1917.

Other experimental poets of the teens included Carl Sandburg, Vachel Lindsay, Marianne Moore, and T. S. Eliot. The above mentioned literary figures are only representative examples of writers involved in the spirit of rebellion. Most of those mentioned were in some way related to the life or work of O'Keeffe.

But more than literature, the visual arts led the revolt against the values of the nineteenth century. As early as 1908, two exhibitions in New York marked a strong challenge to the well-established realist tradition in American art. A group of New York artists called The Eight—Arthur Davies, William Glacken, Robert Henri, Ernest Lawson, George Luks, Maurice Prendergast, Everett Shinn, and John Sloan—held an exhibition at the Macbeth Gallery, while Alfred Stieglitz showed the work of the French modernist, Henri Matisse. The work of The Eight marked a revolution in subject matter, in displaying the unconventional and uglier aspects of urban life. Stieglitz's exhibition of Matisse's paintings marked the beginning of Stieglitz's life-long campaign as proponent and representative of the "modern" spirit, and of an abstract and expressionist art, foreign and American. In 1912 Stieglitz showed an exhibition of children's work at 291 (unheard of previously in the American art world). The show emphasized the importance of spontaneity and individuality in art. Then, in 1913 the famous Armory Show struck its blow in New York City, and traveled subsequently to Boston, Philadelphia, and Chicago. Milton Brown has termed this show "the most important single exhibition ever held in America."[6]

From February 17 to March 15, 1913, the Sixty-Ninth Regiment Armory was thronged with visitors staring wide-eyed, for the first time, at European moderns. The show included works from the late Impressionists—Vuillard, Bonnard; post-impressionists—Cézanne, Van Gogh, Gauguin; Cubists—Picasso, Braque; the Fauves—Matisse, Derain, Vlaminck; and a few pioneer American modernists. There were few German expressionists, and the Italian futurists were excluded. The show was organized by the Association of American Painters and Sculptors, dominated basically by The Eight. Praise, as well as great despair was expressed by the critics and general public. "Marcel Duchamp's *Nude Descending the Staircase* was selected by the press and public as the symbol of the comprehensibility and ridiculousness of the new art."[7] The president of the Association and chief organizer of the show, Arthur Davies, stated that the purpose of the show was to "present modern art 'so that the intelligent may judge for themselves.'"[8] However, the show soon came to be taken as a defense of modernism, which came to be associated with incompetence, immorality, conspiracy, revolution, and anarchy. Arguments, pro and con, concerning the show, became based on philosophical as well as aesthetic grounds. Critics such as Kenyon Cox, Frank Jewett Mather, Jr., Edward Daingerfield, and Royal Cortissoz viewed the exhibition as not only an attack on traditional art but also as an attack upon the order of the world in general. Cox wrote that "the real meaning of this Cubist movement is nothing else than the total destruction of the art of painting . . ."[9] while Mather wrote, ". . . laymen may well dismiss on moral grounds an art that lives in the miasma of morbid hallucination or sterile experimentation, and denies in the name of individualism values which are those of society and life itself."[10]

On the other hand, defenders of modernism, such as the critic Hutchins Hapgood, felt that "modern art in its courageous search for fundamental human experience . . . had a great deal to teach us. His description of modern art as a seeking for instinctive perception of form and abstract expression was not bad for those days."[11] Arthur Dow praised the principle of modernism, claiming that "the history of art was the history of revolutions, that revolutions were evidence of new energy and that experimentation was to be valued."[12] To those who decried revolution, Christian Brinton responded that the development of modernism was an evolutionary rather than a revolutionary process.

To accept this new art was to begin to accept changes in society in general, for the new forms suggested a new way of seeing where the freedom of the individual and his inner instinctual perceptions had come to a fore. Meyer Shapiro described the Armory Show as marking "a point of acceleration"[13] in a revision of the image of the past. No longer was there an absolute known reality and set of laws in art and philosophical thinking. Rather there were a myriad of ways of looking at and using form, space, color, and content in a work of art.

Although the Armory Show did not bring a complete acceptance of modern art, it did bring an exposure to new ways of thinking and seeing. There were converts to the new art such as the collectors Duncan Phillips and Katherine Dreier, and new galleries began to show contemporary art. Following the show, more artists turned to abstraction and semiabstraction. The Armory Show, too, in its emphasis on the individual spirit, marked a further change in the relationship of art and culture to institutions and large organized groups. In the past, the church, state, or aristocracy had served as patron to the arts. Modern art at this time received little organized support from such groups. It seemed particularly difficult in a growing machine age for the public to deal with individual inner freedom and spirituality. Thus support for young struggling artists experimenting with new forms was difficult. It remained for proponents of the new "modern art," such as Alfred Stieglitz, to offer some of these artists both monetary and spiritual support.

"The most important single factor aside from the Armory Show in the birth of the modern spirit, was Alfred Stieglitz, who in his small gallery at 291 Fifth Avenue showed many European pioneers and championed American experimentalists."[14] Stieglitz's gallery became a haven for New York avant-garde artists, writers, and musicians. For many, Stieglitz was a combination of a genius and an impressario who provided spiritual inspiration and, for some, financial support in order that artists respected by Stieglitz be able to pursue their individual creative expressions. Those frequenting his galleries and seeking his advise and respect included Hart Crane, William Carlos Williams, Herbert Seligmann, Paul Rosenfeld, Jean Toomer, Sherwood Anderson, Dorothy Brett, Paul Strand, Lewis Mumford, and Waldo Frank. Those painters who worked steadily with Stieglitz's support, and who comprised the well-known Stieglitz inner circle were John Marin, Arthur Dove, Marsden Hartley, Georgia O'Keeffe, and slightly later, Charles Demuth. To better understand the role Stieglitz played in the development of modern art in America, one must step back a few years before the Armory Show.

In 1902 Stieglitz established the Photo-Secession, a group of photographers, with Edward Steichen. This was an attempt to elevate photography to the realm of the other fine arts, feeling that photography should involve artistic skill rather than merely serving its traditional role as a descriptive or narrative record. American photographers' work—at that time mostly pictorial works—were circulated to prominent American and European exhibitions, thereby winning Stieglitz international acclaim. Stieglitz also started a new periodical, *Camera Work,* an art work in itself with fine graphics and typography that promoted photography as a fine art through its illustrations and articles. By 1908 *Camera Work* not only covered photography but also contained articles about contemporary avant-garde fine arts and literature. *Camera Work* was discontinued in 1917 as a result of the United States' involvement in World War I.

Stieglitz established his first gallery, 291 (first called the Little Gallery of the Photo-Secession), with Edward Steichen in 1905 to further pioneer photography as a fine art, as well as to foster the new modernists. The gallery was a part of Stieglitz's goal to establish

> *. . . a community of artists and critics at 291 whose interaction would generate new discoveries and new statements in the arts. The essence of 291 was indefinable, but its spirit unquestionably shaped the lives of those who gathered there. Behind it all, to be sure, was Stieglitz, but 291 was not a reflection of the proprietor alone, influential though he may have been. He attracted to the gallery a community of kindred souls who generated a special kind of creative electricity that inspired each participant in his or her own way.*[15]

For Stieglitz the purpose of art was the true expression of one's inner self, only to be achieved in an atmosphere of absolute freedom which Stieglitz sought to establish in his gallery. The gallery, however, was not without opposition by traditional and more conservative forces in the New York art world at this time. Critic Thomas Craven blasted 291 as a "bedlam of half-baked philosophies and cockeyed visions" where Stieglitz "shrewdly managed to hold the position of arbiter, to maintain a reputation for superior acumen." Craven also called Stieglitz "a Hoboken Jew without knowledge of or interest in the historical American background."[16]

Stieglitz himself photographed continuously—New York City, the Lake George area, O'Keeffe and other contemporaries, providing endless subject matter for him. With the influence of modern art—cubism and other methods of abstraction—Stieglitz gradually rejected the pictorialism of the Photo-Secession. By the 1910's he began to talk about the "fundamental idea of photography" and started a series of formal and objective photographs from the back window of 291. His continuing search for truth is seen in a statement written for an exhibition in 1921.

> *The Exhibition is photographic throughout. My teachers have been life-long-continuous experiment. Incidentally a great deal of hard thinking. Any one can build on this experience with means available to all. . . .*
>
> *My ideal is to achieve the ability to produce numberless prints from each negative, prints all significantly alive. . .*
>
> *I was born in Hoboken. I am an American. Photography is my passion. The search for Truth my obsession.*[17]

Continuing photographic compositions throughout much of Stieglitz's life were his studies of cloud formations which were to be "equivalents" of man's experiences and a composite portrait of O'Keeffe. In the cloud studies, titled the *Equivalents,* he

> *extended the concept of his photography. . . . The translation of experience through photography, the storing up of energy, feeling, memory, impulse, will, which could find release through subject matter later presenting itself to the photographer, were thus evident. This*

should have ended for all time the silly and unthinking talk to the effect that the photographer
was limited to a literal transcript of what was before him.[18]

A number of his cloud images also bear musical titles such as his *"Music: A Sequence of Ten Cloud Photographs" No. I*, 1922 and *Songs of the Sky*, 1924, indicative of his interest in Kandinsky. (Stieglitz had actually printed an excerpt of Kandinsky's *Concerning the Spiritual in Art* in the July 1912 issue of *Camera Work* and had bought the only Kandinsky work in the Armory Show for $500.)

The beautiful composite portrait of O'Keeffe shows a multi-faceted approach to portraiture. The portrait, done over a period of about thirty years, consists of over two-hundred photographs of various parts of O'Keeffe's body—her hands, her head, and her feet in various settings—indicating her many moods and abilities, as well as the intense and intimate relationship of O'Keeffe and Stieglitz.

The spirit of Stieglitz and his photography did much for the advancement of photography as an art. In 1924 a significant event in the life of photography as a new art form occurred. One of the most conservative museums in the United States at the time, the Boston Museum of Fine Arts, took on a collection of twenty-seven Stieglitz photographs in response to the urging of Ananda Coomaraswamy, curator of Oriental art.

In general, Stieglitz, from 1908 to 1913, promoted his artists and modern art, sacrificing his own work. He also became involved in other periodicals beyond *Camera Work*. To further promote the cause of Modern Art, with Picabia and Marcel Duchamp, Stieglitz founded another periodical *291* in 1915 to present the Dada ideas of these artists. Another journal, short-lived but published about the same time was *Seven Arts*, edited by Waldo Frank. The contributors to *Seven Arts* such as D. H. Lawrence, Theodore Dreiser, Sherwood Anderson, Randolph Bourne, and Willard Huntington Wright, were very close to Stieglitz and his ideas.

When Stieglitz was unable to continue publication of *Camera Work* in 1917, he wrote to Herbert Seligmann, "There is really no *free and fearless* publication of any kind today in this country—Perhaps we'll have to issue an occasional leaflet after all."[19] The result was the publication of *MSS* or *Manuscripts* which included writing by Waldo Frank, William Carlos Williams, Kenneth Burke, and Paul Rosenfeld. In its pages were articles concerning the avant-garde in the arts, with the praise of works such as the music of Edgar Varese and Arnold Schoenberg.

The powerful influence of Stieglitz and the atmosphere created at his galleries were described and documented in a volume compiled in commemoration of Stieglitz's birthday in 1934, by Dorothy Norman, Waldo Frank, Lewis Mumford, Paul Rosenfeld, and Harold Rugg. The volume, *America and Alfred Stieglitz, a Collective Portrait*, contains articles by those closely associated with Stieglitz and records impressions of the preceding twenty years. The prevailing spirit of many of the articles is a deep religiousness and feeling of awe and respect for the world Stieglitz had created in his gallery and through his ideas. Stieglitz is pictured as artist, teacher, and seer who fought for "an American place," an American culture where the artist as an American was free to develop his potential.

Listen to what he has to say, and 'free' is the overtone of almost every word. Free to work,
free to be himself, free to live without selling his soul, these are rough translations of the

eloquent speech which Stieglitz has wielded for years as other men wield weapons. . . . That modern industrialism completely nullifies freedom, that the fathers of the republic were motivated not only by idealism but also by economic determinism . . . does not alter Stieglitz's position.[20]

The importance of a supportive community is also emphasized in these articles.

In the fullest sense of the word every community in America should have its American Place. This would be the true culture center in which people would come together both for personal self-cultivation through creative production and for social participation in the cooperative community.[21]

According to Harold Rugg, Stieglitz continued the tradition of Emerson, Whitman, and Louis Sullivan in striving to "create the tradition of the American Thing" and "an honest Creative America."[22] In his contribution to the volume, William Carlos Williams refers to an emphasis on a "purchased culture" from Europe, as America grew to its urbanization, industrialization, and material wealth in the teens and twenties. Williams and many of Stieglitz's contemporaries felt American culture had become subservient to the power of wealth. But,

Not Stieglitz. . . . The effect of his life and work has been to bend together and fuse, against whatever resistance, the split forces of the two necessary cultural groups: (1) the local effort . . . and (2) the forces from the outside.[23]

The painter Arthur Dove wrote of Stieglitz, "I do not think I could have existed as a painter without that super-encouragement and the battle he has fought day by day for twenty-five years. He is without a doubt the one who has done the most for art in America."[24]

For Stieglitz the artists he fostered were like his children. He stated that he would do anything he could for the artists whom he respected and encouraged, "not in the name of chauvinism, but because one's own children must come first."[25] And to many he was a kind of father figure. Sherwood Anderson wrote in the dedication of *A Story Teller's Story,* "To Alfred Stieglitz, who has been more than father to many puzzled, wistful children of the arts in the big noisy, growing and groping America."[26]

The influence and life-giving force of Stieglitz's work and person on the critics and artists who frequented his galleries lasted until his death in 1946. Stieglitz said of himself in his last years, "At least it can be said of me by way of epitaph that I cared."[27] It is this ultimate care and concern that seemed to have such lasting effects on Stieglitz's surrounding circle.

One must now ask how Georgia O'Keeffe fits into this world of ideas and innovations in the arts that she found in New York prior to America's entry into World War I in 1917. She arrived in a city ripe with ideas and change and absorbed much of that energy, influenced consciously and unconsciously by the temper of those times. O'Keeffe's own personal rebellion against the teaching of men such as William Merritt Chase at the Art Students League, who taught the imitation of the old masters, seems a part of the wider rebellion mentioned before. With the influence of Arthur Dow, O'Keeffe was opened to the possibility of finding something of her own. Dow's teaching, his defense of Modernism and interest in the Oriental arts did greatly alter the course of O'Keeffe's work. Some of O'Keeffe's work, too, reflects Oriental qualities. The Oriental emphasis on simplicity is seen in the relationship of various lines in an early work such as *Blue Lines,* 1916. Further, one finds the Oriental concentration on one subject in a painting such as the "jack-in-the-pulpit" series; and in the flattening of forms in later paintings such as the "patio" series. Daniel Catton Rich describes O'Keeffe's relationship to an Oriental tradition.

> *Concentration like this on one subject is far more likely to be found in the Orient than in the West. In many ways O'Keeffe's approach is closer to Chinese and Japanese traditions of perspective and modeling than to European. She tends to flatten her forms, to design in two dimensions and to eliminate expressive brush strokes. . . . Another Oriental trait is the variation in format. . . .*[28]

Today, according to Calvin Tomkins, the only works of art hanging in O'Keeffe's long white studio in Abiquiu, New Mexico, are two of her own paintings, a 1950 abstraction in blue, black, and white, *Black Rock,* 1971, and an Oriental print by Hiroshige.[29] Not only is O'Keeffe's individual rebellion important, but also important is the fact that O'Keeffe, as a woman, attended an institution of higher education, and indeed, an institution such as Columbia. Women's higher education in terms of professional and academic pursuits was relatively new in America. Only in 1881 had a group of women who were among the first women college graduates, founded the Association of Collegiate Alumnae to encourage women's higher education. In the early twentieth century many Americans still believed in the "cult of feminine domestic sanctity" and "considered higher education for women unnatural and heretical."[30] Although O'Keeffe never graduated from Columbia, the historical opportunity for her to attend, as a woman interested in a career, was important. The push for women's higher education was also part of the woman's movement in general, in the early twentieth century which lead to the passage of the Nineteenth Amendment in 1920, granting women the right to vote. Although there is no real evidence of O'Keeffe's connection (although she is called a "feminist" in a 1929 article[31]) with the women's movement until a statement in 1942 in *Equal Rights,* the official organ of the National Woman's Party, the historical events of the early twentieth century with a strong women's rights movement provided a strong moral support for O'Keeffe. Further, she had the models of strong females in her own family.

O'Keeffe's first show at 291 in 1917 and subsequent entry into the Stieglitz circle also began her contact with writers of the time, who frequented Stieglitz's galleries. O'Keeffe recalls that when the galleries were open there were always artists and writers around. "I never knew how many there would be for dinner. It seemed as though anyone who was around the gallery in the late afternoon would come back afterward."[32] Among the writers with whom O'Keeffe kept up a fairly steady correspondence through the years were fiction writer, Sherwood Anderson; critic-novelist, Carl Van Vechten; critic, Henry McBride; and artist, Dorothy Brett. (Many of these letters are located in the Beinecke library at Yale University.) Much of the correspondence indicates a mutual personal closeness and professional respect on the part of O'Keeffe and her correspondent.

Although the influence on O'Keeffe of some of the writers mentioned previously, such as Ezra Pound, is not found in direct documentation, there are parallels in the revolution in form of the long poem and visual arts, particularly in the paintings of O'Keeffe and some of the other members of the Stieglitz circle. O'Keeffe's work in her various series and changing treatment of one object, such as a clam shell or flower, parallel the metamorphic tradition of the twentieth-century long poem. Her work, too, is clear, precise, and straightforward as suggested by some of the tenets of the imagists.

Many of the writers, artists, and intellectuals whom O'Keeffe either directly or indirectly knew, frequented the salons of Mabel Dodge Luhan or the home of Walter Arensburg.

Who were Mabel Dodge Luhan and Walter Arensburg? A wealthy and flamboyant Buffalo aristocrat, Mabel Dodge was married to the conservative Boston architect Edwin Dodge after the early death of her first husband. They spent many of their years together at an elaborate Italian villa, the villa Curonia outside of Florence, where Mabel constantly entertained artists and writers. Mabel met Gertrude Stein and was immediately drawn to her ideas and the artistic revolution occurring in Paris, which could be seen in the work of painters such as Picasso, Braque, and Matisse. In 1912 the Dodges moved to New York City in order that Mabel's son be able to go to school there. The Dodge's apartment at 23 Fifth Avenue became a haven for radicals and intellectuals. Their salon was probably the first to rival Stieglitz's 291. Those frequenting Mabel Dodge's apartment were from mixed ideological backgrounds. There were the more radical Emma Goldman; labor leader Bill Haywood; some of Stieglitz's young artists, in particular Marsden Hartley and John Marin; Walter Lipmann; Max Eastman, editor of *The Masses*; and the politically radical journalist John Reed. To use Mabel's own words, "Socialists, Trade Unionists, Anarchists, Suffragists, Poets, Relations, Lawyers, Murderers . . . Artists, Modern-Artists . . . and just plain Men all met there, and stammering in an unaccustomed freedom a kind of speech called free, exchanged a variousness in vocabulary called in euphemistic optimism opinions."[33] At the apartment "avant-garde artists from the Stieglitz group argued with the radicals that perennial question of the Rebellion: intensive dedication to art against art for the masses."[34] Dodge herself wrote, often in a rambling journal-like form, or in abstract poems. The beginning of her memoirs, dedicated to Jack Reed, the poet, referred to a quotation from O'Shaughnessy capsulizing the political and artistic sensibility of many of those frequenting Dodges salons.

> *"Yet we are the movers and shakers*
> *of the world for ever, it seems."*[35]

Dodge was also involved in preparations for the Armory Show having become friends with Jo Davidson, the American sculptor, and member of the Association of American Painters and Sculptors, the group that worked on organizing the show. Dodge contributed money to the show and wrote to Gertrude Stein, "I am working like a dog for it. I am all for it."[36]

Mabel Dodge became friendly with both Stieglitz and O'Keeffe, although Stieglitz did not become a frequent visitor to her salons. Dodge's chief importance was as a catalyst in bringing together a variety of vibrant and interesting people, allowing their ideas to mix and overflow in the social security and warmth that her radiant and conversant personality and open apartment provided.

As time passed, Dodge became more and more attracted to socialism and anarchism and was greatly attracted to the charismatic personality and writings of John Reed.

Divorcing her husband, she and Reed lived together for a short period of time. For Dodge, Reed represented the dawning of a new age. She recorded in her memoirs, "'Oh, Reed darling, we are just at the threshold, and nothing is ever so wonderful as the threshold of things, don't you know that?' But this meant nothing to him."[37]

In 1915 Dodge met artist Maurice Sterne and lived with him until their marriage in 1917. Sterne and Dodge left New York in 1917 to live in Taos, New Mexico, an artists' colony then becoming popular for both artists and writers. This marriage lasted only a short time. Dodge finally married the Pueblo Indian, Tony Luhan, whose quieter spiritual interests seemed to complement her more flamboyant personality.

Following Luhan's departure from New York in 1917, O'Keeffe frequently wrote to her. O'Keeffe must have had deep respect for Mabel Dodge Luhan as a person and writer, for at one point she wrote Luhan, expressing a desire for Luhan to write about her painting.

> *What the men can't—What I want written—I do not know—I have no definite idea of what it should be—but a woman who has lived many things and who sees lines and colors as an expression of living—might say something that a man can't—I feel there is something unexplored about woman that only a woman can explore—Men have done all they can do about it.*[38]

Besides Dodge's salons and 291, there was another extraordinary circle of artists and intellectuals interested in avant-garde art forms that revolved around the 33 West 67th Street apartment of Walter Conrad Arensburg, a reporter for the New York *Evening Post,* and literary connoisseur. Arensburg, unlike Stieglitz, was not domineering and was not an artist. Rather he and his wife, Mary Louise Stevens, a genteel young musician from Lowell, Massachusetts, began to collect new and "modern" art following a visit to the controversial Armory Show. Those frequently convening at the welcoming Arensburgs who served food and liquor endlessly, included Marcel Duchamp, Walter Pach, Francis Picabia, Charles Sheeler, Charles Demuth, Arthur Dove, Marsden Hartley, Man Ray, Joseph Stella, Max Eastman, Amy Lowell, William Carlos Williams, and Isadora Duncan. The primary thrust of the group was toward Dada art, primarily due to the great influence of Marcel Duchamp. Nihilistic in orientation, Dada art sought to destroy traditional notions of the art object, as exemplified in works such as Duchamp's "readymades," a series of manufactured objects that he elevated to the level of art by signing or inscribing them and placing them in a museum or gallery. As diverse as the Stieglitz and Arensburg circles might appear, there was no great opposition between the two and some artists such as Hartley, Dove, and Demuth frequented both circles. Emphasis in the Arensburg group tended toward the conceptual and the intellectual, while emphasis in the Stieglitz circle was toward expression of the intuitive and lyrical. Some artists needed and liked both kinds of stimulation. And Stieglitz actually kept Duchamp's ready-made urinal, *Richard Mutt* at 291, where he photographed it.

Arensburg not only fostered the visual arts but was also a literary patron. He financially supported a number of small experimental literary magazines such as the poetry magazine *Others,* where Ezra Pound was greatly publicized, and *The Blind Man,* published in connection with the first exhibition of the Society of Independent Artists in 1917. Unfortunately the latter publication lasted for only two issues.

In the early twenties the Arensburgs abruptly departed for Hollywood, California, leaving behind the legacy of their salons that inspired such free discussion among Americans and Europeans and supported the growing spirit of New York Dada, which indeed faded when the Arensburgs left the city.

The year 1917 and the United States' entry into World War I, marked an artistic and historical breaking point. Stieglitz's gallery 291 closed in 1917 in part due to financial reasons and in part due to the fact that it was difficult to obtain art works from Europe (even though he was becoming more and more interested in American art). O'Keeffe's show was the final exhibition hung at 291. The war was difficult for Stieglitz who loved Germany, being of German origin and having studied there. In 1917, too, the last issue of *Camera Work* was published. The closing of the gallery and ceasing of the *Camera Work* publication was preceded by other rifts in Stieglitz's world only a year or two before. The Photo Secession photographers, Gertrude Käsebier, Clarence White, and Alvin Langdon Coburn broke off relationships with Stieglitz. Other friends, De Zayas, Haviland, and Agnes Meyer started a new gallery, The Modern Gallery, as a commercial branch of 291, thereby weakening Stieglitz's influence and opposing Stieglitz's dislike of commercialism. Thus, 1917 was a grim year for Stieglitz. After the closing of 291 he recalled, "I walked up and down in my overcoat, my cape over the coat, hat on, and still I would be freezing. . . . I had nowhere else to go—no working place, no club, no money. I felt somehow as Napoleon must have felt on his retreat from Moscow."[39] In 1917 Steichen also left New York for France with the U.S. Army and Mabel Dodge Luhan left New York for Taos, New Mexico.

Stieglitz rented a room on a lower floor of 291 Fifth Avenue to have a place to go and did meet frequently with some of his contemporaries and followers at the Far East Tea Gardens, a Chinese restaurant at Columbus Circle.

For Stieglitz to offer O'Keeffe a year to paint in New York in early 1918 was a risk. But it was also an opportunity for a renewed spirit and "fresh air" to enter his life. For Stieglitz, O'Keeffe's work at this time embodied the high and pure ideals he was searching for through art.

O'Keeffe's entry into the New York art world at this time seems to have occurred at an opportune time in history as well as in philosophic and artistic thought. The events and thinking of the early twentieth century, a period of unrest and change, but optimistically rebellious, provided a supportive background for O'Keeffe to develop as an individual. Certainly she was a woman and artist in her own right, but was influenced both consciously and unconsciously by the trends of this period.

Notes

[1]Dore Ashton, *A Reading of Modern Art* (New York: Harper & Row, 1971), p. 152.

[2]John Carey, "D. H. Lawrence's Doctrine," in *D. H. Lawrence—Novelist, Poet, Prophet,* ed. Stephen Spender (New York: Harper & Row, 1973), pp. 124–125.

[3]Letter from O'Keeffe to Anderson (Chicago: Newberry Library, undated).

[4]Wassily Kandinsky, *Concerning the Spiritual in Art,* 1912 (New York: George Wittenborn, 1947), p. 52.

[5]*Ibid.*

[6]Milton Brown, *American Painting from the Armory Show to the Depression* (Princeton: Princeton University Press, 1955), p. 47.

[7]*Ibid.,* p. 49.

[8]John Baur, *Revolution and Tradition in Modern American Art* (Cambridge: Harvard University Press, 1951), p. 6.

[9]Brown, *American Painting,* p. 53.

[10]*Ibid.*

[11]Milton Brown, *The Story of the Armory Show* (New York: Joseph Hirshhorn Foundation, 1963), p. 54.

[12]Brown, *American Painting,* p. 53.

[13]Meyer Shapiro, "Rebellion in Art," in *America in Crisis,* ed. Daniel Aaron (Hamden, Conn.: Archon Books, 1971), p. 205.

[14]H. H. Arnason, *History of Modern Art* (Englewood Cliffs, N.J.: Prentice-Hall, 1965), p. 410.

[15]William Homer, "Alfred Stieglitz and 291," in *Avant-Garde Painting and Sculpture, 1910–25, Exhibition Catalogue* (Wilmington, Del.: Delaware Art Museum, June 1975), p. 90.

[16]Thomas Craven, *Modern Art: The Men, The Movements, The Meaning* (New York: Simon & Schuster, 1935), p. 312.

[17]Herbert Seligmann, "291: A Vision Through Photography," in *America and Alfred Stieglitz, A Collective Portrait,* ed. Waldo Frank (Garden City, N.Y.: Doubleday, Doran and Co., 1934), p. 116.

[18]*Ibid.,* p. 121.

[19]Dorothy Norman, *Alfred Stieglitz: An American Seer* (New York: Random House, 1973) p. 140.

[20]Elizabeth McCausland, "Stieglitz and the American Tradition," in *America and Alfred Stieglitz* p. 228.

[21]Harold Rugg, "The Artist and the Great Transition," in *America and Alfred Stieglitz,* pp. 196–197.

[22]*Ibid.,* p. 196.

[23]William Carlos Williams, "The American Background," in *America and Alfred Stieglitz,* p. 32.

[24]Arthur Dove, "A Different One," in *America and Alfred Stieglitz,* p. 245.

[25]Norman, *Alfred Stieglitz,* p. 119.

[26]Barbara Haskell, *Arthur Dove* (San Francisco: San Francisco Art Museum, 1974) p. 13.

[27]Norman, *Alfred Stieglitz,* p. 229.

[28]Daniel Catton Rich, "Georgia O'Keeffe, Forty Years of Her Art," *Exhibition Catalogue,* Worcester Art Museum, Massachusetts, October 4–December 4, 1960, pp. 3–4.

[29]Calvin Tomkins, "Profiles–Georgia O'Keeffe," *New Yorker,* March 4, 1974, p. 61.

[30]Roberta Wein, "Women's Colleges and Domesticity, 1875–1918," *History of Education Quarterly* XIV (Spring 1974): 31.

[31]Robert H. Coates, "Abstraction-Flowers" *New Yorker,* July 6, 1929, p. 48.

[32]*Ibid.,* p. 47.

[33]Mabel Dodge Luhan, *Intimate Memories,* Vol. III (New York: Harcourt Brace, 1936), p. 83.

[34]Henry May, *End of American Innocence* (New York: Alfred Knopf, 1959), p. 312.

[35]Mabel Dodge Luhan, *Intimate Memories,* Vol. III, Preface.

[36]Mabel Dodge, quoted in Donald Gallup, ed., *Flowers of Friendship* (New York: Alfred Knopf, 1953), p. 71.

[37]Luhan, *Intimate Memories,* p. 213.

[38]Georgia O'Keeffe, Letter to Mabel Dodge Luhan, 1925 (New Haven: Yale University, Beinecke Library).

[39]Norman, *Alfred Stieglitz,* p. 134.

Chapter Two
Celebration and Isolation, 1918–1929

Excitedly greeted by Stieglitz in New York in 1918, O'Keeffe took up residence and painting in the small studio apartment of Stieglitz's niece Elizabeth at 114 East 59th Street. Attracted by the spirit and work of O'Keeffe, Stieglitz began to spend much time at the little studio. He soon moved out of his home at 1111 Madison Avenue, leaving his wife of twenty-four years, Emmeline, and his daughter, Kitty. He moved in with O'Keeffe, who, in her unconventional way, had no qualms about living with another woman's husband. The two lived in the tiny studio for two years until the rent was raised and they moved to rent-free rooms in a brownstone at 60 East Sixty-fifth Street owned by Stieglitz's younger brother Leopold, an internist, who greatly admired O'Keeffe's paintings. Their summers, until 1929, were spent at Lake George, New York, where Stieglitz's family estate was located. At times, Stieglitz's large and talkative family became too much for O'Keeffe and she would escape to her studio. But both O'Keeffe and Stieglitz did some stirring work during those summers such as: her *Lake George With Crows,* 1921; *My Shanty—Lake George,* 1922, *Corn Dark,* 1924, the corn being from O'Keeffe's garden; and *Lake George Window,* 1929; and his *Dancing Equivalent, Music No. 1, Lake George,* 1922; *First Snow and Trees,* 1922; and the *Little House,* 1923.

The budding and flowering of O'Keeffe's and Stieglitz's relationship and of their art work—his photography and her painting—must be seen in the context of the wider environment, for theirs was a special world, operating sometimes in isolation from and sometimes in unison with larger events.

The eleven years between the end of the war with Germany, and the signing of the Armistice on November 11, 1918 and the stock market crash in the fall of 1929 was a distinct era: the twenties were filled with fun and flamboyance, but marred by a dark side of disillusionment and growing economic problems. Following the signing of the armistice there was great celebration and New York was a bubble of color, jazz rhythms, and dancing flappers as the pace of life quickly accelerated. Americans gradually turned inward though, after this "war to end all wars," for there was disenchantment with the thought of becoming further involved with foreign affairs after Woodrow Wilson's League of Nations was rejected. As America turned inward after the war, there were broken-down values and a strange world of technology and urbanization to face. And so the "lost generation" began, with little of the optimistic crusading spirit of the intellectuals in the prewar years. The years directly following the war, with the Red Scare, Palmer raids, various labor strikes and race riots, and the ratification of the Eighteenth Amendment, marked the beginning of the age of prohibition or the "jazz age," as the twenties came to be called. Warren Harding's economics of "normalcy" and foreign policy of isolation seemed to bring little more than the Teapot Dome scandal and increased paranoia to the nation. The Ku Klux Klan increased its membership across the nation with Blacks, Jews, and Catholics, as its victims. The murder trial, six long years of appeals, and final horrible execution in 1927 of a poor Massachusetts shoemaker, Nicola Sacco, and fish peddler, Bartolomeo Vanzetti, corresponded to the fear and persecution of radicals in the United States that began with the Palmer raids. With the indictment of John Scopes, a high school biology teacher in Tennessee, the teaching of evolution became a crime. In many eyes "the trial was a battle between Fundamentalism on the one hand and twentieth-century skepticism (assisted by Modernism) on the other."[1] Characters of the decade included "the stony Coolidge and the bloody Al Capone, the clergyman discoursing on spiritual principles in advertising, and the booster proclaiming that Rotary was manifestation of the Divine."[2]

Since neither war nor domestic occurrences brought any genuine peace or re-established values for Americans, many sought escape in leisure activities. And so came a quickened pace in American life with increased use of the radio, movies, and automobile, increased publication of sex magazines, and increased practice of bootlegging. Frederick Allen described many Americans as similar to Lady Brett Ashley in Ernest Hemingway's *The Sun Also Rises*.

> *They could not endure a life without values, and the only values they had been trained to understand were being undermined. Everything seemed meaningless and unimportant. Well, at least one could toss off a few drinks and get a kick out of physical passion and forget that the world was crumbling. . . . And so the saxophones wailed and the gin-flask went its rounds and the dancers made their treadmill circuit with half-closed eyes, and the outside world, so merciless and so insane, was shut away for a restless night. . . .*[3]

Many writers of the time probed into the middle-class environment and American self-deceptions. Sinclair Lewis's *Main Street* and *Babbitt* were published and Upton Sinclair wrote *The Goose Step*. F. Scott Fitzgerald's and Ernest Hemingway's work portrayed much of the atmosphere and feeling of the twenties. "In general, novelists of the period were realists who dealt with the commonplace American scene. Their literature was a literature of anger and self-deception."[4]

Poets, as well as novelists, produced a significant body of literature during the twenties. Among those writing were Hart Crane, Wallace Stevens, and William Carlos Williams. (These poets worked in the teens as well.) These poets' work reflected American's turn inward and the desire to define and understand the American experience. The uncertainty of the twenties produced a desire for cultural and local identity. D. H. Lawrence wrote of the general psychic spirit in America.

> *. . . every continent has its own great spirit of place. Every people is polarized in some particular locality, which is home, the homeland. Different places on the face of the earth have different vital effluence, different vibration, different chemical exhalation, different polarity with different stars: call it what you like. But the spirit of place is a great reality.*[5]

The subject matter of many poets was very American. Williams believed strongly in the American locale, insisting that the universal exists only in the locale, that there were "no ideas but in things." Williams was concerned with immediate experience of an object by the poet. Past, present, and future became one in the intensity of experience. For him there was a sense of growth or flowering in this moment of intense experience. A "radiant gist" (Williams' term) became present in the object. Williams' subjects were primarily people and scenes from the American landscape.

In 1925 Williams published *In the American Grain,* his account of American history, which was quite influential for other poets and artists of his time. Although poorly written as a scholarly study of history, Williams adamantly sets forth his view of American history. His heroes were men such as Columbus, Daniel Boone, Aaron Burr, Walt Whitman, and Edgar Allan Poe, who continually sought new worlds. Williams indicted the Puritans as destroyers of anything new and condemned men such as Alexander Hamilton as a usurer. Although the book sold poorly, it was praised by D. H. Lawrence, Hart Crane, Charles Sheeler, Alfred Stieglitz, and Martha Graham. Stieglitz took the name of his gallery, An American Place, from the book.[6] Although most of Williams' most famous work, *Paterson,* was not published until the forties, he worked on the poem most of his life. As a long poem, it contains many of the structural qualities mentioned earlier, concerning Pound's long poems, particularly in the sense of metamorphosis and use of accretive imagery. The central theme of the city of Paterson, New Jersey, becomes intertwined with the other predominant images of the poem—Sam Patch, the poet Paterson, the divorced women, the river, the rocks. Through the fragments of local details, Williams hoped for the reader to see more general relationships, to become more perceptive, less indifferent to the surrounding world.

Williams was closely associated with Stieglitz and his circle as evidenced by the thesis of an entire study, *The Hieroglyphics of a New Speech* where Bram Dikstra explores the relationship of Williams to the Stieglitz circle. Williams was close friends with precisionist painters Sheeler and Demuth and approached subjects in a manner similar to the precisionists in a search for "the reality beyond the actuality" of a subject. Demuth actually dedicated one of his most important paintings, *I Saw the Figure 5 in Gold,* to Williams. The painting was based on one of Williams' poems, "The Great Figure." Sheeler was "the American artist whom Williams most specifically praised for realizing his local materials in a universal way."[7] Williams' ideas about the American condition were to some extent influenced by writers such as D. H. Lawrence, and the *Seven Arts* critics such as Waldo Frank, Randolph Bourne, Van Wyck Brooks, and Paul Rosenfeld,[8] all of whom were friends or admirers of Alfred Stieglitz.

Hart Crane expressed a view of history similar to Williams. His major work, *The Bridge,* handles a myth of a nation concerning the past, present, and future of America. The various settings in Crane's poem include the Brooklyn Bridge, Virginia, and New England. The poem covers various periods in time—the eras of Columbus, Pocahontas, Rip Van Winkle, and the twenties. Always there is a sense of bridges crossed or of bridges that need to be crossed. Both Crane and Stieglitz believed in the importance of intuitive perception, and that art should record such perceptions. Stieglitz created his "equivalents" and Crane created his "ultimate harmonies"[9] believing that the reality of an object could symbolize an inner emotional state.

Hart Crane occasionally read his poetry at Stieglitz's gallery and corresponded with

Stieglitz. Stieglitz wrote to Crane in 1923, "We're after Light—ever more Light. So why not seek it together—as individuals in sympathy in a strong sentimental spirit—as men— not as politicians."[10] And Crane once exclaimed to Stieglitz, "I am your brother always."[11]

Although O'Keeffe was not directly involved in the frenetic social and economic life of the twenties, she was closely associated with the artists and thinkers who espoused new forms and content in their art. In general, the exuberant experimental spirit in the art world of the teens lost momentum, and the Armory Show as catalyst had lost its power for artistic change. The mood of the nation did not provide stimulus for a number of artists who actually fled to Europe. But a few remained, steadfastly devoted to the cause of modernism. Among those were Alfred Stieglitz, the artists of his inner circle, such as Marsden Hartley, John Marin, Arthur Dove, Charles Demuth, and as of her arrival in New York, Georgia O'Keeffe.

Stieglitz's and O'Keeffe's relationship blossomed quickly. In 1924 they were married, shortly after Stieglitz divorced his wife. Although the two were very different in person- ality—he, gregarious from an urban, European-oriented background; she, quiet, from the rural American heartland—they were both committed to their own work and each other's work and strove for excellence and purity. Both were also committed to Amer- ica, she perhaps more strongly because of her upbringing. O'Keeffe had no desire to go to Europe at this time. The influence of Stieglitz, professionally on O'Keeffe and the support he gave her, is to be seen as an important factor in her development and recognition as an artist. Stieglitz's and O'Keeffe's close relationship as husband and wife and as professionals is documented by the intimate photographs that comprise Stieglitz's composite portrait of O'Keeffe begun in the teens, by some of O'Keeffe's paintings,[12] various statements of O'Keeffe and Stieglitz, (although the Stieglitz–O'Keeffe corre- spondence is sealed until 2020), and statements of those who knew both O'Keeffe and Stieglitz. O'Keeffe herself writes of the relationship,

> The relationship that Stieglitz and I had was really very good, because it was built on something more than just emotional needs. Each of us was really interested in what the other was doing. I think what he did in photography was one of the great documents of the period. Of course, you do your best to destroy each other without knowing it—some people do it knowingly and some do it unknowingly. But if you have a real basis, as we did, you can get along pretty well despite the differences.[13]

In some of O'Keeffe's correspondence to the critic Henry McBride, who also became a close friend of hers, she wrote of her relationship with Stieglitz, and her concern for being the best. "I don't even mind being called names, but I don't like to be second or third or fourth. I like being first if you noticed at all. That's why I get on with Stieglitz— with him I feel first—and when he is around and there are others he is the center and I don't count at all."[14] One also sees here a touch of jealousy on O'Keeffe's part. Stieglitz, as a somewhat possessive counterpart, wanted to keep much of O'Keeffe's work for himself and often refused to sell some of it.

In a letter to Henry McBride toward the end of Stieglitz's life, O'Keeffe wrote of Stieglitz, "Aside from my fondness for him personally I feel he has been very important for something that has made my world for me."[15]

And what happened to Stieglitz's work during the twenties? Although he did not have a gallery during the years 1918–1925, he did gather a small number of new allies about him such as Carl Zigrosser, Louis Kalonyme, William Carlos Williams, Hart Crane, Paul Rosenfeld, and D. H. Lawrence. The Lawrences were in America from about 1922 to 1925. They had been convinced by Mabel Dodge Luhan, a greater admirer of Lawrence, to visit America and the Southwest. Apparently O'Keeffe never met Lawrence, but that she liked and respected Lawrence's work from his articles in *Seven Arts* onward is evident from statements of Herbert Seligmann.[16] When Lawrence's *Lady Chatterley's Lover* was published in the late twenties, Herbert Seligmann wrote a favorable review of it in the *New York Sun* which cost him his job there. Both Stieglitz and O'Keeffe liked Lawrence's book, and as "Lawrence was interested to have Georgia O'Keeffe's opinion, she also wrote approvingly."[17]

Buoyed by his marriage to O'Keeffe and the success of a group show, "Seven Americans," where works by Marin, Dove, Hartley, O'Keeffe, Strand, Demuth and Stieglitz himself were shown in 1925, Stieglitz opened a new gallery, The Intimate Gallery, in Room 303 in the Anderson Galleries building at 489 Park Avenue, in December of 1925. With this gallery Stieglitz hoped to perpetuate the spirit of 291, but focused on selling the work of the small group of American artists in his circle. Like a number of other artists and writers during the twenties, Stieglitz was concerned with finding an artistic definition of America and felt that support of individual American artists would result in a more easily understood collective American spirit. He wrote in 1923 to Paul Rosenfeld:

> That's why I'm fighting for Georgia. She is American. So is Marin. So am I. Of course by American I mean something much more comprehensive than is usually understood, if anything is really understood at all. . . . But there is America—Or isn't there an America. Are we only a marked down bargain day remnant of Europe? Haven't we any of our own courage in matters 'aesthetic'? Well, you are on the true track and there is fun ahead.[18]

Some of Stieglitz's own photography documented his search for an American identity. His *Spiritual America,* a photograph of the flank and harness of a workhorse is both concrete and abstract. The formal, abstract composition as well as content image are both enticing to the eye and mind. His photographs of his artist friends serve as documents of these important artistic figures. Stieglitz's most important photographic work during the twenties, though, is his beginning of his well-known cloud images, *The Equivalents.* Through these photographs Stieglitz hoped to carry out the idea that abstract shapes and colors could express abstract thoughts or sensations. The clouds images are simultaneously abstract and realistic with no ground appearing and no horizon line. Stieglitz wrote of the clouds:

> In looking at my photographs of clouds, people seem freer to think about the relationships in the pictures than about the subject matter for its own sake. . . . My photographs are a picture of the chaos in the world, and of my relationship to that chaos. My prints show the world's constant upsetting of man's equilibrium, and his eternal battle to re-establish it.[19]

Stieglitz wrote to a number of his contemporaries concerning his excitement about the new photographs. To Hart Crane he wrote in September of 1923:

> . . . it was great excitement—daily for weeks . . . I had told Miss O'Keeffe I wanted a series of photographs which when seen by Ernest Bloch (the great composer) he would exclaim:

Music! Music, May, why that is music! . . . . and Bloch saw them—what I said I wanted to happen happened verbatim.[20]

Some forty years later, O'Keeffe herself was to do a series of cloud paintings as if she were above the clouds.

Stieglitz's photographic and gallery work had to be somewhat curtailed after he suffered from a heart attack in 1928 from which he never fully recovered. Although the Intimate Gallery was somewhat financially successful, the Anderson Galleries building was sold in the fall of 1929 and Stieglitz was forced to close the gallery. He was not interested in opening another gallery but at the urging of O'Keeffe and his friends, who helped raise money, he opened a new gallery, An American Place, in December 1929 at 509 Madison Avenue, Room 1710. He continued the non-commercial, almost religious spirit of 291 and the Intimate Gallery. New exhibitors were included, European as well as American, such as George Grosz, Ansel Adams, Eliot Porter and William Einstein. As in his own work and as at his other galleries, Stieglitz again created an atmosphere of integrity and intensity. To a visitor at his gallery, Stieglitz once vehemently stated, "Man, can't you figure it out for yourself? I am trying to sustain life at its highest, to sustain a living standard for the artist, to permit every moment to live without isms, fashions or cults attached. This place is a living center even when it is deserted."[21]

O'Keeffe had yearly exhibitions of her new work at both the Intimate Gallery and An American Place.

During the twenties, O'Keeffe's most noted works were her large flower images, organic and lyrical; and her paintings of New York City, often hard-edged and geometrically precise. Her first big flower painting was completed in 1924, the year she was married. The blown-up flower images in particular received controversial critical responses, often equating the works with sexual imagery. O'Keeffe intensely disliked such criticism. (In-depth discussion of O'Keeffe's paintings and critics' writings occurs in Parts II and III.)

There were often reciprocal influences among Stieglitz and the circle revolving about him, including O'Keeffe. Although O'Keeffe denies any direct influence of photography on her work, the close-up images of some of her works, such as the flower paintings, suggest the sharp-focused, close-up images made possible with a camera, and being done by photographers such as Paul Strand, Edward Steichen, and Edward Weston. Works such as Weston's *Shell,* 1927 (George Eastman House) or *Lotus,* 1922 are very similar to O'Keeffe's large flowers. O'Keeffe would have had numerous opportunities to see such photographs and know the photographers since they were all close associates of Stieglitz. Indeed, in 1900, Stieglitz had bought the first photographs Steichen had sold at five dollars each. Strand's work was shown at 291 as early as 1916, and Weston became friends with Stieglitz and Sheeler starting in 1922.

Gradually O'Keeffe became good friends with a number of artists and writers frequenting Stieglitz's galleries, as well as with the inner circle, consisting of Marin, Dove, Hartley and Demuth. With the support and encouragement of members of the Stieglitz circle, O'Keeffe was very productive during these years. There were times, though, when she had to prove herself to "the boys." She has referred to doing *My Shanty—Lake George,* 1922, to prove to the boys she could work with a dark palette. Of all the artists in the Stieglitz inner circle, O'Keeffe was perhaps closest to Arthur Dove in both personal friendship and professional respect.[22] O'Keeffe said of Dove, "I discovered and picked him out before I was picked out and discovered. Where did I see him? A reproduction in a book. The Eddy book I guess, a picture of fall leaves. Then I trekked the streets looking for others."[23] The only work Dove hung in his houseboat home was an early O'Keeffe drawing, *Mona*. Both O'Keeffe and Dove drew heavily on nature for their images and seemed to attempt to portray the very essence of an object or scene in their work. Both O'Keeffe and Dove also painted visual equivalents of sound if one may judge by their titles. For example, Dove painted *Music*, 1913, *Sentimental Music*, 1917, and *Chinese Music*, 1923, while O'Keeffe painted *Blue and Green Music*, 1919 and *Music—Pink and Blue I*, 1919. Dove's and O'Keeffe's concern and respect for one another provided a continuing source of mutual support and inspiration.

O'Keeffe also became friendly with Charles Demuth. O'Keeffe speaks of a close friendship with Charles Demuth at the time.

> *Demuth was very elegant, too. He was also more amusing than any of the other artists I knew. . . . In my memory, he is the only artist who was any fun to be with. We were always going to do a large picture together—a flower painting—but we never did. . . . He always had lunch with Stieglitz and me when he came to town, and we always enjoyed it.*[24]

Demuth actually paid tribute to O'Keeffe in his 1924 *Poster Portrait of O'Keeffe*. In their friendship, O'Keeffe and Demuth provided a mutual respect and support for one another.

Charles Demuth and Charles Sheeler were involved with a group of painters at this time known as the "immaculates" or "precisionists," whose work was a creative compromise between realism and abstraction. The terms immaculate or precisionist describe the precise technique of the sharp-edged and simplified forms in the compositions. Much of the subject matter of these painters was the American landscape, both industrial and rural. The "immaculately patterned pictures" of this group "became, therefore a comprehensible expression of American life and the first important bridge between native tradition and the modern vision."[25] The chief painters in this group were Charles Sheeler, Charles Demuth, Louis Lozowick, Niles Spencer, and Georgia O'Keeffe, although O'Keeffe didn't like to be classed with any group. Martin Friedman remarks that "the vitality of this painting is in its insistent logic and discipline through which the familiar object—a building, complex machine, or even a flower—is stripped of its ultimate, stripped and presented with astonishing lucidity."[26] The influence of Cubism and photography is seen in much of the work. O'Keeffe and Sheeler came to represent the two main currents of the group.

"For the most part, O'Keeffe's images of a monumentalized natural world are concerned with primal forces of creation and decay. In contrast, Sheeler's architectural and mechanical subjects are chaste celebrations of the more immediate and tangible spirit of modern technology."[27]

O'Keeffe's chief subjects in nature in the twenties were flowers, leaves, and Lake George scenes. But O'Keeffe also painted scenes of the urban landscape. From 1926 to 1929 she painted scenes from the windows of Stieglitz's Intimate Gallery and from her apartment in the Shelton Hotel overlooking New York City's East River. She also painted abstractions during the twenties.

The precisionist painters continued painting after the twenties, but during this decade they seemed to be most a group, in their interest in the architectural forms of the city, although there was never any desire to promote a cause or theory on the part of the artists. Always, though, even in the years following the twenties, there was an allegiance to the object painted and its essential structure. Ironically, the precisionists "may have to some degree precipitated the decline of avant-garde fortunes in the twenties and thirties, when they sought to apply Cubist methods to indigenous subject matter."[28]

O'Keeffe thus found support in her milieu, in the twenties in both the Stieglitz circle and precisionist group, which at times overlapped.

Although O'Keeffe was not directly involved with the general frenetic life of the twenties in New York, she was closely associated with the artists and thinkers who espoused new form and content in their art and such associations were reflected in some of her work. Indeed, O'Keeffe and some of the poets were similar in their approach to subject matter, use of imagination, and new language of form, whether visual for O'Keeffe, or verbal for the poets. For example, she, as William Carlos Williams did, seemed to uncover "the radiant gist" or sparkling essence of an object.

In the summer of 1929 O'Keeffe, at the urging of Mabel Dodge Luhan, made a summer trip to New Mexico with Rebecca Strand, Paul Strand's wife. She stayed in Taos with Luhan and was forever captivated by the majesty of the New Mexican terrain, the wide, expansive space of red earth and blue sky.

The radiant New Mexican sunlight was particularly alluring for O'Keeffe. O'Keeffe, as other artists and writers since the end of the nineteenth century, was immediately drawn to the Taos and Santa Fe area. As early as 1914 a Taos Society of Artists had been organized and by 1929 there was a well-established art community there. That summer O'Keeffe, for the first time in years, met people outside Stieglitz's domain—personalities such as: Spud Johnson, a young poet and Luhan's secretary; Ansel Adams, then a beginning photographer working for the Sierra Club; and Daniel Catton Rich, then at the Art Institute of Chicago. In 1943, Rich was responsible for the first large-scale retrospective exhibition of O'Keeffe's work in Chicago. In 1960 another major retrospective of O'Keeffe's work was held at the Worcester Art Museum, Worcester, Massachusetts, under Rich's direction.

For part of that summer of 1929 O'Keeffe stayed with Dorothy Brett, an English aristocrat and painter who had been friends with members of the Bloomsbury group and had followed the Lawrences to New Mexico. O'Keeffe visited Brett at Kiowa Ranch, a gift to the Lawrences from Mabel Dodge Luhan. While there, O'Keeffe was enthralled by a giant pine tree under which she watched the stars in the black void that was the sky in that infinite New Mexican terrain. The tree remained in her memory and shortly thereafter she painted her well-known *Lawrence Tree*, 1929.

O'Keeffe could not forget New Mexico and thereafter she summered in New Mexico while Stieglitz stayed at Lake George. The decision to leave Stieglitz each summer was often difficult for O'Keeffe. In various letters to her friends one finds mention of her inner struggle. She wrote to Blanche and Russell Matthias, "If I can keep up my courage and leave Stieglitz I plan to go west . . . for two months. It is always such a struggle for me to leave him."[29] In a letter to Stieglitz himself one finds an example of O'Keeffe's intense involvement with the New Mexican landscape and her desire to share her feelings, as well as her love and concern for Stieglitz.

At five I walked—I climbed way up on a pale green hill and in the evening light—the sun under clouds—the color effect was very strange—standing high on a pale green hill where I could look all round at the red, yellow, purple formations—miles all around—the color intensified by the pale grey green I was standing on. It was wonderful—you would have loved it too—Just before I went to walk I had two letters from you—. . . You sound lonely—and I wonder should I go to the lake and have two or three weeks with you before you go to town—I will if you say so—Wire me and I will pick right up and start.[30]

In the fall of 1929 O'Keeffe was back in New York filled with the strength and inspiration gained when she was in New Mexico. That vibrancy of spirit was soon to be somewhat marred by the events of October and November. On October 29, 1929, the panic of the stock market crash began a new era for America—the Depression years. Until 1929 most Americans felt there would be no limit to future money-making and growth of technology in the United States. New Yorkers were afraid. " 'I'm afraid, every man is afraid,' confessed Charles H. Schwab of United Steel. 'I don't know, we don't know whether the values we have are going to be real next month or not.' "[31] In the midst of the waves of bankruptcy, Stieglitz and O'Keeffe remained remarkably calm, always convinced of the power of their own creative strength, individually and collectively. They continued onward in their work, relatively undaunted by the problems besetting the business community, and in December 1929, as previously mentioned, Stieglitz's new gallery, An American Place was quietly opened.

The twenties thus ended on the terrifying note of the stock market crash. But the decade had brought a deepening of spirit on the part of many artists and writers, particularly those associated with the Stieglitz circle. Explorations in defining the American experience, in both abstract and concrete terms had succeeded on a variety of levels. As the reality of the oncoming Depression became more vivid, O'Keeffe, Stieglitz, and their associates were fortunately able to maintain their equilibrium, and continued to make strong visual statements.

Notes

[1]Frederick Allen, *Only Yesterday* (New York: Harper & Row, 1931), p. 168.

[2]Oliver Larkin, *Art and Life in America* (New York: Rinehart and Co., 1949), p. 372.

[3]Allen, *Only Yesterday,* p. 100.

[4]Haskell, *Arthur Dove,* p. 47.

[5]*Ibid.*

[6]James Guimond, *The Art of William Carlos Williams* (Chicago: University of Illinois Press, 1968), p. 92.

[7]*Ibid.,* p. 55.

[8]*Ibid.,* p. 66–67.

[9]Alfred Stieglitz, letter to Hart Crane, July 27, 1923, Lake George, in Sara Greenough, *Alfred Stieglitz* (Washington, D.C.: National Gallery of Art, 1982), p. 235.

[10]Dorothy Norman, *Alfred Stieglitz: An American Seer* (New York: Random House, 1973), p. 228.

[11]R. W. B. Lewis, *The Poetry of Hart Crane* (Princeton: Princeton University Press, 1967), p. 122.

[12]Seligmann, interview January 17, 1975, New York City.

[13]Tomkins, "Georgia O'Keeffe," p. 47.

[14]Henry McBride papers, Archives of American Art, Smithsonian Institution, n.d.

[15]Calvin Tomkins, "Georgia O'Keeffe," *New Yorker,* March 4, 1974, p. 47.

[16]Herbert Seligmann, interview at his apartment, New York City, January 17, 1975, and *Alfred Stieglitz Talking* (New Haven: Yale University Library, 1966), pp. 135–143.

[17]Armin Arnold, *D. H. Lawrence and America* (London: Linden Press, 1958), p. 157.

[18]Sara Greenough, *Alfred Stieglitz* (Washington, D.C.: National Gallery of Art, 1982), p. 212.

[19]Dorothy Norman, *Alfred Stieglitz: An American Seer* (New York: Random House, 1973), p. 161.

[20]Alfred Stieglitz, quoted in Sara Greenough, *Alfred Stieglitz,* p. 207.

[21]Stieglitz, quoted in Norman, *Alfred Stieglitz,* p. 136.

[22]Haskell, *Arthur Dove,* p. 13.

[23]*Ibid.,* p. 13–14.

[24]Tomkins, "Georgia O'Keeffe," p. 44.

[25]John Baur, *Revolution and Tradition in Modern American Art* (New York: Macmillan Company, 1958), p. 7.

[26]Martin Friedman, *The Precisionist View in American Art* (Minneapolis: Walker Art Center, 1968), p. 13.

[27]*Ibid.,* p. 14

[28]Brown, Hunter, Jacobus, Rosenblum, and Sokol, *American Art* (Englewood, N.J.: Prentice-Hall, 1979), p. 443.

[29]Georgia O'Keeffe, to Blanche and Russell Matthias, n.d., Beinecke Library.

[30]Georgia O'Keeffe, letter to Alfred Stieglitz, n.d., Whitney Museum files New York: Whitney Museum of American Art.

[31]Carl N. Degler, *Out of the Past, The Forces That Shaped America* (New York: Harper & Row, 1959), pp. 381–382.

Chapter Three
The American Scene, 1930–1946

In February of 1930 O'Keeffe opened a new show of work, inspired by her New Mexican visit, at An American Place. Some of her most well-known images including *Black Cross, New Mexico,* 1929 and *Ranchos Church, Taos,* 1929 appeared in that show. *The Black Cross* was inspired by the crosses of the Penitente Indians. *The Ranchos Church* was inspired by the west-end of the mission church of St. Francis of Assisi at Ranchos de Taos. Both illustrated O'Keeffe's sensitivity to important elements of life in New Mexico and the Southwest.

In March of 1930 D. H. Lawrence died. O'Keeffe and Stieglitz mourned with Dorothy Brett. In the larger world there was a more widespread mourning as the dark cloud of the Depression set in. Industrial stagnation, bank failures, and rising unemployment brought despair to hundreds of Americans.

The Depression was described as "showing man as a senseless cog in a senselessly whirling machine which is beyond human understanding and has ceased to serve any purpose of its own."[1] Gone was the sense of individualism of the teens and twenties. Instead, there was a sense of social mindedness and concern for economic and social salvation for the nation. More than ever did Americans seem to seek a cultural identity. Writers such as John Dos Passos, Erskine Caldwell, James Farrell, and John Steinbeck dealt more with problematic social environments. Among the poets, Archibald MacLeish, in *Panic,* a radio drama about the crash, and Edna St. Vincent Millay in *Conversation at Midnight,* turned to social and political themes. In drama, playwrights such as Robert Sherwood in *Petrified Forest,* Maxwell Anderson in *Winterset,* and Thornton Wilder in *Our Town* wrote of their time and people. Marxist communism, too, became more popular among the intellectuals. Frederick Allen wrote,

> . . . one man in three at a literary party in New York would be a communist sympathizer, passionately ready to join hands, in proletarian comradeship, with the factory hand or sharecropper whom a few years before he had scorned as a member of Mencken's 'booboisie'. . . .[2]

Public despair concerning conditions in America was symbolized in 1932 by reaction to the kidnapping of Charles Lindbergh's child. Lindbergh had become a national hero with his transatlantic flight in 1927.

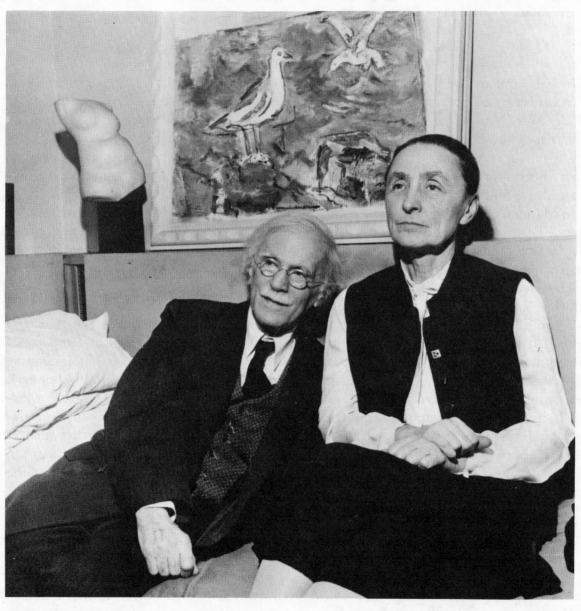

O'Keeffe and Stieglitz at An American Place in the Forties. The Bettmann Archive Inc.

Not only did domestic events threaten Americans' senses of security, but so, too, did events abroad. In 1933, the Nazis burned the German Reichstag and Hitler was elected Chancellor of Germany. The threat of war became even more imminent as the thirties went on.

Promises of change in the United States came in 1932 with the election of Franklin Roosevelt and his subsequent New Deal legislation. In 1935 within the Works Progress Administration, the Federal Art Project was begun, giving employment to artists. Much of the art for this project and by other artists in America consisted of social realist and American scene painting. Artists painting in this vein included Thomas Hart Benton, Grant Wood, Raphael Soyer, and John Steuart Curry. Artists such as Philip Evergood, Ben Shahn, and William Gropper, conveyed political messages in their painting. The desire for the integration of art and life became greatly increased.

During the Depression years the tradition of realism was revived, and may be seen as an extension of the Ashcan School. Within the realist revival there were two areas of development. One focused on American scenes—in the city and in rural environments. Two such predominant painters were Edward Hopper and Charles Burchfield. Hopper's paintings of eerie street scenes and isolated houses depicted an ugly loneliness in American life. Many of Burchfield's paintings of the American landscape convey a sense of bleakness. Often he portrayed the lifestyle of small midwestern towns that Sinclair Lewis and Sherwood Anderson had written about. More programmatic in approach were painters such as Thomas Hart Benton and John Steuart Curry, who were aided by the very conservative writings of the critic Thomas Craven, who saw American history and mythology as a way to attack abstract and modern art.

The other form of American realism in the thirties was a more strident social protest in the work of artists such as Ben Shahn, Jack Levine and Philip Evergood. Ben Shahn's work serves a good example of American realism. Shahn, one of the most prolific of the W.P.A. muralists, did a number of social and political statements. One large protest statement he painted in 1931–32 was a series of twenty-three paintings dealing with the trial and execution of Nicola Sacco and Bartolomeo Vanzetti, Italian immigrants convicted of a murder that many felt they did not commit.

In the thirties a number of black artists emerged such as Romare Beardon and Jacob Lawrence. Black imagery was viewed as an extension of American scene painting and as a form of social protest.

The Depression period also brought a return to more primitive expression, as evidenced in the work of a Louis Eilshemius or John Kane. O'Keeffe greatly admired Eilshemius, who had studied at the Art Students League as she had, and abandoned his academic training. O'Keeffe wrote to critic Henry McBride of a visit to see Eilshemius' work, "I have been at Eilshemiuses. I saw St. Joan. . . . Shaw and Strindberg made very deep impressions on me but not deeper if as deep as my visit to Eilshemius."[3]

Yet not all of the art created in the thirties was realist oriented and socially minded. Artists such as O'Keeffe and members of the Stieglitz circle who were part of the first wave of modernism before 1920 continued to paint much as before. Indeed, those artists "associated with Stieglitz retained their belief in the efficacy of individual enrichment over communal action and declined to participate in the W.P.A. Projects."[4] Other artistic directions of the thirties involved structural abstraction in work of artists such as Josef Albers, Ilya Bolotowsky, Burgoyne Diller; expressionist abstraction—Milton

Avery, Hans Hofmann, de Kooning; or surrealism and magic realism—Peter Blume, Ivan Albright. The formation of the American Abstract Artists Organization in 1936 provided some support for artists moving toward abstraction. The group included artists Ibram Lassaw, Burgoyne Diller, Ashile Gorky, Stuart Davis, Willem de Kooning, Alice Mason and George L. K. Morris. There was a wide variety of abstract styles with constructionist, cubist, expressionist, and biomorphic elements in the work of these artists. Writings of some of these artists such as Stuart Davis and Balcombe Greene who wrote for the radical journal *Art Front,* indicate that abstraction was seen as a moral force as important as the social realists. The very activity of abstract painting was seen as an elevating force. O'Keeffe was not a part of this group. Indeed, George L. K. Morris, painter of strict geometric abstractions, attacked her bone paintings, stating in *Partisan Review* that "your lack of technical equipment and your lack of taste lay naked and raw."[5]

Although O'Keeffe's work of the thirties did not reflect the social mindedness or strict regionalism of much of the art of the time, her particular attachment to the New Mexico region beginning in 1929, as seen in her paintings and verbal statements, illustrates her brand of regionalism as she depicts many facets of the Southwestern lifestyle and terrain.

As were the poets, O'Keeffe was concerned with a sense of the American experience, although she cannot really be considered a regionalist or American scene painter in the sense of Benton or Curry. Herbert Seligmann described O'Keeffe's work as "entirely and locally American," and that through her work "American aspects are identified and made personal."[6] O'Keeffe's America was seen in such paintings as *Barn with Snow,* 1934, *Grey Hills II,* 1936, *Jimson Weed,* 1938, *Black Cross,* 1929, *Pedernal and Red Hills,* 1936, and *Cow's Skull, Red White and Blue,* 1931. With a touch of irony, O'Keeffe has commented on her work on *Cow's Skull, Red White and Blue:*

> *I was quite excited over our country and I know that at that time almost any one of those great minds (intellectuals and artists in the East) would have been living in Europe if it had been possible for them. They didn't even want to live in New York—how was the Great American Thing going to happen? So as I painted along on my cow's skull on blue, I thought to myself "I'll make an American painting. They will not think it great with the red stripes down the sides—Red, White and Blue, but they will notice it."*[7]

Doris Bry wrote of the public coming to see "a series of unique paintings of their own country, that in their variety transcended any regional painting, and to wonder at the artist's statement of the natural world."[8] A 1957 letter from a Whitney Museum curator stated, "The work she (O'Keeffe) has produced in New Mexico is among the most original expressions of a distinctly American subject matter without any of the chauvinistic tendencies of regionalism."[9] O'Keeffe felt America was an important place to work in those years. She spoke of the years following her arrival in New York City and her conversations with various intellectuals of the time. "They would sit around and talk about the great American novel and the great American painting, but some would have stepped across the ocean and stayed in Paris if they could have. Not me, I had things to do in my own country."[10]

In 1931 O'Keeffe painted her first bone paintings and continued to paint many such paintings, as well as other aspects of the New Mexican landscape, except during a serious illness in the middle of the decade. Some associated the bone paintings with the rise of surrealism because of the unusual juxtaposition of objects such as flowers and cow skulls floating on the picture plane. But O'Keeffe denies such. "I was in the Surrealist show when I'd never heard of Surrealism."[11] Others associated the skull paintings with death, particularly because of her serious illness in the mid-thirties. O'Keeffe vehemently denied these allegations as well. In 1932 she traveled to the Gaspé country in Canada and remained there for a short while painting Canadian barns and crosses. Some of the Canadian barns are good examples of a continuing precisionist tendency in O'Keeffe's work. The clean architectural forms of paintings such as *Stables,* 1932 and *White Canadian Barn II,* 1932, have a timeless quality and reflect a sense of purity and permanence.

In 1932 O'Keeffe also participated in a mural competition held by the Museum of Modern Art to select designs for the walls of Radio City Music Hall. (The murals were originally to be done by the Mexican Diego Rivera and some other foreigners, but a number of Americans protested vehemently.) O'Keeffe's mural design, *Manhattan,* similar to some of her paintings of the New York skyline, was selected to be executed on the walls and ceiling of the second-mezzanine powder room. Stieglitz, unfortunately, was greatly opposed to O'Keeffe's doing any such mural, disliking intensely the whole mural movement and the notion of democratizing an artform. The mural project was a source of severe tension between O'Keeffe and Stieglitz. Ignoring his authority, O'Keeffe set out to work on the mural only to have the cloth upon which she was to paint separate from the wall due to poor workmanship. O'Keeffe broke down completely from the tension and was unable to complete the mural. She was admitted to Doctors Hospital, for treatment of psychoneurosis, where she remained for seven weeks. Japanese painter Yasuo Kuniyoshi eventually painted the murals for the room.

Perhaps another source of pressure for O'Keeffe during the early thirties was the rising number of women artists receiving recognition, including O'Keeffe's own sister Ida. The number recognized was still considerably small, but things were changing. Five women artists were elected into the National Institute of Arts and Letters between 1930 and 1932. O'Keeffe herself was elected into the Institute in 1949 and received its Gold Medal for painting in 1970. In 1932 and 1933 Anna Hyatt Huntington and Cecilia Beaux were appointed to the American Academy of Arts and Letters. Florine Stettheimer, a fanciful figurative artist, was acclaimed by critic Henry McBride among others. The New Deal programs also employed a number of women artists, such as Alice Neel and Lee Krasner, who were just establishing themselves as artists. These artists were seen somewhat as threats to O'Keeffe's number one place. Yet conversely, the growing recognition of women artists perhaps made it easier for O'Keeffe to continue on her way through the oncoming decades.

During the decade O'Keeffe also did some commercial work, needing, as many people during the Depression did, to earn some extra money. But she did not compromise her own work. She worked for the Steuben Glass company and traveled to Hawaii in 1939 for the Dole Pineapple Company. For Steuben Glass she designed a lovely, open lily to be engraved on the bottom of some large crystal bowls, which were to sell for $500 each. O'Keeffe had various disagreements with the Dole company. She wanted to live with the pineapple workers in Hawaii but was told that it was against company policy. She also painted a papaya tree for the company which was rejected as being the product of a rival company. O'Keeffe finally painted a pineapple acceptable to Dole when she was back in New York, after the company had a fresh pineapple shipped to her from Hawaii.

In the thirties O'Keeffe and Stieglitz also began to develop close friendships outside their own sometimes tumultuous relationship. O'Keeffe became friends with Jean Toomer, a young black writer, whose wife had died of cancer. Toomer was best known for his novel, *Cane,* set in the American South and published in 1923. She and Toomer were not lovers but O'Keeffe trusted him greatly. He seemed to answer an inner need for her after her stay in Doctors Hospital. In a letter she wrote to Toomer she opened up a great deal. Important, too, is the analogy she drew between herself and the tilled earth—Her roots thus continued to be in the black soil of the American heartland where she was born.

> *My center does not come from my mind—it feels in me like a plot of warm moist well tilled earth with the sun shining hot on it. . . . It seems I would rather feel starkly empty than let anything be planted that cannot be tended to the fullest possibility of its growth . . . my plot of earth must be tended with absurd care. . . . By myself first—and if second by someone else, it must be with absolute trust. . . . It seems it would be very difficult for me to live if it were wrecked again just now.*[12]

During these years Stieglitz was becoming noticeably older. Often in poor health, he spent much of his time on a cot he kept in the back of An American Place. He continued to photograph, with difficulty, until 1937. During the thirties his photographs changed from the lovely free-floating clouds of the twenties to the colder geometric forms of New York's skyscrapers. The Depression made it difficult too, to foster and sell art that was not "socially" oriented. Yet his strength of spirit prevailed and he continued to fight for his cause of modern art and freedom of expression for the individual. He became close friends with young Dorothy Norman, still in her twenties, who became business manager of the gallery in 1933 and did much to keep the gallery alive. Norman did much to help Stieglitz, taking care of clerical items and more importantly, raising money for the gallery. In 1933 the lease for the gallery was actually put in Norman's name. Stieglitz photographed Norman as he had O'Keeffe, although he did not produce such a voluminous complex portrait of Norman as he had of O'Keeffe. Stieglitz also taught Norman to photograph. As a result, there are some excellent photographs of Stieglitz and An American Place during these years. He also arranged for the publication of some of Dorothy's poems. Norman, in turn, brought out an arts magazine *Twice a Year: A Journal of Literature, the Arts and Civil Liberties,* which she dedicated to Stieglitz. The magazine, begun in 1937, was published throughout the next decade. There was speculation about the nature of Stieglitz's and Norman's relationship. "When asked many years later if her relationship with Stieglitz was romantic, intellectual or spiritual, Dorothy responded, 'It was all of those.'"[13]

Whatever the nature of Norman's and Stieglitz's relationship was, it was close and this was upsetting to O'Keeffe. At one point she accidentally received a letter from Stieglitz meant for Dorothy Norman. These years marked the beginning of a change in O'Keeffe's and Stieglitz's relationship. In many ways the thirties were hard years for O'Keeffe as the Depression years were for the rest of the country. Yet she was able to rally in periods of bleakness. A letter to Dorothy Brett in the thirties indicated her continuing strength. " . . . my feelings about life is a curious kind of triumphant feeling about—seeing it bleak—knowing it so—and walking into it fearlessly because one has no choice—enjoying one's consciousness—I may seem very free—a cross between a petted baby and a well-fed cow—but I know a few things."[14]

O'Keeffe and Stieglitz never lost faith in each other's work although Stieglitz had to stop photographing in 1937 due to ill health. Years later O'Keeffe was to write, "For me he was much more wonderful in his work than as a human being. . . . I believe it was the work that kept me with him—though I loved him as a human being. . . . I put up with what seemed to me a good deal of contradictory nonsense because of what seemed clear and bright and wonderful."[15] Stieglitz continued to remain the primary support of O'Keeffe as an artist, and realized he must not oppose such things as her trips to New Mexico which were crucial to her survival as an artist. In 1936 the couple moved from the Shelton to a penthouse apartment at 405 East Fifty-fourth Street so O'Keeffe could have more working space, even though Stieglitz disliked the idea of change. By then Stieglitz was often bedridden and O'Keeffe most likely paid the rent from the sales of her paintings. Now it was O'Keeffe who needed to support Stieglitz as he had once done for her. O'Keeffe found it increasingly difficult to leave Stieglitz. In her letters to Stieglitz in the summer of 1937, one finds statements such as, "You sound a bit lonely up there on the hill—It makes me wish that I could be beside you for a little while—I suppose the part of me that is anything to you is there—even if I am here."[16]

Despite changes in their relationship, O'Keeffe and Stieglitz appear to have remained very close to each other.

By the late thirties the United States' economy seemed to be on the mend and O'Keeffe's work was selling fairly well. In 1938 she was awarded an honorary doctorate from the College of William and Mary in Williamsburg, Virginia, the only degree she had except for her high school diploma. In 1938 the Nazis also annexed Austria and Czechoslovakia. Artistic discussion at An American Place and at O'Keeffe's and Stieglitz's apartment was frequently interrupted to turn on the radio to hear the latest news from Europe. Stieglitz, with his European heritage, was again more concerned than Georgia about the oncoming war.

In 1939 the decade came to a close with the opening of the Museum of Non-Objective Art by Solomon Guggenheim, the first television broadcast, and the beginning of World War II with the German invasion of Poland. In that year O'Keeffe again suffered from nervous exhaustion and was ordered to bed. Fortunately she recovered more quickly than previously in 1933. In that year O'Keeffe was also chosen as one of the twelve outstanding women of the past fifty years along with Eleanor Roosevelt and Helen Keller by the New York World's Fair Tomorrow Committee. With this award O'Keeffe's spirits were buoyed and by many she was considered the most well-known and successful female artist in America. By this time O'Keeffe had well developed her own style and continued to work in her own "ism." As Daniel Catton Rich was to write four years later, "Seen on the whole, her art betrays a perfect consistency. It has undergone no marked changes of style but has moved outward from its center. In over a quarter of a century in painting, O'Keeffe has only grown more herself."[17]

Feeling that she was far from the forces of war, O'Keeffe journeyed once again to New Mexico in 1940, this time to purchase Ghost Ranch north of Abiquiu. Built out of mud and straw bricks with hand-carved lintels, the house, patio, and eight acres surrounded by National Forest land was a wonderful retreat for O'Keeffe. That summer O'Keeffe painted her first paintings of the first home she had ever owned.

Gradually she renovated her new home to be the simple, aesthetic environment she desired, with few superfluous details. Predominant in the house were her collections of bones, rocks, shells, feathers, etc. that were so important in her work. By 1943 almost every room contained large panes of glass to bring the magic of the desert world inside.

O'Keeffe had hoped she was far from the war in New Mexico when the Japanese bombed Pearl Harbor and America entered the war in December of 1941. But twenty miles from her was the Los Alamos atomic research laboratory and, at times, men arrived at the ranch on weekends to look around. Still lukewarm toward the war, O'Keeffe was surprised to be awarded an honorary Doctorate of Letters along with General Douglas MacArthur, by the University of Wisconsin in 1942. Besides the bombing of Pearl Harbor, 1941 also brought the death of Sherwood Anderson, author and friend of O'Keeffe and Stieglitz. In that same year Henri Bergson, the philosopher and writer whose writings on intuition and time had influenced many such as Stieglitz and his circle, also died. And O'Keeffe's friend Florine Stettheimer died a few years later. In these war years O'Keeffe was also concerned about the status of women, although she felt she had relatively little in common with most women and actually preferred to be with men. Her artwork had become her children and she therefore had little to say to women to whom mothering and domestic details were a major part of their lives. But disliking traditional sex roles, in 1942 O'Keeffe wrote an endorsement for the National Woman's Party, which was attempting to get an equal rights amendment passed. A number of years later she stated, "I think it's pretty funny that women have always been treated like Negroes in this country and they don't even know it. Even when you tell them, they won't listen."[18]

The deaths of war and of friends, though, could not mar the success of O'Keeffe's first full-scale retrospective at the Chicago Art Institute in 1943. The sixty-one O'Keeffe paintings—her flowers, her landscapes and her bones—were a wonderful change for viewers weary of the war. All the critics were not favorable but most spoke in glowing terms. Wrote one reviewer, "Find the abstraction which is filled with lovely green running from dark to light, with cream and pale pink balancing its beauty, and you will find it hard not to remember the poet's admonition—'beauty is its own excuse for being.'"[19]

Throughout the war years O'Keeffe continued to divide her time between New York and New Mexico. In 1942 she and Stieglitz had moved to a smaller place nearer An American Place at 59 East Fifty-fourth Street so Stieglitz could walk to the gallery should taxis be unavailable. O'Keeffe had also thought ahead to the possibility of wartime fuel rationing and wanted a place with a bedroom small enough to heat with an electric heater. Unfortunately, few people came to the gallery during the war, and Stieglitz only showed Marins, Doves, and O'Keeffes. But the gallery was Stieglitz's lifeblood and he still spent most of his days there. During the war, Manhattan disturbed O'Keeffe more than usual with the air raid drills and blackouts. Basically she returned each winter for Stieglitz. As he aged rapidly and needed her help, there seemed to be fewer tensions between the two. As she once told a friend, "We agree on the important things."[20] She wrote to Henry McBride,

> I see Alfred as an old man that I am very fond of—growing older—so that it sometimes shocks and startles me when he looks particularly pale and tired. . . . Aside from my fondness for him personally I feel that he has been something that has made my world for me—I like it that I can make him feel that I have hold of his hand to steady him as he goes on.[21]

The war finally ended in 1945. That same year O'Keeffe bought a second house, an abandoned hacienda in Abiquiu, New Mexico. Captivated by the door, and interaction of spaces in the building, O'Keeffe used this as the subject of a number of her patio paintings such as *In the Patio I*, 1946, *In the Patio IV*, 1948, and *Patio with Black Door*, 1956. In letters to Henry McBride at this time one sees how important this land and house were to her—"You know I never feel at home in the East like I do here." On buying the house she wrote, "I think it's wonderful. I've always had an odd feeling that it was mine."[22] As with Ghost Ranch, O'Keeffe had the place renovated and added large panes of glass. From her all-white studio she could see the expansive Chama River Valley.

She returned to New York again that winter and in the spring of 1946 had another major exhibit at the Museum of Modern Art. It was the first such retrospective for a woman painter at this museum. Henry McBride wrote a review of the show for the *New York Sun* which, despite his friendship with O'Keeffe, O'Keeffe did not like. He referred to her "stardom" and her success as a "woman artist"[23] not simply as an artist.

O'Keeffe was glad to return to Abiquiu that summer. Worried about Stieglitz's health, she left him with a housekeeper. A few weeks after arriving in Abiquiu in June of 1946, O'Keeffe received a telegram that Stieglitz, having suffered a stroke, was in critical condition in Doctors Hospital. She took the next plane east to find him already in a coma. Stieglitz died peacefully on July 13, 1946 at the age of eighty-two. O'Keeffe was then fifty-nine. A small and quiet funeral service was held after O'Keeffe searched diligently for a pine coffin. There was no music nor spoken statements, as Stieglitz had requested. One could only recall the hours of silence Stieglitz had posted in his galleries and the religious spirit he fostered there. Georgia took Stieglitz's ashes to Lake George and buried them ceremoniously near the lake. Within a few months of Stieglitz's death, Marin had a heart attack and Arthur Dove died. O'Keeffe returned to Abiquiu in the fall of 1946 for spiritual sustenance.

With the death of Stieglitz an era was thus ended, not only for O'Keeffe but also for the art world. Stieglitz's daily battle for the Early American moderns' paintings, for photography, for the freedom of individual intuitive artistic expression, and for his continuing support of O'Keeffe owed much to Stieglitz and to the world she found in New York, particularly in the teens and twenties. O'Keeffe and Stieglitz inspired each other with their invincible spirits and continuous striving for creative excellence. It is this milieu of the avant-garde thinking of the first half of the century, and of persons surrounding O'Keeffe, such as Stieglitz and his circle, that greatly influenced O'Keeffe in the establishment of her own "ism." Within this supportive atmosphere her strength and creativity bloomed. With such a foundation, she was able to continually follow her own instincts and vision.

Notes

[1] Frederick Allen, *Since Yesterday: The Nineteen Thirties in America* (New York: Harper and Brothers Publishers, 1940), p. 55.

[2]*Ibid.,* pp. 158–159.

[3]Georgia O'Keeffe, Undated letter to Henry McBride, Henry McBride Papers, Archives of American Art.

[4]Haskell, *Arthur Dove,* p. 69.

[5]George L. K. Morris, "Art Chronicle: Some Personal Letters to American Artists Recently Exhibiting in New York," *Partisan Review,* March 1938.

[6]Herbert Seligmann, "Georgia O'Keeffe, American," *Manuscripts,* March 1923, p. 10.

[7]Georgia O'Keeffe, *Georgia O'Keeffe* (New York: Viking Press, 1976), no p.

[8]Doris Bry, "Georgia O'Keeffe," *Journal of the American Association of University Women* 34 (January 1952): 79.

[9]Letter from the Whitney Museum to D. Cogswell, Mt. Holyoke College, 1957, Whitney Museum files.

[10]Edith Evan Asbury, "Silent Desert Still Charms Georgia O'Keeffe, Near 81," *New York Times,* 1970, (n.d.) Whitney Museum Files.

[11]Lloyd Goodrich, Doris Bry, *Georgia O'Keeffe.* New York: Whitney Museum of American Art, 1970, p. 24.

[12]Georgia O'Keeffe, Letter to Jean Toomer, January 18, 1934, Nashville: Fisk University Library.

[13]Laurie Lisle, *Portrait of an Artist: A Biography of Georgia O'Keeffe* (New York: Seaview Books, 1980), p. 200.

[14]Georgia O'Keeffe to Dorothy Brett, n.d., Beinecke Library.

[15]Georgia O'Keeffe in *Georgia O'Keeffe: A Portrait by Alfred Stieglitz* (New York: Metropolitan Museum of Art, 1978), Introduction.

[16]Georgia O'Keeffe, From eight letters from O'Keeffe to Stieglitz, July 29 to September 30, 1937, *Exhibition Catalogue,* An American Place, 1937–38.

[17]Daniel Catton Rich, *Georgia O'Keeffe* (Chicago: Art Institute of Chicago, 1943).

[18]Grace Glueck, "It's Just What's in My Head," *New York Times,* October 18, 1970.

[19]Eleanor Jewett, "O'Keeffe Show Unexcelled in Beauty, Color," *Chicago Tribune,* January 31, 1943.

[20]Laurie Lisle, *Georgia O'Keeffe,* p. 261.

[21]Georgia O'Keeffe, Letter to Henry McBride, McBride Collection, Archives of American Art, Smithsonian Institution.

[22]Georgia O'Keeffe, Undated letters to Henry McBride, McBride Papers, Archives of American Art.

[23]Henry McBride, "O'Keeffe at the Museum," *New York Sun,* May 18, 1946.

Chapter Four

After the War, After Stieglitz—1947 to the Present

After Stieglitz's death, O'Keeffe, as sole inheritor and executor of his entire estate, was faced with the task of distributing and cataloguing his collection of art works including hundreds of photographs and approximately fifty thousand letters. With the help of a diligent young secretary, Doris Bry, O'Keeffe finally completed the task by 1949. The bulk of the collection went to the New York Metropolitan Museum and to the Art Institute of Chicago, and an archives was set up at the Beinecke Rare Book and Manuscript Library at Yale University for Stieglitz's letters and papers. Smaller components of the collection were given to other institutions such as Fisk University in Nashville, Tennessee. O'Keeffe also organized two exhibitions of his collections—at the Museum of Modern Art in 1947 and the Art Institute of Chicago in 1948. The settling of Stieglitz's estate was finally completed and O'Keeffe left for Abiquiu in the spring of 1949, very pleased she had just been elected to the National Institute of Arts and Letters, of which only ten percent of those elected were women. She did attempt to keep An American Place going, but found she could not replace Stieglitz. In 1950 she exhibited some of her own new paintings there, which marked the final exhibition. The opening of her show was a sad occasion for members of the Stieglitz circle and those who had known and worked with both Stieglitz and O'Keeffe.

Stieglitz's death and O'Keeffe's move to New Mexico on a full-time basis greatly changed her world. The milieu in which she lived and worked became much narrower and quieter. The stimulus of the New York intellectual and artistic world and the specific influences of Stieglitz, members of his circle, and other associates had been very important for O'Keeffe in her earlier years. Her work had budded, blossomed, and was now in its full maturity. At sixty-one O'Keeffe had those years of experiencing New York and tasting New Mexico behind her as a firm foundation upon which to wend her own way. She was more than ready to return to the land, to the quietness of a more rural existence. Her paintings came to reflect her less-complicated life in the simplified flattened forms that began to appear in works such as the "Patio" paintings. The New Mexican terrain, or what O'Keeffe collected in that terrain, became predominant subject matter.

As the forties ended and gave way to the silent fifties, O'Keeffe looked for someone to take over the business aspects of arranging exhibitions and selling her work which Stieglitz had always done, thereby protecting her from the frequent harshness of the commercial end of the art world. She finally reached an agreement with Edith Halpert, a well-known dealer of Russian descent, who fostered modern American artists at her Downtown Gallery which she had begun in 1926 in Greenwich Village. Stieglitz had actually loaned some of his artists' works to her for group shows in the thirties. Doing well, Halpert had moved to East Fifty-first Street near Fifth Avenue. Halpert had represented artists such as Charles Sheeler, Max Weber, and Ben Shahn and had recently taken on the works of Dove, Demuth, and Marin. O'Keeffe was again the only woman represented, which was to her liking. O'Keeffe's first show there in 1952 received little acclaim. O'Keeffe did not seem concerned and seemed content to return to her New Mexico retreat.

Although O'Keeffe was not as productive in the late forties and during the fifties as she once had been, it is important to view her work in comparison to what was going on in the avant-garde art world of New York at that time to realize how strongly O'Keeffe maintained the identity of herself as a person, and of her work. Losing the support of Stieglitz and a bygone world, she could easily have been influenced or tempted by the experiments of the avant-garde. She could have returned to the more academic painting of her early training, or she could have given up painting altogether as she had done from 1908 to 1912. But O'Keeffe was O'Keeffe and intended to remain that way.

What, then, was happening in New York that O'Keeffe, although she was in New Mexico much of the time, saw emerging in the wider world?

During the war, when the Nazis had occupied France, a number of artists from the School of Paris, such as painters Léger, Chagall, Dali, and sculptor Jacques Lipschitz, had come to New York. With such emigration the School of Paris lost momentum and Paris was no longer the alluring art center that had attracted so many American artists in the earlier part of the century. Focus began to switch to America. Although the dominant trend in American art in the thirties had been social realism, a few artists, as mentioned earlier, continued to experiment with abstraction. Peggy Guggenheim, at her Art of This Century Gallery in New York, began to show some of those European and American artists. Between 1943 and 1946 artists such as Jackson Pollock, Mark Rothko, Clyfford Still, Hans Hofmann, and Robert Motherwell had their first solo shows and the seeds of abstract expressionism and the New York School were sown. After the W.P.A. project declined, many of these artists found themselves living in New York in near-poverty but believing greatly in the expressive and reductive qualities of abstraction. The postwar years brought a sense of personal crisis to a new generation with existentialist concerns. (Works such as Camus' *The Stranger* had already been out for several years, having been published in 1942.) Robert Motherwell wrote of these young artists' concerns, "The need is for felt experience—intense, immediate, direct, subtle, unified, warm, vivid, rhythmic."[1] Thus, the very act of painting with large, slashing backstrokes on heroic large-size canvases became important and the term "action painting" was coined in 1951 by critic Harold Rosenberg. The automatism of surrealism appealed to many of these artists, as the role of chance, risk, and large gestures became inherent in the painting act. Self-definition and confrontation with the existential world was felt to be possible through the painting process. The need for a shared community was felt by these artists as was the case for Stieglitz's artists. There was no Stieglitz as catalyst, but many of these artists met frequently in the evenings at The Club, located at 35 East Eighth Street, and Hans Hofmann had established his well-known school on West Eighth Street. These painters sought a new statement of an American mythology and search for identity that had begun with the American scene painters. While Thomas Hart Benton, the great American scene advocate and also Jackson Pollock's teacher, painted realistic scenes of an American nature and landscape, and while O'Keeffe painted intuitive and lyrical abstractions of nature, Pollock identified himself with nature saying "I am nature."[2] Important for Pollock was to be in his painting as a part of nature; and at the same time reflect an emptiness in nature. Benton, O'Keeffe, and Pollock, although very different, all reflect aspects of a romantic imagination where nature, instinct, and the unconscious are directly or indirectly involved in the process of making the paintings. By 1947 there was little recognizable subject matter in Pollock's work and his drip paintings had become symbols of a new American avant-garde.

Although O'Keeffe never did abstract expressionism per se, her work from the 1950's onward was of a larger and larger scale as were the abstract expressionists'. She portrayed, in her own way, the vastness and sense of infinity that a number of New York School artists sought. She also flattened her forms, as advocated by artists such as Gottlieb, Rothko, and Newman who wrote, "We favor the simple expression of the complex thought. We are for the large shape because it has the unequivocal. We wish to reassert the picture plane. We are for flat forms because they destroy illusion and reveal truth."[3] O'Keeffe never espoused any program or theory as seen in the manifesto-like letter by Gottlieb, Rothko, and Newman to the *New York Times* that appeared in art critic Edward Alden Jewell's column as early as June 13, 1943. But the sense of vastness in a painting such as O'Keeffe's *From the Plains II,* 1954 contains some of the same sensibilities of a painting such as Barnett Newman's *Vir Heroicus Sublimis,* 1950–51 or Rothko's *No. 22, 1950,* 1950.

In 1958 O'Keeffe did exhibit fifty-three small watercolors, done with a very rapid but lyrical gesture, in 1916 and 1917 at the Downtown Gallery. The spontaneous washes of these watercolors were in many ways similar to the larger gestural works of Pollock and de Kooning. O'Keeffe's work, though, was viewed more for its historical content and was basically overshadowed by the very large-scale abstract expressionist work. Following this show O'Keeffe withdrew even more from the art scene.

O'Keeffe's work is perhaps best seen in terms of content in relationship to some of the concerns of the New York School as being part of a continuing concern for American artists to capture the essence of the American landscape and its infinite extensions, which has slowly evolved through the history of American art, reaching an extreme point of abstraction with the abstract expressionists.

Although less productive in the fifties as a painter, O'Keeffe, for the first time, did some extensive traveling. In 1953 she traveled to Europe for the first time, visiting France and Spain. At the Louvre, O'Keeffe was attracted to the Fra Angelicos and the Buddhist sculptures, and at the Prado she was drawn to the Goyas, particularly the lighting. She loved the Spanish bullfights and returned to Spain the next year for three months. She did not want to return to France and did not even want to meet Picasso.

In the spring of 1956 she journeyed to Peru for three months, and traveled through the high Andes country, attracted by the wilderness of the terrain. One of the few paintings that remain or are known about from her travels, is of the Andes, *Misti-A Memory* done in 1957.

The year 1959 found O'Keeffe at age seventy-one on a three-and-one-half-month trip around the world, including a seven-week stay in India. She looked forward in particular to the Orient and visited Tokyo, Hong Kong, and Taiwan among other places in the Far East. O'Keeffe loved, as she had as a student of Arthur Dow, seeing the Japanese prints, being drawn to the peaceful harmony and fine craftsmanship of them. She said of her trip to Japan, "Japan did not seem new to me. It was as if I'd known it before. The first time I saw Fuji, it was white, over water. It was glorious."[4] It is interesting that O'Keeffe found aspects of her very own Abiquiu landscape to be similar to some of the Japanese prints. She has remarked, "Sometimes the light hits the mountains from behind and front at the same time, and it gives them the look of Japanese prints, you know, distances in layers."[5]

The area O'Keeffe seemed to like least was the city of Rome, finding the elaborate ornamentation and oversized scale of the Baroque and Christian art to be "vulgar." As she strongly stated, "The cherubs on the wall of the Vatican—dreadful. Those big naked things. Bigger than a man. Everything in Rome was like that to me—extraordinarily vulgar."[6] It is not surprising that when O'Keeffe had the opportunity to travel again in 1960 she returned to Japan and did not go to Europe. Following her trip around the world, O'Keeffe began her very beautiful "sky-above-the-clouds" paintings. Her airplane trips also inspired her "river" paintings, such as *It was Yellow and Pink, III,* 1960, where ribbons of vibrant yellow flow through the pink landscape. Some of these paintings contain the blues of a waterway, while in others, O'Keeffe's imagination has transformed the shapes into bold color areas.

O'Keeffe's air travel coincided with the world's entry into the Space Age. In 1957 Russia launched the first earth satellites, Sputnik I and II. In 1958 the United States launched the first moon rocket, which although it failed to reach the moon, traveled seventy-nine thousand miles from earth. The year 1959 saw the Russian Lunik actually reach the moon.

On earth, in the United States, there were more reactionary events that must have disturbed O'Keeffe. In 1957 the desegregation crisis in Little Rock, Arkansas, became so acute that President Eisenhower had to send in paratroopers to forestall violence. In 1959 the U.S. Postmaster General Summerfield banned D. H. Lawrence's *Lady Chatterley's Lover* (which had favorably impressed O'Keeffe on its publication) from the mails on grounds of obscenity. (The ruling was reversed in 1960 by the Circuit Court of Appeals.) Thus, by 1960 O'Keeffe's world had greatly widened again as she used her newfound perceptions and perspectives in her work. For a woman in her seventies, born in the horse-and-buggy era, her sense of adventure and ability to transform what she saw to artistic expression was extraordinary. Much of her new work, based on her flying experiences, was shown in 1960 in a retrospective exhibition organized by Daniel Catton Rich at the Worcester Art Museum in Worcester, Massachusetts, where Rich had become director. In the catalogue, Rich referred to the great consistency of O'Keeffe's vision. "Her work shows a complete organic youth. There have been no sudden reversals, no abrupt shifts of style. It has always had the same lucidity, the same elegance, the same renunciations and the same inner richness, regardless of theme or period."[7]

Following her Worcester show, O'Keeffe exhibited for the last time at the Downtown

Gallery in the spring of 1961. O'Keeffe and Halpert had had mounting tensions growing between them. O'Keeffe finally broke with Halpert in 1963. She took on Doris Bry, who had helped settle Stieglitz's estate, as her agent.

Continuing her interest in rivers, O'Keeffe took a number of trips down the sometimes tumultuous Colorado River, exhilarated by the sights and sounds, shapes and colors of the river and its banks. Among those with her on the first trip were Eliot Porter, some of whose work Stieglitz had collected, and Tish Frank, a granddaughter of Mabel Dodge Luhan. Some of the old ties to O'Keeffe's world before Stieglitz's death were thus renewed.

While O'Keeffe painted her dream-like rivers and images of simplified roads, and her flattened patio in the sixties, the art world at large was rebelling against the abstract expressionists in the forms of the pop artists, op artists, minimalists and color field painters. Pop art forms were stimulated by an interest in mass media and pop culture. Radios blared pop tunes such as "Itsy Bitsy Teeny Weeny Yellow Polka Dot Bikini" and "Let's do the Twist," and by 1960 there were 85 million television sets in the United States as compared to 105 million in Great Britain, two million in West Germany, and 1.5 million in France. Pop artists took the banal themes and objects of everyday life and elevated them to the realm of art through parody and often irreverence. Andy Warhol's soup cans and Roy Lichtenstein's blown-up comic strip frames were indeed different from O'Keeffe's paintings of objects in the everyday world. O'Keeffe's feathers, flowers, shells, and bones became even more poetic in the face of the cold, commercial images of the pop artists.

Although O'Keeffe did not do the bold color field paintings of a Morris Louis or Kenneth Noland where color became the subjects of the painting, some painters such as Kenneth Noland and Paul Feeley have admitted that O'Keeffe has been a strong influence on their work.[8] O'Keeffe's concern for color, frontality, openness, and symmetrical sensitivity was admired by these artists. In particular, Feeley used a watercolor technique he had picked up from O'Keeffe whereby each colored area was separated from the next by a thin margin of unpainted surface. As Noland worked on his concentric circles of color, he took much interest in O'Keeffe's centrifugally designed flower images in a piece such as *At the Rodeo*, 1929, an enlargement of a Mexican Indian ornament. One can also find great similarity between some of the ovoid shapes and saturated colors of Ellsworth Kelly's early work and the openings in O'Keeffe's pelvis paintings, i.e., *Pelvis Series, Red with Yellow*, 1945. O'Keeffe, in return, admired Kelly's pure colors and precise forms. In these instances O'Keeffe became the influence rather than the influenced.

The minimalist painters and sculptors searched for reductive essential forms and rejected any type of pictorial illusionism. Many of the works tended to be monochromatic, and oriented toward pure geometric shapes, such as the cube or square, and were sometimes referred to as primary structures. Donald Judd's piece of eight stainless forty-eight-inch cubes, 1968 or Frank Stella's shaped canvas, *Ileana Sonnabend* of 1963 illustrated this new sensibility.

O'Keeffe's work in the sixties, particularly the patio paintings, has some definite affinity with the minimalists. The works tend to be large and simple in format, with few outlines, with an emphasis on large, flat, reductive colored areas. In *Patio with Red Door*, forty-eight by eighty-four inches, 1960 O'Keeffe has taken the simple shapes of the door and stepping stones and reduces them to their essence. She has set the shapes in a floating,

expansive field that evokes a feeling of infiniteness. O'Keeffe's exquisite color gradations, where the graded reds and pinks of the door are picked up further in the row of
rectangles and the landscape strip at the top, add a special refinement to the piece.
O'Keeffe's work, however, differs from the minimalists in that much of her work from
the sixties evokes a mystical sense, as her forms balance themselves in a boundless field,
headed toward infinity.

Perhaps the most monumental work done during the sixties was the *"Sky Above the
Cloud"* series. The culmination of this series, *Sky Above Clouds IV*, 1965, an eight by
twenty-four foot mural, is the largest work O'Keeffe has ever done. There is a sense of
fading away in these cloud works and a lovely sense of rhythm that carries the viewer
from one shape to another. There is also an interesting ambiguity in some of these sky
works with the introduction of a horizon line that suggests that the blue sky might be
water. The viewer becomes enveloped in the primal forces of air and/or water.

O'Keeffe's concern with the sky and outer spaces in the sixties is a way of confronting
the dawning Space Age in a reassuring, almost classical manner. For O'Keeffe, achievements in outer space were a way of living out man's dreams, an important achievement.
When asked in 1960 her feeling about man orbiting the earth for the first time, she
replied, "Flying around the world so fast to me seems a dream, even if I know it is
probably a reality. I was three and one half months flying around the world. . . . To do it
in a day seems a dream."[9]

O'Keeffe continued her air trips through the late sixties. She traveled to Greece,
Egypt, and the Near East in 1963, to England and Austria in 1966, and to Vienna again in
1969 to see the Lipizzan horses a second time.

In 1966 she had another retrospective exhibition at the Amon Carter Museum. With
ninety-six works, the show received much acclaim. In particular, her large-scale cloud
piece was hailed as monumental by many. With this show O'Keeffe was back in the
public eye again, with a variety of articles being written about her. She received several
more awards, as well, and in 1963 she was elected to the American Academy of Arts and
Letters, where she was one of five women. In 1966 she was elected to the American
Academy of Arts and Sciences.

O'Keeffe's last major retrospective was held at the Whitney Museum of American Art
under the direction of Lloyd Goodrich. The show traveled to Chicago and San Francisco.
Originally planned for 1969, it finally opened in October of 1970 because O'Keeffe
insisted on having the largest floor in the museum for her show. The large cloud painting
could not be taken upstairs, so it hung on the first floor. And it stayed in Chicago,
because it would not fit through any door of the San Francisco museum. The show set
new attendance records for exhibitions of American painters.

By the 1970's the definition of art in America had greatly expanded. Art was no longer
a tangible object to be found in a museum. This decade was a time of pluralism in the
huge variety of experiments in the visual arts and in the breaking of boundaries between
traditional art forms. There was photo-realist art, land art, performance art, body art,
process art, conceptual art, video art, and so forth. Representative of the change in the
notion of what art was, were pieces such as: Christo's *Running Fence*, 1976, a twenty-
four-and-a-half mile, eighteen foot high translucent fabric fence erected in northern
California by students and engineers after considerable political and sociological negotia-
tions with citizens and officials in the countryside where the fence was erected; or a Vito

Acconci piece where he treated his body as a "place" by creating a sore on his arm from continuous rubbing and having it photographed periodically over the period of an hour. As the seventies progressed and disillusionment following Watergate set in, many artists turned to more narcissistic, biographical types of statements. The "I/Me Generation" was in play. (In contrast, the late sixties performance and conceptual art pieces were often more violent, public events; reflective, to some extent, of the seemingly neverending Vietnam War.)

Seen against the background of these radical changes in the very nature of art, O'Keeffe's work, in its continuing individual consistency and strength of image and technique, seems all the more remarkable. During the early seventies O'Keeffe did a series of paintings of black rocks that she had collected near her house. For her they had become a "symbol" of "the wideness and wonder of the sky and of the world. They have lain there for a long time with the sun and the wind and the blowing sand making them into something that is precious to the eye and hand—to find with excitement, to treasure and to love."[10] The rocks in paintings such as *Black Rock With Blue III,* 1970 or *Black Rock With Blue Sky and White Clouds,* 1972, stand like Zen statues, at one with their world, representing a solidity and magical calmness.

Due to failing eyesight, a tragic loss to any artist, during the seventies O'Keeffe was not able to work as prodigiously as she had in the sixties. In 1971, at the age of eighty-four, O'Keeffe faced the terrible fact that her vision was blurred. After visiting many eye specialists she found she had lost her central vision and retained only her peripheral sight, a common occurrence in old age. She found she needed more help around the house. Fate answered in the arrival of a young potter, Juan Hamilton, at her door one fall day in 1972. He asked if she had any odd jobs for him to do. Brought up under Hispanic influence until the age of fifteen, Hamilton, recently divorced, had come to work at the nearby Presbyterian Conference Center under the guidance of Jim Hall, a friend of Hamilton's parents. Checking on Hamilton's credentials, O'Keeffe hired him (somewhat impulsively, since she had turned away many young men and women with similar requests) to do odd jobs. Somehow drawn to Hamilton's creative skills, O'Keeffe soon hired him on a full-time basis. Hamilton taught her how to make hand-built clay pots and O'Keeffe was excited by the tactile qualities of the clay that compensated for her failing eyesight. O'Keeffe wrote of her experience with the clay,

> *The pots that he made were beautiful shapes—very smooth. . . . I rolled the clay and coiled it—rolled it and coiled it. I tried to smooth it and I made very bad pots. He said to me, 'Keep on, keep on—you have to work at it—the clay has a mind of its own! . . . I finally have several pots that aren't bad, but I can't yet make the clay speak—so I must keep on.'"[11]*

It is interesting to note that a number of Hamilton's and O'Keeffe's pots look somewhat like O'Keeffe's rock paintings.

O'Keeffe never felt completely comfortable with ceramics and in 1976 was inspired to paint again after a trip to Washington, D.C. with Hamilton, concerning some of Stieglitz's uncatalogued photographs. The resulting series, *A Day With Juan* have less subtle color gradations but do not lack O'Keeffe's spirit. In 1977 she painted a series of watercolors based on a trip to a friend's farm in New Jersey. O'Keeffe has continued to courageously paint, asking her housekeeper to read paint labels which she would memorize on her way back to her studio.

O'Keeffe was also persuaded by Hamilton and Viking Press to write a book. The book, published in 1976, a large luxurious edition of fine color plates and accompanying text by O'Keeffe, contained works never before shown publicly. It was itself a work of art.

O'Keeffe also wrote the Introduction to a book of Stieglitz's photographs of her which was published in 1978 in conjunction with an exhibit of the photographs at the Metropolitan Museum in New York. In that Introduction one sees O'Keeffe's continued belief in the power of Stieglitz's work, as well as further insight into her relationship with Stieglitz.

> . . . his power to destroy was as destructive as his power to build—the extremes went together. I have experienced both and survived, but I think I only crossed him when I had to—to survive.
>
> There was a constant grinding like the ocean. It was as if something hot, dark and destructive was hitched to the highest, brightest star.
>
> For me he was much more wonderful in his work than as a human being. I could see his strengths and weaknesses. I put up with what seemed clear and bright and wonderful.[12]

The presence of Juan Hamilton has added much to O'Keeffe's world in recent years. She has made more public appearances, although she has turned down many interview requests. Perhaps the most poignant public appearance was in a documentary film by Perry Miller Adato of National Educational Television, aired on O'Keeffe's ninetieth birthday in 1977. Both O'Keeffe and Hamilton have enjoyed each other's creative abilities and influences and have been good companions for each other in times of need. There has been much speculation about their relationship—that they are married, that they are lovers, that he is a surrogate son, that their relationship is based solely on mutual artistic interests. Both have denied that they are married.[13] Hamilton owns an adobe cottage with a skylit studio on top, about three miles away from O'Keeffe, and works for O'Keeffe. Both continue to work productively on their own artwork.

O'Keeffe has rewritten her will to include Hamilton, who has been named executor instead of Doris Bry.[14] In 1977 O'Keeffe dismissed Bry as her agent and sued successfully to get her photographs and paintings from Bry. Bry countersued O'Keeffe, claiming she was more than an agent and should be entitled to more than a twenty-five percent agent's fee. She also sued Hamilton, claiming "malicious interference," for 13 million dollars. Hamilton countersued for Bry's damaging his name.

The exact nature of O'Keeffe's and Hamilton's relationship is perhaps not as important as the fact that O'Keeffe has been able to continue to work well into her nineties, continuing to produce work of excellence with the encouragement and assistance of Hamilton. Indeed at ninety-four, inspired and assisted by Hamilton, O'Keeffe completed a large-scale sculpture, a medium she abandoned in 1917. The piece, *Abstraction,* an eleven foot spiral of painted cast aluminum, appeared in a sculpture show "Twenty American Artists" at the San Francisco Museum of Modern Art during the summer of 1982. The spiral form is reminiscent of some of O'Keeffe's paintings such as her shell pieces, i.e., *Shell I,* 1928 or *At the Rodeo,* 1929. This spiral, in its looming black three-dimensionality, appears more dramatic and muscular than O'Keeffe's two-dimensional curvilinear forms. The piece was the first public exhibition of a sculpture by O'Keeffe.

O'Keeffe at ninety-four traveled to see the show, experiencing many of the works with her hands because of her poor eyesight.

Thus age has not daunted O'Keeffe's creative drive and spirit. Her New Mexican milieu has continued to be a stimulus to her, although she sometimes appears remote to the approximately one hundred fifty towns-people of Abiquiu. The town of Abiquiu is still steeped with Indian traditions. The people still heartily celebrate the birth of two saints, Santa Rosa and Santa Tomas, holidays which are more important than Christmas. O'Keeffe takes pride in the fact that her house is almost as old as the town itself.

The allure of New Mexico's light and land has continued to attract artists to Taos and Santa Fe. Today there is much more of a commercial aspect to the area than when O'Keeffe first arrived there. The old Mabel Dodge Luhan place became the headquarters for Dennis Hopper and his desert riders in 1973, as a pop and tourist culture began to make its presence felt.

In general there are a variety of approaches to art by the numerous artists who now live in the Santa Fe area. In the older art centers there is an interest in a regional experience, dealing with a primitive and ritualistic iconography that reflects various Southwest Indian cultures. There are those who are concerned specifically with landscape motifs, inspired by the color and space of the New Mexican terrain; and there are those who carry on the mainstream concerns of the avant-garde New York and Los Angeles art worlds, although there is relatively little conceptual art done. Artists now also center around Albuquerque and Roswell, and the University of New Mexico art department attracts a large number of students. Besides O'Keeffe, two artists, Andrew Dasburg and Raymond Jonson, have been the most well-known artists in New Mexico. Jonson, in his nineties, has been known for his pioneering use of an airbrush to achieve atmospheric effects. Dasburg, whose work hung beside Duchamp's *Nude Descending the Staircase* in the Armory Show in 1913, had returned to the cubism of his early years in a series of rhythmic landscapes, done in the years before his death in 1979. Yet Dasburg and Jonson received little attention outside New Mexico for much of the century. O'Keeffe was the New Mexican artist known outside the state. Today there appears to be a growing national interest in a Southwestern art, perhaps due in part to the work of O'Keeffe. There appears to be a new regional flowering that could not have been done on either coast. Myths of the Old West, and images of the new West have emerged in the work of artists such as John Fincher, Ken Saville, and John Wenger.

O'Keeffe is not active in the New Mexican art scene, but she has been inspired by many of the same aspects of the New Mexican land and culture that have inspired some of the young emerging artists. Although there is a growing commercialism in the area, one must ultimately come to grips with the spirit of the place. As one critic once wrote, ". . . if you stay in New Mexico, sooner or later you have to come to terms with the earth, the sky, the mountains and the pervasive spirit of the place. To be sure, symbols of pop culture and American progressivism are pushing up against the traditional horizon— . . . but there aren't any wild west shows here, and the adobe culture of the Southwest still hugs the earth."[15]

In 1929 O'Keeffe had stated with awe and wonder, "No one told me it was like this."[16] Today the magic of her milieu still remains for her. She still climbs the ladder to her roof and soaks in the view of the majestic valley around her. The thought of losing her beautiful countryside to death is difficult for her. "When I think of death, I only regret that I will not be able to see this beautiful country anymore, unless the Indians are right and my spirit will walk here after I'm gone."[17]

Thus O'Keeffe continues to live and work with the same strength of purpose she possessed as a young girl, when she first decided to become an artist. Her drive, her talent, and her hard work, coupled with the support and influence of people and places in her milieu, have through the years brought O'Keeffe to where she is today. Without the continuing support and encouragement she received, particularly in her early years, and particularly from Alfred Stieglitz and his contemporaries, O'Keeffe might have remained a little-known artist in Texas. The various worlds in which O'Keeffe has lived and traveled, providing artistic and intellectual stimulus and inspiration, have indeed influenced O'Keeffe's development. As Dore Ashton wrote, ". . . the history of art and literature is filled with statements . . . affirming the artist's sense of being shaped by the epoch in which he performs his art. The 'time' of an artist makes itself felt, even if only as tyranny against which the artist reacts."[18] And through her work O'Keeffe has given back to the world statements of the power of time and place integrated with the power of her genius and nerve. As she herself stated, "If my painting is what I have to give back to the world for what the world gives to me, I may say that these paintings are what I have to give at present . . . what I have been able to put into form seems infinitesimal compared with the variety of experience."[19]

Notes

[1]Brown, Hunter, Jacobus, *American Art,* p. 477.

[2]Brian O'Doherty, *American Masters, The Voice and The Myth of Art* (New York: E. P. Dutton, 1982), p. 105.

[3]Ellen Johnson, ed., *American Artists on Art From 1940 to 1980* (New York: Harper & Row, Icon edit., 1982), p. 14.

[4]Mary Lynn Kotz, "Georgia O'Keeffe at 90," *ARTnews,* December 1977, p. 38

[5]Beth Coffelt, "A Visit with Georgia O'Keeffe," *San Francisco Sunday Examiner and Chronicle,* April 11, 1971, p. 20.

[6]Charlotte Willard, "Georgia O'Keeffe," *Art in America,* October 1963, p. 94.

[7]Daniel Catton Rich, "Georgia O'Keeffe, Forty Years of Her Art," Catalogue, Worcester Art Museum, October, 1960.

[8]E. C. Goosen, "O'Keeffe," *Vogue,* March 1, 1967, p. 224.

[9]Katherine Kuh, *The Artist's Voice* (New York: Harper & Row, 1962), p. 202.

[10]Georgia O'Keeffe, *Georgia O'Keeffe* (New York: Viking Press, 1976), no p.

[11]*Ibid.*

[12]Georgia O'Keeffe, *Georgia O'Keeffe, A Portrait by Alfred Stieglitz* (New York: Metropolitan Museum of Art, 1978), Introduction.

[13]Laurie Lisle, *Portrait of an Artist,* p. 324.

[14]*Ibid.*

[15]Duncan Pollock, "An Earthbound Iconography," *Art in America,* July–August 1943, p. 99.

[16]*Ibid.*

[17]Henry Seldis, "Georgia O'Keeffe at 78: Tough Minded Romantic," *Los Angeles Times West Magazine,* January 22, 1967.

[18]Dore Ashton, *A Reading of Modern Art,* p. 152.

[19]Doris Bry, "Georgia O'Keeffe," *Journal of the American Association of University Women* 34 (January 1952): 79.

II. THE CRITICS AND THEIR BACKGROUND

Throughout her work there is a dual conception of nature: a nature as the painter herself; and nature as an unfailing companion with whom she converses in terms of wonderful precision, intimacy, and shades of meaning. In subject matter she turns her back on humanity, but there is love in her work, courage, strength, devotion. . . . Hers is a world of exceptional intensity: bones and flowers, hills and the city, sometimes abstract and vigorous, sometimes warm and fugitive. She created this world; it was not there before; and there is nothing like it anywhere.

James Thrall Soby, *The Saturday Review,* July 6, 1946.

I think I'd rather let the painting work for itself than help it with the word.

Georgia O'Keeffe, "Exhibition of Contemporary American Painting and Sculpture," University of Illinois, 1955.

"What an artist does with his influences, how well he absorbs, distills and translates them into the context of his own work, tells his story."[1] As O'Keeffe has told her "story" through the years with her paintings, the critics have responded to that story in a variety of ways. O'Keeffe has received good reviews, bad reviews, and reviews with extreme interpretations of her work. Some of the criticism, particularly that pertaining to what has been called sexual imagery in her work, O'Keeffe has vehemently denied, saying the critics are only talking about themselves. Because of some of the extreme statements about her work, O'Keeffe has often withdrawn from the public eye. Some talk about her as a desert recluse, but O'Keeffe has always been in touch with the wider world around her. Because some of the critics' writings have led to diverse interpretations of O'Keeffe's work it is important to better understand the nature of those writings, in order to penetrate the critical mythology that surrounds much of O'Keeffe's work, particularly in relation to "the feminine experience" and her work.

Upon reading the criticism written about O'Keeffe's work from 1916 to the present, it appears that the criticism falls into three major topical areas: 1) the feminine experience, 2) the questions of symbolism and translation of O'Keeffe's art, and 3) the relationship of nature to O'Keeffe's work. Because of the nature of O'Keeffe's paintings, there is some overlapping of topical areas within the critical writings. The following pages are written with the intent of delineating each topical area as clearly as possible and establishing the basic historical and/or philosophical viewpoint(s) related to each area in order to more clearly understand the critics' writings, and thereby better understand O'Keeffe and her work, and their relationship to the public at various points during her career. The critics' opinions cited here are, in general, representative of the body of critical literature dealing with a particular topic in relation to O'Keeffe's work.

Notes

[1]Alexandra Johnson, "An Influence On Oneself," *Christian Science Monitor,* November 15, 1977, p. 24.

Chapter Five
The Feminine Experience

"Finally a woman on paper!"[1] Such were the words uttered by Alfred Stieglitz at his gallery 291, upon first seeing some of O'Keeffe's drawings, which were secretly brought to him in 1916 by O'Keeffe's friend, Anita Pollitzer. As previously indicated, O'Keeffe had her first show at 291 in 1917 and thereafter continued to paint and exhibit regularly. These words of Stieglitz marked the beginning of a critical mythology concerning the feminine experience that began to surround O'Keeffe's work, particularly in the twenties and thirties, through the writings of her critics. Elizabeth McCausland, art editor of the *Springfield Republic,* retrospectively described O'Keeffe as becoming "enshrined as goddess of the female."[2]

To better understand the climate in which the critics dealt with O'Keeffe's feminine imagery, it is necessary to first mention the position of American women in general, prior to, and simultaneous to the critics' writing. Early steps toward reform in women's rights officially began with the three-day Seneca Falls Convention in 1848. Held in Seneca Falls, New York, the convention was for the purpose of discussing the social, civil, and religious rights of women. The early women's rights movement showed little interest in getting the vote. Rather, interest was in gaining control in property holdings, earnings, divorce procedures, opportunity for education and employment, and in changing the concept of female inferiority, inherent in established religion. With the coming of the twentieth century and growth in technology and urbanization in America, women became more involved in America's labor force as factory workers, office workers, and in various social services. The legal position of women in terms of property rights, earnings of married women, and so forth, varied from state to state with the greatest area of backwardness existing in the South due to the slow recovery from the Civil War. With the increasing number of women workers, the push for women's suffrage grew. The struggle for suffrage had its peaks and valleys in the fifty-three years that passed from the time of the first state suffrage referendum held in Kansas in 1867, to the final ratification of the Nineteenth Amendment in 1920. Thus, the early twentieth century was a time of great change concerning the status of women.

At the same time in this early part of the century Freud's ideas became prevalent. As a result there was increased thought and discussion concerning sexuality, the sub-conscious, and the role of women. Many of O'Keeffe's critics reflect this concern for sexuality and the role of women in their writing.

Further, one must examine the position of women artists prior to the period in which

O'Keeffe began to work to better understand O'Keeffe's and her critics' positions. A few to be considered in comparison are; Angelica Kaufmann (1741–1807), Elizabeth Vigée-Lebrun (1755–1842), Berthe Morisot (1841–1895), Mary Cassatt (1844–1926), Cecilia Beaux (1863–1942), and Marie Laurencin (1885–1956). Kaufmann and Lebrun were both daughters of painters and chiefly did portrait work for the patronage they received, as did most male painters of the time. Lebrun was a friend of Marie Antoinette, and Kaufmann centered her work in Rome and London. Kaufmann also painted religious and classical subjects. Paintings of the Madonna, Virgil, Achilles, and Paris were typical subject matter of the time. As Lebrun and Kaufmann, Beaux did not really blaze any new trails but painted in the accepted style of the time. She mainly painted portraits of various heroes of her time such as Theodore Roosevelt, Georges Clemenceau, and Lord Beatty. Both Cassatt and Morisot were from fairly wealthy families and both were influenced by the work of the French impressionists. Mary Cassatt's world was one of mothers and children, the prime subject matter for many of her paintings. Cassatt spent much of her time in Paris, although she was American, being drawn to the circle of the French impressionists, and influenced by her friend Edgar Degas. Using similar subject matter and expressing a similar femininity based in the world of women and children was the French, Berthe Morisot. Her paintings often portrayed the leisure world of teas and strolling through well-kept gardens, experienced by many of the middle-class women and children of the time. Morisot came under the influence of Manet, and she, like Cassatt, dealt with some of the problems of light and color that concerned the French impressionists. Another French painter of the early twentieth century whose fragile studies of young girls contrast with the healthy figures of Morisot and Cassatt was Marie Laurencin. Laurencin's studies of young girls suggested a feminine perspective of fragility and secretness. Upon graduating from school Laurencin was advised not to paint, but to learn to play the mandolin. It was only on attending the Académie Humbert, where she met Braque, that she continued to paint with his encouragement. Both Braque and Laurencin quickly left the Académie, both interested in pursuing the radical cubist experiments that Picasso had initiated. Subsequently she met Picasso and Apollinaire through Braque, and continued to meet with such artists regularly in the cafés of Montmartre.

Important to the success of each of these women was the financial and moral support each received from various sources, as well as a strong personality and determination to continue painting. All but one of these women were in secure financial situations, each coming from relatively affluent families. Only Vigée-Lebrun faced money problems during her childhood years. Each also had a mentor who provided artistic and spiritual stimulation.

In general, the number of recognized women artists in art history is relatively few. Indeed it has only been in the twentieth century that women have been admitted into life drawing classes where the model was nude. In the nineteenth century it was felt that greatness in art was something only men could pursue. The words of artist Vanburgh to his student Olive illustrate the equation of the artist with a strong masculinity. "I said it was impossible for a woman to become an artist—I mean a great artist. Have you ever thought what that term implies? . . . A gentleman—we artists are the friends of kings. . . . A man of iron will, indomitable, daring, and passions strong. . . . Last and greatest, a man who, feeling an artist should *be,* by nature."[3]

Those women who did become at all successful often had to fight harder than men for any type of recognition and sometimes took on a masculine mode of dress, as did Rosa Bonheur, who usually wore men's clothing.

O'Keeffe was thus born into a world where women artists received little or no recognition. How did women painters in America express themselves prior to the twentieth century? To better understand the relationship of O'Keeffe's work to other American women artists before and of her time, it is helpful to have an understanding of the general trends in American women artists' work in the eighteenth and nineteenth centuries.

In America in the late eighteenth century, the chief medium for women painters was miniature painting. In a catalogue for a 1965 exhibit of women artists in America from 1707 to 1964 at the Newark Museum, curator William Gerdts described the "preciousness of form, emphasis upon charm and delicacy, rather than upon power and strength,"[4] of miniature paintings as a typical expression of the time. Some women did still lifes and some concentrated on sculpture.

Toward the end of the nineteenth century more women began to do portraits and figurative painting, particularly domestic scenes and images of women and children. The work of these earlier women artists in general reflected a genteel, delicate, and somewhat sentimental sensibility. Most works did not evoke a sense of strength, monumentality, or power.

The word feminine, as ascribed to painters prior to the twentieth century and prior to O'Keeffe, usually referred to a daintiness, delicacy, or preciousness, and/or reflected the popular style of the time, or circle in which the women painters moved. There is little evidence to validly link the works of Lebrun, Kaufmann, Morisot, Cassatt, Laurencin, O'Keeffe, or even later Louise Nevelson, Helen Frankenthaler or Bridget Riley, to one meaning of feminine. As Linda Nochlin writes, "In every instance women artists and writers would seem to be closer to other artists and writers of their own period and outlook than they are to each other."[5] O'Keeffe is a first to follow her deepest instincts and cast off some of the influence of previous education and upbringing.

It is interesting to note that almost none of the women painters, including O'Keeffe in the history of art until recent years, have overtly dealt with the male or female body and its sexuality. Reflecting on this phenomena, Linda Nochlin, in speaking of the nineteenth century in particular, writes, "This is, of course, not the result of some calculated plot on the part of men, but merely a reflection in the realm of art of woman's lack of her own erotic territory on the map of nineteenth-century reality. Man is not only the subject of all erotic predicates, but the customer for all erotic products as well, and the customer is always right. Controlling both sex and art, he and his fantasies conditioned the world of erotic imagination as well."[6] In another essay Nochlin states that women artists did not deal with certain subjects, nor frequently achieve excellence, due to society's institutions and education. As indicated, women in general did not have access to nude models for drawing. "As late as 1893, 'lady' students were not admitted to life drawing at the official London Academy, and even when they were, after that date, the model had to be 'partially draped.'"[7]

Indeed, works such as the nude *Olympia* by the male Manet in 1863 evoked very hostile comments when first exhibited at the salon of 1865. "A Woman 'more or less naked and leering at the spectator with a conscious impudence . . . brutal vulgarity and coarseness . . . as surprising as it is disgusting. . . .'"[8] The expression of almost any type of overt or previously unexpressed sexuality in painting, has evoked somewhat controversial responses throughout history until recent years.

For O'Keeffe the position of women and women artists has appeared to be important to her at various points in her career, as one reads her various statements concerning her having to initially prove herself to "the boys"—some of the other members of the Stieglitz circle. For example, she states, "At first the men didn't want me around. They couldn't take a woman artist seriously. I would listen to them and I thought, my, they are dreary. I felt much more prosaic but I knew I could paint as well as some of them who were sitting around talking."[9]

Being near Greenwich Village in New York in the twenties, O'Keeffe was most certainly privy to the strong women's rights movement at work during the teens and twenties. Her friendship with Mabel Dodge, who had strong feminist and socialist leanings, would have brought her into contact with the ideas of women such as Crystal Eastman, Henrietta Rodman, Ida Rauh, Neith Boyce, and Susan Glaspell. All wanted to *do* something to give women the same opportunities as men, and not be tied to the home—quite radical thinking for the time.

Although O'Keeffe did not like to be put in a box as "a woman artist" and sometimes actually preferred the company of men to passive women, she disliked continuing traditional sex roles. And in 1942 she wrote an endorsement for the National Woman's Party which was trying to get an equal rights amendment passed.

The role of women in general, of women artists in particular, and the attitudes toward sexuality, thus, were in a state of flux in the early part of the twentieth century. O'Keeffe's critics began writing in this milieu. Many critics referred to a feminine and sexual imagery in O'Keeffe's work. It was this so-called "feminine imagery" in O'Keeffe's work that has evoked much controversy.

Foremost among the critics and artists writing about the feminine imagery were Paul Rosenfeld, Herbert Seligmann, Lewis Mumford, and Marsden Hartley. These four men were close friends and admirers of Alfred Stieglitz and somewhat influenced by his thinking. Sherman Paul, in an Introduction to Rosenfeld's *Port of New York,* describes Rosenfeld's loyalty to Stieglitz and his surrounding group. "As an art critic Rosenfeld was almost exclusively the interpreter of the painters in Stieglitz's group. He was fiercely loyal to Stieglitz, filially bound to him . . . and the courage and faith with which he espoused the cause of art were comparable to Stieglitz's, drawn from the belief in the value of art that both profoundly shared: 'the bridge of consciousness of self, to life, and through that to new life and creation again.'"[10] What were Stieglitz's ideas concerning the feminine experience? The following words of Alfred Stieglitz in a conversation with Dorothy Norman, soon after O'Keeffe's first show, exemplify his position, and indicate the power O'Keeffe's art held for him.

> When Woman desired to paint—or model—she went to Man to be taught. . . . She attempted to become what her teacher was to her. . . . In the past a few women may have attempted to express themselves in painting. . . . But somehow all the attempts I had seen, until O'Keeffe, were weak because the elemental force and vision back of them were never overpowering enough to throw off the Male Shackles. . . . In short if these Women who produced things which are distinctively feminine can live side by side with male produced Art . . . we will find that the underlying aesthetic laws governing the one govern the other—the original generating feeling merely being different. . . . Woman is beginning—the interesting thing is she has actually begun.[11]

For Stieglitz the intensity and immediacy of feeling and experience was strikingly feminine. More strikingly male, historically speaking, for Stieglitz, was the overemphasis on mind and theory. F. S. C. Northrop linked Stieglitz's thoughts with Plato's work, as he described Stieglitz's interpretation of one of O'Keeffe's early works, *Abstraction No. 11, The Two Blue Lines*, 1916. "Long ago, Plato in his *Timaeus* identified the mathematically designated 'theoretic component' in things with the male principle in the universe and the intuitive 'aesthetic component' with the female principle. This is precisely the interpretation which Alfred Stieglitz, the informed student of Georgia O'Keeffe's art, places upon her *Abstraction No. 11, The Two Blue Lines*: the one blue line represents the female aesthetic component in things. And the common base from which they spring expresses the fact that although each is distinct and irreducible to the other, both are united.[12] Northrop further mentioned this intuitive aesthetic component in the art of one such as Georgia O'Keeffe as conveying "the aesthetic immediacy of things without intellectually added references and interpretations."[13]

Stieglitz's and O'Keeffe's own relationship as husband and wife, as evidenced in Stieglitz's composite portrait of O'Keeffe and some of O'Keeffe's paintings, appeared to be a good balance of masculine and feminine qualities as discussed by Northrop. In personality Stieglitz represented the more intellectual in his love of ideas and stimulating conversation. O'Keeffe, less gregarious, appeared more intuitive in both her work and her ways of thinking. Stieglitz's composite portrait of O'Keeffe indicates a deep respect and feeling of intimacy for O'Keeffe, as well as a strong intellectual and emotional life on the part of the photographer, Stieglitz, and his subject, O'Keeffe.

In general, progress for Stieglitz was to be found in the expression of the very inner being of the individual. For him a sense of completion lay in the combination of so-called masculine and feminine principles with dominance of the individual's intuitive spirit. Stieglitz saw modern art as a weapon to fight against the nineteenth-century values and materialism of the majority of Americans interested only in realistic or academic art. Through his daily battles for the cause of modern art, Stieglitz hoped to raise the artistic consciousness of the general public.

Stieglitz's ideas concerning masculine and feminine, and modern art influenced a number of critics. In studying the nature of some of the various critical writings it is therefore necessary to keep in mind Stieglitz's thinking and influence.

What, then, were the various positions held concerning O'Keeffe's feminine imagery? Some opinions expressed were quite disparaging, as represented in the words of Samuel Kootz.

> *Much of her earlier work showed a womanly preoccupation with sex, an uneasy selection of phallic symbols in her flowers, a delight in their nascent qualities. O'Keeffe was being a woman and only secondarily an artist. Assertion of sex can only impede the talents of an artist, for it is an act of defiance, of grievance, in which the consciousness of these qualities retards the natural assertions.*[14]

In contrast Kootz mentions O'Keeffe's later works (although he isn't specific, except for mentioning "some vibrant crosses") where her intelligence has come to the fore, "where she is becoming more aware of the peculiar laws of a picture, and so, inevitably on the way to becoming a better painter."[15] For Kootz the role of intellectual experience was of prime importance. For him, progress in aesthetics, and indeed in society itself, was to be in the advancement from expression of an emotional life to purely intellectual thought.

Unlike Stieglitz, he saw the expression of sexuality, the senses, and intuition, as a regression in communication.

At the other extreme were the critics who lavished praise on O'Keeffe's work in highly poetic language. In 1927 Lewis Mumford wrote, "She has beautified the sense of what it is to be a woman; she has revealed the intimacies of love's juncture with purity and absence of shame that lovers feel in their meeting; she has brought what was inarticulate and troubled and confused into the realm of conscious beauty, where it may be recalled and enjoyed with a new intensity."[16] In his 1931 book, *The Brown Decades,* he wrote further, "She is the poet of womanhood in all its phases: the search for the lover, the reception of the lover, the longing for the child, the shrinkage and blackness of the emotions when the erotic thread has been lost, the sudden effulgence of feeling. . . . Without painting a single nude, without showing a part of the human body, she has magnificently embodied passion, sexual life, womanhood, as physical elements and as states of soul."[17] Mumford unfortunately gave no specific examples or explanations of his statements except that of the "filling of a large canvas with the corolla of a flower," and that O'Keeffe's work might serve as evidence of the issues of the day if Sherwood Anderson's novels and Freudian psychologists' papers were burned. It is difficult to ascertain what exactly Mumford meant by "sense of what it is to be a woman," but certainly his conception went beyond a physical sexual interpretation to the "states of soul." Mumford was concerned with basic, emotional needs of life versus the mechanical routines in which he felt society was caught. He referred to the importance of the role of the artist in society. In his 1927 article he compared O'Keeffe to Matisse in stating that "the pure artist is always more deeply in touch with life."[18] Throughout much of his career Mumford has criticized our society's overemphasis on progress—defined as technological advancement—which he seemed to associate with masculine qualities. In a more recent article in the *New Yorker* Mumford reflected on the past seventy years of American culture,

> . . . the myth of the machine, the basic religion of our present culture, has so captured the modern mind that no human sacrifice seems too great provided it is offered up to the insolent Marduks and Molochs of science and technology. . . . But even at their best all these improvements, however helpful, remain peripheral: they fail to do justice to man's central concern, his own humanization.[19]

For Mumford the expression of "feminine qualities"—the basic emotional needs of life, above and beyond the mechanical routines and technological advancement—is the only way to man's humanization. And for Mumford, a universal humanization is the optimum goal, and a sign of social progress. To Mumford, the expression of an artist such as O'Keeffe begins to reach that goal.

Herbert Seligmann, a contemporary of Mumford and friend of Stieglitz, wrote of O'Keeffe in 1923,

> O'Keeffe has made the ocean, wave, or sky, flower, or fruit herself. She has added to America's chronicle hitherto unattempted truths of a woman's sensibility. It is in terms of the identity in her statement that all her works are related to each other and to life.[20]

Ten years later Seligmann referred to O'Keeffe as a "Woman in Flower," in the title of an article. He began his article by writing, "Let us concede that what Georgia O'Keeffe commits to canvas is not 'painting.' Suppose it is called woman in flower. Or let us say she has found new terms for the bright edge of pain, the suffusing mystery of sensation stated in visual terms, the experiences of mortal flesh that range the depths of spiritual exaltation."[21] Seligmann's highly poetic language seems in keeping with the intensity of some of O'Keeffe's work. His opening statement that what O'Keeffe "commits to canvas," etc., leads us immediately away from the formal aspects of painting such as color, composition, "historical" style, that are often a part of art criticism, to the realm of experience, on both the part of the artist and of the viewer. This tendency to step away from in-depth analysis of formal aspects of O'Keeffe's work is typical of many of O'Keeffe's critics in the twenties and thirties.

Seligmann's description of an expression of an intensity of experience is akin to John Dewey's ideas of art as an intensified, fulfilled experience as described in his book *Art as Experience,* which was written about the same time, 1934. Dewey wrote, "Experience is the result, the sign, and the reward of that interaction of organism and environment which, when carried to the full, is a transformation of interaction into participation and communication. . . Ultimately there are but two philosophies. One of them accepts life and experience in all its uncertainty, mystery, doubt, and turns that experience upon itself to deepen and intensity its own qualities—to art and imagination."[22] For Seligmann the whole being became involved in O'Keeffe's and Stieglitz's art—"as it is not the ear alone which listens, so it is not the eye alone which sees."[23] And for Seligmann, involvement with O'Keeffe's work became a type of religious experience, no matter what the religion.

Seligmann mentioned little about method and rarely gave specific data from actual paintings to back up general statements. In referring to method, Seligmann wrote of "the intense innocence and incandescent purity of these utterances, made possible and real by immaculate craftsmanship."[24] The terms innocent, purity, and immaculate related directly to the somewhat popular notion of the time that a woman was related to the innocence and purity of nature. In an interview in January of 1975 Seligmann made use of his 1933 term, "immaculate craftsmanship," several times. He felt O'Keeffe's work had continued to deserve such a description. Seligmann held, too, that the positive critics' opinions concerning O'Keeffe's expression of a "woman's experience," were still valid. For Seligmann, the most important aspect of the "woman's sensibility," of the "woman in flower," was the ability to feel the immediacy and/or intimacy of any given experience and for O'Keeffe, to express such in newly found visual terms. Seligmann was very close to Stieglitz's position, which is not surprising, since Seligmann spent hours and hours in Stieglitz's gallery as audience, friend, and unpaid secretary. (For further details of Seligmann's impressions and experiences in Stieglitz's gallery see his book, *Alfred Stieglitz Talking.*)

A further admirer of Stieglitz was Paul Rosenfeld, a popular literary, art, and music critic who wrote prolifically during the twenties and thirties. Sherman Paul describes Rosenfeld as a romantic and humanist. ". . . in his belief in the primacy of the heart; for though he is classic in his desire to see the external world clearly, he knew that the intellect could not fully capture the rhythms of life. . . ."[25] Rosenfeld was viewed by many as one of the most warmly regarded critics of his generation. He wrote much of O'Keeffe in his *Port of New York.* Concerning his feelings about O'Keeffe's work as the expression of a woman, he wrote,

There are spots in this work wherein the artist seems to bring before one the outline of a whole universe, a full course of life: mysterious cycles of birth and reproduction and death expressed through the terms of a woman's body. . . . Whether it is the blue lines of mountains reflecting themselves in the morning stillnesses of lake-water, or the polyphony of severe imagined shapes she has represented; whether deep-toned, lustrous, gaping tulips or wicked, regardful alligator pears; it is always as though the quality of the forms of a woman's body, the essence of the grand white surfaces, has been approached to the eye, and the elusive scent of unbound hair to the nostril . . . the paintings of Georgia O'Keeffe are made out of the pangs and glories of earth lived largely.[26]

The expression of life passionately lived was mixed with, what appears to be for Rosenfeld, a sexual relationship with the soil and land, that involved passion and tenderness. (In a later essay on "Mozart the Romantic," Rosenfeld described the romantic feeling for nature as feminine.)

Another critic of the time, Louis Kalonyme, also associated the soil and earth with sexual forces.

The world she [O'Keeffe] paints is maternal, its swelling hills and reclining valleys are pregnant with a beauty born of a primeval sun. The sun's rays' points piercing the human forms of the earth give birth through her to singing flowers which are fragrant chalices of a golden radiance. . . She reveals woman as an elementary being, closer to the earth than man, suffering pain with passionate ecstasy, enjoying love with beyond good and evil delight.[27]

In Rosenfeld's and Kalonyme's association of sexuality and rhythms of the soil, one is reminded immediately of D. H. Lawrence's work. It is no surprise that Rosenfeld was an admirer of Lawrence as were O'Keeffe and Stieglitz.[28]

Further in O'Keeffe's capacity as a woman to express the immediacy of her experience, according to Rosenfeld, was her ability to deal with opposing forces—"far upon near, hot upon cold, bitter upon sweet"[29]—in content and style to create a new reality. "She is not conscious of a single principle without becoming aware of that contrary which gives it life."[30] Rosenfeld placed O'Keeffe in a Hegelian world of thesis, anti-thesis, and synthesis, the synthesis being the new reality O'Keeffe created with her paintings. But whereas Hegel spoke mainly of larger historical forces, Rosenfeld dealt with the individual experience of O'Keeffe.

Although Rosenfeld dealt largely with O'Keeffe's experience as a woman, he, as Mumford, stressed the importance of the artist's vision, the artist being seen since the days of Romanticism in the nineteenth century as a unique genius with imaginative creative power operating on the fringe of society. "What she [O'Keeffe] herself within herself is, where she is woman most, becomes apparent to her, because of her artist's vision, in external objects."[31] The role of the artist for Rosenfeld was not to "espouse the cause of 'the world' and defend its special interests. These special interests have everlastingly been those of power and booty. . . ."[32] Rather the artist was to "become the impassioned advocate of things produced out of feeling: things having the quality of life and awakening feeling and bringing men into touch with its divine source and object. . . ."[33] Thus for Rosenfeld the power of O'Keeffe's expression as a woman was closely related to the vision of the artist and to a relationship with the soil. In general, Rosenfeld himself was not as oriented toward larger social forces, as Stieglitz, Mumford, or Seligmann. The intense, private expression of the artist was more important.

The last of those critics and artists closely associated with Stieglitz to be considered in detailed discussion here is Marsden Hartley, who painted and wrote some art criticism. In a 1920 essay that O'Keeffe reportedly disliked greatly, Hartley wrote, "with Georgia O'Keeffe one takes a far jump into volcanic crateral ethers, and sees the world of a woman turned inside out and gaping with deep open eyes and fixed mouth at the rather trivial world of living people. . . . Without someone to steady her, I think O'Keeffe would not wish the company of more tangible things than trees."[34] Hartley, although basically respecting O'Keeffe in his writing, pictured O'Keeffe as an almost incurable romantic and purist. "She is far nearer to St. Theresa's version of life as experience than she could ever be to that of Catherine the Great or Lucrezia Borgia. Georgia O'Keeffe wears no poisoned emeralds. She wears too much white; she is impaled with white consciousness."[35] It is extremely questionable whether O'Keeffe's life of experience approached the life of Spanish contemplative nun, St. Theresa. The importance of Hartley's analogy lies in the psychic energy and mysticism that Hartley attributed to each woman.

In a later article in 1936, Hartley's statements suggested that the qualities of mystic, artist, and woman were interlocked in O'Keeffe's womanly expression. "Artists and religionists are never very far apart . . . . but she [O'Keeffe] remains the same as always—just what she is, a woman, having a woman's interests, a woman's ardours in pursuit of the sense of beauty—a woman's need of getting at her own notion of truths—she is never struggling for manpower of man equality—she has no need of such irrelevant ambitions—she has never made a cult of her own intensified intuitions—she is even free from the laudations that have been lavishly heaped upon her—she is a woman, utterly free."[36] Many other critics have also used the term mystic in describing O'Keeffe, i.e., Edward Alden Jewell's description: "The painting is autobiographical as thoroughly as it is mystical. Each picture might be called a portrait of the artist herself."[37]

Although Hartley basically respected O'Keeffe as an individual, as a woman, he saw the world progressing from the particular expression of individual emotions as O'Keeffe's "feminine" expression, to the universality of "masculine" reason. "It is not the idiosyncrasy of an artist that creates the working formula, it is the rational reasoning in him that furnishes the material to build on. . . . I cannot but return to the previous theme which represents my conversion from emotional to intellectual notions; and my feeling is of what use is a painting which does not realize its esthetical problem? . . . I would rather be sure that I had placed two colors in true relationship to each other than to have exposed a wealth of emotionalism gone wrong in the name of richness of personal expression."[38] Rosenfeld, Mumford, Seligmann, and Hartley represent a very emotional approach to O'Keeffe's work, most likely because they were so closely associated with the Stieglitz circle at the time and were influenced by Stieglitz's thinking.

Other critics dealt with the feminine experience in O'Keeffe's work in a less subjective manner. Helen Appleton Read's and Edmund Wilson's writings are good examples. Read described Hartley's 1920 essay as "hysterical exaggeration,"[39] and attempted to explain the frequent emotional reactions, positive and negative, to O'Keeffe's work. "Granting that much of this is hysterical exaggeration, and granting that such an interpretation of O'Keeffe's work must influence everyone who has read it into seeing in her paintings Freudian complexes and suppressed desires, nevertheless even without having read it, I think that the most casual gallery frequenter would find some disturbing emotional content in her work. They are in some way an expression on canvas of an intense emotional life which has not been able to express itself through the natural channels of life. But distinctly they are not unhealthy or morbid."[40] Unlike a Hartley, Read spent more time dealing with specific subject matter, various still lifes, and referred to the living qualities that O'Keeffe impared to the apples, pears, lilies, and leaves. Unlike the other critics, Read attempted to squarely deal with previous opinions that women couldn't be artists. As a woman, Read felt it important to deal with this issue. "Astuter critics and psychologists than Moore have claimed that woman can never be a true creative artist; that she can only create life. Perhaps that is what O'Keeffe meant when she said: 'Wise men say it isn't art! But what of it, if it is children and love in paint?' There it is, color, form, rhythm. What matter if its original be aesthetic or emotional?"[41]

Edmund Wilson used less poetic or explosive language than many of the critics in his reaction to O'Keeffe. In 1925, describing her "feminine intensity" he contrasted the work of male and female artists. "Male artists, in communicating this quality [intensity] seem usually merely to import it to the representation of external objects . . . that is, something detachable from themselves; whereas women imbue the objects they represent with so immediate a personal emotion that they absorb the subject into themselves."[42] Wilson, detached from the Stieglitz circle, felt Stieglitz's power over others was sometimes too manipulative, but he did respect Stieglitz. Wilson describes Stieglitz as "something of a mesmerist,"[43] and writes of some of his visits to Stieglitz's gallery. "My admiration for these artists was genuine, but if I had not been subjected to Stieglitz's spell, I might have discussed them in different terms."[44]

The above then, are representative examples of the early critical writings chiefly concerned with the feminine experience in O'Keeffe's work. In general, for these critics the meaning of feminine involved the expression of the immediacy and intimacy of an experience without intellectualizing or theorizing upon that experience. For some of the more positive critics, O'Keeffe's feminine expression was bound to her vision as an artist, as a mystic, or to her relationship with nature. The meaning of feminine as related to O'Keeffe's work for these early critics was quite different from the more traditional definition that equated femininity with passiveness, delicacy, decorativeness, and domesticity.

In the forties some of the criticism became less emotional and less subjective, and dealt with the feminine experience by placing O'Keeffe in a political perspective, relating to the woman's movement. In 1945 Carol Taylor of the *New York World Telegram* wrote of an interview with O'Keeffe. "She [O'Keeffe] revealed herself as something of a feminist, but of the kind that discusses the subject over tea cups, not from a soap box."[45] In 1942 O'Keeffe did write a statement for the paper *Equal Rights,* the official organ of the National Woman's Party, in favor of the Equal Rights Amendment. Since the forties O'Keeffe has received publicity and honors from various colleges and political institutions—at the New York World's Fair of 1939–1940 she was chosen as one of the twelve outstanding women of the past fifty years. In 1945 she was honored by the National Press Club as one of the twelve outstanding women of the year. In 1965 she was honored by the New Mexican Senate for her outstanding achievements in painting.

Since the forties, there have continued to be statements concerning the association of O'Keeffe's forms with sexual forms, particularly in paintings such as *Music—Pink and Blue I,* 1919 or *Black Iris,* 1926. But there has been little of the highly poetic and emotional language of the earlier critics. In general, most of the criticism concerning the controversial feminine experience was written in the twenties and thirties.

The quite emotional reactions to this "woman on paper" reflects to some extent the early twentieth-century period of unrest, experimentation, and change in all of the art forms, and society at large, as well as interest in psychology and sexuality brought about by Freud's writings. O'Keeffe herself has denied any type of sexual interpretation by the critics, and has stated, "The critics are just talking about themselves, not about what I am thinking."[46] Concerning her flower paintings, to which much of the feminine, sexual interpretations refer, O'Keeffe has written,

> *Still—in a way—nobody sees a flower—really—it is so small—we haven't time—and to see takes time like to have a friend takes time. If I could paint the flower exactly as I see it no one would see what I see because I would paint it small like the flower is small.*
>
> *So I said to myself—I'll paint what I see—what the flower is to me but I'll paint it big and they will be surprised into taking time to look at it—I will make even busy New Yorkers take time to see what I see of flowers.*
>
> *Well—I made you take time to look at what I saw and when you took time to really notice my flower you hung all your own associations with flowers on my flower and you write about my flower as if I think and see what you think and see of the flower—and I don't.*[47]

Who does one believe, O'Keeffe or her critics, concerning the interpretation of the feminine experience in her work? The answer appears to lie in a combination of the opinions of both. In some ways the critics were talking about themselves. The highly emotional, at times almost ecstatic, language of some of the critics of the twenties and thirties reflected a large degree of personal involvement with Stieglitz—his ideas and in O'Keeffe's work—and in their own writing. These writings did, at times, become extensions of the critics themselves. The intense personal involvement reflected, too, a personal commitment to a change in the established American order, particularly on the part of those connected with the Stieglitz circle. Some of the critics as Mumford, were also general cultural critics and hoped to change the public's consciousness through their writing. A number of the critics mentioned also projected what they wanted, or feared to see, in their writing. A quotation by Leo Katz concerning some of the critics' very personal reactions to O'Keeffe's works, expressed such a viewpoint.

> *Her art has made passionate friends as well as passionate enemies. It has made friends because there were those who longed to see things expressed which no one had ever had the courage or ability to express before—things which delicately interpreted the true inner nature of human-kind. It has made enemies from feelings which they feared to see opened, lest their own hollow and hypocritical equilibrium be destroyed.*[48]

The highly poetic and often beautiful language of the more emotional responses such as the words of a Rosenfeld, Hartley, or Mumford, can be criticized for its exaggeration and lack of specific examples to back up broad statements about O'Keeffe's work. Too infrequently did the critics deal with specific paintings or with O'Keeffe's own words about her work although O'Keeffe's statements are relatively few in number. At times the critics, particularly those associated with the Stieglitz circle, seemed to be writing or talking for each other. The sometimes complex and very rich language usually appeared for a select group rather than the general public. Many of the critical articles appeared in such magazines as *Vanity Fair, Camera Work, Creative Art,* and *Manuscripts* which were considered somewhat avant-garde for the time. In general, the reader of some of these critical writings must accept these critical opinions upon faith.

Yet these critics, particularly those praising this woman on paper cannot be entirely discounted. Even today, some critics, in a less extreme fashion than the earlier critics, point to an underlying sexuality and feminine experience in the intensity and depth of O'Keeffe's paintings. Lloyd Goodrich, Robert Hughes, and Douglas Davis, are among those who have expressed such an opinion. It seems impossible to deny the communication of the new language of forms of O'Keeffe and the emotional response that is evoked in most viewers upon seeing some of her paintings. Particularly in the association of femininity with the ability to experience on an immediate and intimate level—no matter what the level of experience—and directly express such an experience, do some of the critics appear apt in their appraisals. A feeling of an overall sexuality in the finest sense of the word, that portrays the depths of human experience, is emitted in many of O'Keeffe's paintings through her treatment of subject matter in her unique colors, forms, and sense of movement. It is unfair, though, to interpret paintings such as the flower paintings strictly in terms of a particular sexual act or experience. (An in-depth discussion of selected paintings, including the flower paintings, occurs in Chapter Eight.) A statement by Herbert Seligmann perhaps best places O'Keeffe's work in a proper perspective in terms of an historical, intellectual, and emotional meaning of "feminine" for O'Keeffe's work.

> The intensities of O'Keeffe (as expressed in her personality and her work) established her as the essential reality which the so-called feminist movement—now partially at least historic—was groping for and about.[49]

Notes

[1]Elizabeth McCausland, "Georgia O'Keeffe in a Retrospective Exhibition," *Springfield Republic,* May 26, 1946, p. 6c.

[2]*Ibid.*

[3]Dinah M. Craik, *Olive* (London: Chapman & Hall, 1850), p. 161.

[4]William Gerdts, "Women Artists of America 1707–1964," *Exhibition Catalogue* (Newark, N.J.: Newark Museum, 1965), pp. 9–10.

[5]Linda Nochlin, "Why Have There Been no Great Women Artists?," in *Art and Sexual Politics,* ed. Thomas Hess and Elizabeth Baker (New York: Collier Books, 1971), p. 4.

[6]Linda Nochlin, "Eroticism and Female Imagery in Nineteenth Century Art," in *Woman as Sex Object,* ed. Linda Nochlin and Thomas Hess (New York: Newsweek, Inc., 1972), p. 10.

[7]Nochlin, "Why Have There Been No Great Woman Artists?" p. 24.

[8]Gerald Needham, "Manet, Olympia, and Pornographic Photography," in *Woman as Sex Object,* p. 81.

[9]Dorothy Seiberling, "Horizons of a Pioneer," *Life,* March 1, 1968, p. 52.

[10]Sherman Paul, Introduction to *Port of New York* by Paul Rosenfeld (New York: Harcourt Brace, Inc., 1924), p. xvi.

[11]Dorothy Norman, *Alfred Stieglitz,* pp. 137–138.

[12]F. S. C. Northrop, *The Meeting of East and West* (New York: Macmillan Co., 1946), p. 163.

[13]*Ibid.*

[14]Samuel Kootz, *Modern American Painters* (Norwood, Mass.: Brewer & Warren, Inc., 1930), p. 49.

[15]*Ibid.*

[16]Lewis Mumford, "O'Keeffe and Matisse," *The New Republic,* March 2, 1927, p. 16.

[17]Lewis Mumford, *The Brown Decades* (New York: Macmillan Co., 1931), pp. 244–245.

[18]*Ibid.*

[19]Lewis Mumford, "Reflections—Prologue to Our Time," *New Yorker,* March 10, 1975, p. 50.

[20]Seligmann, "Georgia O'Keeffe, American," p. 10.

[21]Herbert Seligmann, "A Woman in Flower," *Exhibition Catalogue,* January–February 1933, p. 1.

[22]John Dewey, *Art as Experience* (New York: G. P. Putnam's Sons, 1934; Capricorn Books, 1958), pp. 22, 34.

[23]Seligmann, "A Woman in Flower," p. 1.

[24]*Ibid.*

[25]Sherman Paul, Introduction to *Port of New York,* p. xx.

[26]Paul Rosenfeld, *Port of New York,* pp. 204–206.

[27]Louis Kalonyme, "Georgia O'Keeffe: A Woman in Painting." *Creative Art,* January 1928, p. 40.

[28]Herbert Seligmann, *Alfred Stieglitz Talking* (New Haven: Yale University, 1966), pp. 135, 143.

[29]Rosenfeld, *Port of New York,* p. 199.

[30]*Ibid.*

[31]*Ibid.,* p. 208.

[32]*Ibid.,* p. xxxvii.

[33]*Ibid.,* p. xxxviii.

[34]Hartley, "Georgia O'Keeffe," pp. 31–32.

[35]*Ibid.,* p. 31.

[36]Marsden Hartley, "A Second Outline in Portraiture," *Exhibition Catalogue,* An American Place, January 4–February 27, 1936, pp. 5–7.

[37]Edward Alden Jewell, "O'Keeffe: 30 Years," *New York Times,* May 11, 1946, p. 6x.

[38]Marsden Hartley, *Creative Art,* June 1928, p. 22.

[39]Helen Appleton Read, "Georgia O'Keeffe—Woman Artist Whose Art is Sincerely Feminine," *Brooklyn Eagle,* March 2, 1924, p. 4.

[40]*Ibid.*

[41]*Ibid.*

[42]Edmund Wilson, *The American Earthquake, A Documentary of the Twenties and Thirties* (Garden City, N.Y.: Doubleday/Anchor Books, 1958), p. 98.

[43]*Ibid.,* p. 101.

[44]*Ibid.*

[45]Carol Taylor, "Miss O'Keeffe, Noted Artist is a Feminist," *New York World Telegram,* March 31, 1945, p. 29.

[46]Douglas Davis, "Return of the Native," *Newsweek,* October 12, 1970, p. 105.

[47]Georgia O'Keeffe, *Exhibition Catalogue,* An American Place, January 22–March 17, 1939, pp. 2–3.

[48]Leo Katz, *Georgia O'Keeffe, Portfolio of Twelve Paintings* (New York: Knight Publishing, Inc., 1937), p. 1.

[49]Mahoriri Sharp Young, *Early American Moderns* (New York: Watson-Guptil, Inc., 1974), p. 52.

Chapter Six
Symbolism

Much of the critical writing pertaining to O'Keeffe's work refers to the symbols and symbolism in her painting. Before discussing the nature of some of these critical writings it is necessary to understand the concepts and growth of Symbolism as a movement in the early twentieth century. In America, an important prophet of symbolism was Edgar Allan Poe. Poe's insistence on the approximation of music in poetry and resulting spiritual effect became important in the work of the French symbolists such as Mallarmé, Rimbaud, and Baudelaire in the late nineteenth century. The French symbolists, in general, were reacting to a mechanistic view of nature and social conception of man held by the naturalists. Important, instead, for the symbolists was the expression of the emotions and sensations of the individual. Each poet's symbols were quite individual, for it was the ". . . poet's task to find, to invent, the special language which will alone be capable of expressing his personality and feelings. Such a language must make use of symbols: what is so special, so fleeting and so vague cannot be conveyed by direct statement or description, but only by a succession of words, of images, which will serve to suggest it to the reader."[1] The metaphors and images used were to approximate the abstract flow of music. "By invoking, alluding, suggesting, never speaking with prose directness, its language moving toward a life of its own, the poem will begin to express what is beyond speech."[2] Further, symbolism was an approach to a higher reality beyond everyday experience. In many ways it reflected the ideas of Hegel and Schopenhauer. It also paralleled the thinking of Henri Bergson who felt that this higher reality could best be reached through intuitive forces expressed in a work of art. Through their work, the Symbolists hoped to preserve the purity and autonomy of art. The artist was to disappear somewhat from his work. "Though art does not reproduce the objective world, the work itself must be objective, not subjective. . . . The objective image becomes increasingly palatable until it reaches the stage of epiphany or complete aesthetic existence."[3] The artist became a type of hero who descended into the mind to then express his vision of reality.

The following words of Baudelaire summarize some of the symbolist concerns.

> *What is pure art according to the modern idea? It is the creation of an evocative magic containing at once the object and subject, the world external to the artist and the artist himself. Every piece of sculpture, painting or music evokes the sentiments and the dreams which it sets out to evoke . . . reasoning and deduction are the province of the printed book.*[4]

Many of O'Keeffe's critics felt they had found that evocative magic in some of her works.

In general, the Symbolist can be seen as a kind of romantic in holding that the human mind is capable of actively constructing the world we perceive and "does not merely reflect the given forms of external objects."[5] The symbol is a key to the relationship of the mind and the surrounding world. (In contrast to the French symbolist work that tends to suggest or evoke, is the notion of a fixed specific symbol or body of symbols such as the cross for Christianity or the stars and stripes for the United States.) The language of some of O'Keeffe's critics as well as poets, such as Wallace Stevens and Hart Crane, reflected a definite knowledge of the French Symbolist movement.

The Symbolist movement was to have growing influences on the twentieth-century art world. The idea that a work of art was the expression of the inner spirit of the artist rather than strict observation of nature occurred not only in the work of symbolist artists but also appeared in a variety of formats, in the works of the twentieth-century expressionists, Dadaists, surrealists, and later abstractionists. O'Keeffe and her critics worked within the context of this expanding symbolist force.

Symbolist painters such as Odilon Redon, Gustave Moreau, and Paul Gauguin, sought a new content based on emotion and intuition rather than intellect. Gauguin turned to the exotic mysteries of the Tahitian people and in his synthetism advocated a synthesis of form and color with the intuitive, primitive forces he observed in the Tahitian culture. Redon, as Gauguin, was influenced by Oriental art and also admired the early nineteenth-century Goya etchings which were filled with fantasy and distortion. Redon frequently explored the world of dreams and his work has been considered a direct link between nineteenth-century romanticism and twentieth-century surrealism.

Matisse and the Fauves, as well as the expressionists carried forth the symbolist tenet that color should be used independently of its traditional use, i.e., a horse could be blue. Thus, color became expressive and structural, as well as descriptive in the work of art.

The rise of surrealism was, to a large extent, influenced by the ideas of the nineteenth-century French poets Rimbaud and Comte de Lautreamont. The surrealists, as Rimbaud, were concerned with the exploration of dreams, the subconscious, automatism, and chance. André Bréton's 1924 *Manifesto of Surrealism,* influential for both literature and art, reflected Rimbaud's ideas. The growth of surrealism in painting took two routes. One direction, organic surrealism or biomorphic surrealism, advocated automatism, where thoughts would be automatically expressed without rational control by the mind or intellect. The earlier work of some of the Dada artists, emphasizing chance and automatism, is also reflected in this branch of surrealism. Painters represented in this group were Miró, Masson, and Matta. The other direction called superrealism or naturalistic surrealism dealt more with the use of recognizable objects in strange contexts to represent the subconscious. Painters in this group included Pierre Roy, Salvador Dali, Yves Tanguy, René Magritte, and Paul Devaux.

The growth of these twentieth-century art movements, particularly surrealism, were important for O'Keeffe's critics who often found themselves caught up with the latest movement at the time.

Many of O'Keeffe's critics were well-aware of the symbolist tenets and later outgrowths of the movement. The work of Redon was one of the most recognized at the Armory Show. Picabia and Duchamp were, for a time, closely associated with Alfred

Stieglitz and his circle with their Dada publication *391*. O'Keeffe herself recalls afternoon tea with Marcel Duchamp. "I finished my tea, and Duchamp got up from his chair and took my teacup from me with the most extraordinary grace—with a gesture so elegant that I've never forgotten."[6] Like Redon, O'Keeffe was also an admirer of Goya's works.[7] That the critics were familiar with surrealist works was evident by frequent references to surrealism. American artists such as Man Ray, Peter Blume, and Joseph Cornell were attracted to surrealism and the exploration of the dream image, particularly in the thirties. In 1939 and 1940, respectively, Yves Tanguy and Salvador Dali moved to the United States.

The growth of the symbolist influence was thus important for many of O'Keeffe's critics. Their writings came to reflect many of the symbolists' literary and artistic language and beliefs as well as outgrowths of these beliefs.

In reading the early criticism surrounding O'Keeffe's work one finds frequent analogies of music to O'Keeffe's paintings, as advocated by the symbolists. O'Keeffe's work was often described as the ideal French symbolist poem might be. Indeed, her work has been called poetry, with a "robust physical language speaking to the senses."[8] William Fisher wrote in 1917,

> . . . of all things earthly it is only in music that one finds any analogy to the emotional content of these drawings, to the gigantic swirling rhythms and the exquisite tendernesses so powerfully and sensitively rendered—and music is the condition toward which according to Pater all art constantly aspires. Well, plastic art in the hands of O'Keeffe seems now to have approximated that.[9]

In 1927 Lewis Mumford wrote,

> What distinguishes Miss O'Keeffe is the fact that she has discovered a beautiful language, with unsuspected melodies and rhythms, and has created in this language a new set of symbols; by these means she has opened up a whole area of human consciousness which has never, so far as I am aware, been so completely revealed in either literature or in graphic art.[10]

While in 1937 Leo Katz wrote, "Yet there is so much music in Georgia O'Keeffe's work it suggests that the era of a great woman composer may not be far off."[11] A decade later a reviewer wrote, "Each one [painting] had the contrived spontaneity of music and each the melody of line and color meant more than the bones, blossoms, skyscrapers, barns, crosses, and canyon walls she used for lyrics."[12] In reference to music, O'Keeffe herself has said, "Singing has always seemed to me the most perfect means of expression. Since I cannot sing, I paint."[13] O'Keeffe is also reported to presently have a very large record collection, with Monteverdi as one of her favorites. The best of her hi-fi system is in her studio.[14]

Mumford's suggestion of a new language implicit in O'Keeffe's work was restated by Mumford and by other critics in reference to O'Keeffe's paintings. The idea of, and search for a new, purer language, particularly that approximating music, was a leading concern of the French symbolists, as well as American poets such as Wallace Stevens, Ezra Pound, and William Carlos Williams. Mumford wrote further in 1931, "Miss O'Keeffe has done more than paint: she has invented a language, and has conveyed directly and chastely in paint, experiences for which language conveys only obscenities."[15] Herbert Seligmann wrote of the "new terms" O'Keeffe had found for the "bright edge of pain, the suffusing mystery of sensation stated in visual terms, the experiences of mortal flesh that range the depths of spiritual exaltation."[16]

The descriptions of O'Keeffe's ability to express the intensities of human experience are akin to Stieglitz's *Equivalents,* and Stieglitz's feeling that the cloud photographs were responses to the chaos of men's experience. Seligmann wrote of these photographic statements by Stieglitz, "He [Stieglitz] made clear with a new clarity that the symbols employed in the arts, if they convey anything at all, communicate the profoundest and most exquisite intensities of which highly gifted, sensitive men and women are capable."[17] Barbara Rose felt that Paul Rosenfeld's description of Stieglitz's photographs showed an understanding of O'Keeffe's, Marin's, and Dove's work as well.[18] "The images are spontaneous, complete transpositions into the visual and tactile field of the ineffable sensuous unities, ordinations, wholes and worlds that have constituted the content of the photographer's experience. . . In the form of relationships of shape and line and color they symbolize the harmonies of living matter, restlessly yearning, aspiring, struggling to reach beyond itself. . ."[19] Stieglitz himself wrote of his Equivalents, "My photographs are a picture of the chaos in the world and of my relationship to that chaos. My prints show the world's constant upsetting of man's equilibrium and his eternal battle to reestablish it."[20]

O'Keeffe's paintings have been described as "symbolic equivalents," by such critics as Herbert Seligmann[21] and much later by Barbara Rose. Rose has written "Like Marin, Hartley, and Dove, O'Keeffe found in nature symbolic equivalents for inner emotional states. She did not think of abstracting from nature, but of symbolizing nature's generative force."[22]

In the forties a number of critics dealt with a mystical quality in O'Keeffe's new symbolic language. Edward Alden Jewell, art critic for the *New York Times* wrote, "that Georgia O'Keeffe is in the ultimate sense a mystic. Her works, so much of it, at any rate, is charged with a spirit of universality."[23] James Soby wrote in 1946 "Sometimes her painting seems an art of psychic confession, an inner recital of symbolic language, like the murmur of acolytes."[24]

For critics such as Soby there was a sense of religious spirit in O'Keeffe's work, in the sense of Paul Tillich's idea of "ultimate concern." Seligmann referred to the response in "truly religious people" to the "innocence and incandescent purity"[25] in O'Keeffe's work. Louis Kalonyme spoke of the "pureness" of O'Keeffe's symbols because there were no obvious physical or literary associations.[26]

The critics' feeling that O'Keeffe's work represented a new, evocative and, at times, mystical language also reflected some of the ideas of the painters associated with Stieglitz. As Matthew Baigell writes, "Animated by the belief that art should express ideas rather than things, they gave form to feeling by means of an abstract artistic language. They would have agreed with Ernest Fenollosa, the Orientalist and art educator whose influence had already been felt, when he wrote in 1906 'The self that we find is something far deeper than the froth of personality, something that belongs to all free spirits, as to nature.' "[27]

A question arising in viewing O'Keeffe's artistic language for several of the earlier critics was the problem of translation to a verbal language. Mumford wrote, "Indeed, Miss O'Keeffe's world cannot be verbally formulated; for it touches primarily on the experiences of love and passion."[28] For Seligmann, too, there appeared to be ultimately no translation for some of O'Keeffe's paintings. "For some of these heights of intense being, Georgia O'Keeffe has found new realization incapable of translation into words as music is untranslatable."[29] Much later, Doris Bry wrote, "Shapes, lines, and colors are used to make statements that cannot be said in words, for no words have yet been written that are the equivalents of what is wonderful in a wonderful painting. Paintings are first for the eye, and the deeper apprehension which may lie beyond. The word is only for the mind; and never quite seems to catch up with the essential trueness of the silent eye."[30]

Doris Bry's above words, "the word is only for the mind," point to the importance of the individual instincts and individual language of the artist, for which Stieglitz continuously worked. O'Keeffe herself spoke often of the need for the art work to stand for itself without a verbal expression or analysis—"I think I'd rather let the painting work for itself than help it with the word."[31] O'Keeffe's new visual language also contained an alluring ambivalence attractive to a number of the critics. They saw in her work the possibility of multiple realities from the portrayal of realistic, concrete objects to a sense of the universal. As Doris Bry wrote, "So the paintings of the mountains are the mountains, but go beyond the particular mountain; the flower paintings are and are not flowers."[32]

Besides O'Keeffe, other artists of Stieglitz's circle felt there was no direct translation of their work. ". . . Stieglitz had insisted that images were not translatable into words. Dove, too, maintained that painting 'should necessitate no effort to understand.' Marin may have expressed their attitude most succinctly in advice to a friend: 'Don't everlastingly read messages into paintings—there's the Daisy—you don't rave over or read messages into it—you just look at that bully little flower—isn't that enough!'"[33] O'Keeffe herself wrote very early, "I found that I could say things with color and shapes that I couldn't say in any other way—things I had no words for."[34] The critics closely associated with Stieglitz's circle articulated for the public these artists' feelings about the problems of translation of their paintings.

Besides those writings reflecting the French symbolist tenets of the creation of an evocative language of the artist's personal symbols, other writings have referred to particular symbols in O'Keeffe's work, ascribing particular meanings to particular images. Frequent was the association between O'Keeffe's flower forms and sexual symbolism—that the enlarged flower forms were representative of body forms as discussed in the previous section. Rather than associating the flowers with specific body forms, critics such as Read, felt the fruits or flowers were "symbols of life."[35]

Some critics felt the appearance of bones and skulls in O'Keeffe's paintings signified death with overtones of crucifixion.[36] Some attributed the skulls and death-like imagery to the long illness O'Keeffe suffered in the thirties. Others described the pictures as depressing. A New York Sun critic wrote in 1932, "Miss O'Keeffe's cure for the depression is to wallow in depression."[37] Elizabeth McCausland thought the bone paintings became "fetishes" as the bones took on magical qualities for O'Keeffe.[38] For other critics the skulls appeared as symbols of O'Keeffe's beloved northern New Mexico landscape.[39]

O'Keeffe's work has also been identified with surrealism, particularly what was called naturalistic surrealism, because of the strange juxtaposition of unrelated objects in some of her paintings such as the combination of deer skulls and desert flowers. The floating skulls and flowers at times suggested a dream-life, intuitive world that the surrealists aspired to portray. Royal Cortissoz wrote of an exhibition in 1936, "In one of her pictures here the *Ram's Head—White Hollyhock Hills, New Mexico* she seems to be deviating in the cul-de-sac of Surrealism."[40] For some, O'Keeffe's work was a new branch of surrealism, more subtle, more personal. Mumford wrote, "O'Keeffe uses themes and juxtapositions no less expected than those of the surrealists, but she uses them in a fashion that makes them seem inevitable and natural, grave and beautiful."[41] More recently Daniel Catton Rich wrote, "O'Keeffe constructs such works [those often described as Surrealist] as a poet might construct a sonnet by building up a pattern of seemingly unrelated images which crystallize into a unity."[42] Lloyd Goodrich disagreed completely with those critics connecting O'Keeffe's work with surrealism. "In any case, her art differed fundamentally from Surrealism. It had no relation to psychoanalysis, no conscious use of the subconscious, no deliberate irrationality. Its imagery was simpler, and closer to the world of nature. And she showed none of the surrealists' desire to 'épater le bourgeois.' "[43]

O'Keeffe herself has responded to any surrealist implications in her work, "I was in the Surrealist show when I'd never heard of Surrealism—I'm not a joiner and I'm not a Precisionist or anything else."[44] As for other symbolist interpretations of her work, O'Keeffe also denies such. In answer to a question from Katherine Kuh in a 1960 interview, "Has the idea of symbolism been tacked onto your work by others?" O'Keeffe responded, "Certainly, I've often wondered where they got the idea and what they were talking about."[45] O'Keeffe goes on to refer to a statement she made in 1944 concerning why she did the pelvis bone paintings. "When I started painting the pelvis bones I was most interested in the holes in the bones—what I saw through them—particularly the blue from holding them up in the sun against the sky as one is apt to do when one seems to have more sky than earth in one's world—They were most wonderful against the Blue—that Blue that will always be there as it is now, after all man's destruction is finished."[46] In a 1974 interview with Calvin Tomkins, O'Keeffe again denied symbolist tendencies such as her bones signifying death. In reference to the painting *Horse's Skull with Pink Rose*, 1931, O'Keeffe explained to Tomkins that she had a collection of artificial flowers, which the Spanish people in her part of the country used for funeral decorations. " 'I was looking through them one day when someone came to the kitchen door,' she said. 'As I went to answer the door, I stuck a pink rose in the eye socket of a horse's skull. And when I came back the rose in the eye looked pretty fine, so I thought I would just go on with that.' "[47] In a 1939 catalogue statement O'Keeffe does mention the word symbol, referring to the bones, but merely as representations of the desert.

> I have wanted to paint the desert and I haven't known how. I always think that I cannot stay with it long enough. So I brought home the bleached bones as my symbols of the desert. To me they are as beautiful as anything I know. To me they are strangely more living than the animals walking around—hair, eyes and all with their tails switching. The bones seem to cut sharply to the center of something that is keenly alive on the desert even tho' it is vast and empty and untouchable—and knows no kindness with all its beauty.[48]

O'Keeffe's use of the word "symbols" is similar to the poetic term "synecdoche," or use of a part to represent the whole. For her the bones as symbols became vehicles to represent her feeling for her beloved desert world. It is ironic, that for her, the bones communicated the desert's life, rather than death.

O'Keeffe's denials of a symbolist intent in her work has been mainly in reference to specific symbols attributed to her work, as the sexual symbolism of her flowers or the death symbolism of her bones. She also has objected to being placed in the box of an artistic "movement" by critics, as in the above statement concerning surrealism. More true to the work of O'Keeffe is the feeling of some critics that O'Keeffe's work is its own "ism," created through her "symbolist" language.

O'Keeffe has not appeared to take issue with those critics whose writings reflected some of the ideas of the French Symbolist movement. The assertion that O'Keeffe's work is a new language, for some, approximating music, appears to be a fairer appraisal of her work.

In general, those critics dealing with various types of symbols and outgrowths of symbolism in O'Keeffe's work reflected the more general philosophical artistic and literary thinking of the time—Symbolism has been seen as a descendant of the Romanticism of the eighteenth and early nineteenth centuries. Baudelaire had defined Romanticism as "a mode of feeling," something within the individual, "intimacy, spirituality, color, aspiration toward the infinite."[49] Thus the symbolist is a kind of romantic with emphasis on the individual's intuitive experience and expression. Symbolism was an approach to reality that "transcended physical experience," and that "reality could be achieved only through intuitive experience expressed particularly in the work of art."[50] The critics dealing with various forms of symbolism in O'Keeffe's work and in attempting to analyze and appraise the inner spirit of the artist, can be seen as part of a continuing line of late nineteenth- and twentieth-century artistic thought from the symbolist artists to the expressionists, Dadaists, surrealists, and later abstractionists.

Notes

[1]Edmund Wilson, *Axel's Castle* (New York: Charles Scribner's Sons, 1931), p. 21.

[2]Richard Ellmann and Charles Feidelson, eds., *The Modern Tradition* (London: Oxford University Press, 1965), p. 12.

[3]Ellmann, *The Modern Tradition,* p. 13.

[4]Charles Baudelaire, "Philosophic Art," *The Painter of Modern Life and Other Essays,* Translated, ed. by Jonathan Mayne (London: Phaidon Press, 1964), p. 204.

[5]*Ibid.,* p. 7.

[6]Tomkins, "Georgia O'Keeffe," p. 44.

[7]*Ibid.,* p. 64.

[8]Goodrich, *Georgia O'Keeffe,* p. 22.

[9]William Fisher, *Camera Work,* nos. 49–50, (June 1917), p. 5.

[10]Mumford, "O'Keeffe and Matisse," p. 16.

[11]Leo Katz, *Georgia O'Keeffe, Portfolio of Twelve Paintings,* p. 1.

[12]"Austere Stripper," p. 74.

[13]*Ibid.*

[14]Tomkins, "Georgia O'Keeffe," p. 61.

[15]Mumford, *The Brown Decades,* p. 245.

[16]Seligmann, "A Woman in Flower," p. 1.

[17]*Ibid.*

[18]Barbara Rose, *American Art Since 1900, A Critical History* (New York: Praeger Publishers, 1967), p. 50.

[19]Paul Rosenfeld, "The Boy in the Dark Room," in *America and Alfred Stieglitz,* pp. 86–87.

[20]Norman, *Alfred Stieglitz,* p. 161.

[21]Seligmann, "A Woman in Flower," p. 1.

[22]Rose, *American Art Since 1900,* p. 47.

[23]Jewell, "O'Keeffe: 30 Years," p. 6x.

[24]James Soby, "To the Ladies," *Saturday Review of Literature,* July 6, 1946, p. 14.

[25]Seligmann, "A Woman in Flower," p. 1.

[26]Kalonyme, "Georgia O'Keeffe: A Woman in Painting" p. 37.

[27]Matthew Baigell, *A History of American Painting* (New York: Praeger Inc., 1971), p. 195.

[28]Mumford, "O'Keeffe and Matisse," p. 16.

[29]Seligmann, "A Woman in Flower," p. 1.

[30]Doris Bry, "Georgia O'Keeffe," p. 80.

[31]Georgia O'Keeffe, Catalogue, "Exhibition of Contemporary American Painting and Sculpture," University of Illinois, 1955.

[32]*Ibid.*

[33]Rose, *American Art Since 1900,* p. 46.

[34]Georgia O'Keeffe, *Exhibition Catalogue,* Anderson Galleries, January–February 1923, p. 1.

[35]Read, "Georgia O'Keeffe—Woman Artist Whose Art is Sincerely Feminine," p. 4.

[36]Tomkins, "Georgia O'Keeffe," p. 50.

[37]"Skeleton on the Plain," *New York Sun,* January 2, 1932, p. 23.

[38]McCausland, "Georgia O'Keeffe in a Retrospective Exhibition," p. 6c.

[39]Henry Geldzahler, *American Paintings in the Twentieth Century* (New York: Metropolitan Museum of Art, 1965), p. 132.

[40]Royal Cortissoz, *New York Herald Tribune,* January 12, 1936, p. 13.

[41]Lewis Mumford, "The Art Galleries—Autobiographies in Paint," *New Yorker,* January 8, 1936, p. 29.

[42]Daniel Catton Rich, "Georgia O'Keeffe," *Exhibition Catalogue,* Worcester Art Museum, October 4–December 4, 1960, p. 5.

[43]Goodrich, *Georgia O'Keeffe,* p. 24.

[44]Katherine Kuh, *The Artist's Voice,* p. 202.

[45]*Ibid.,* p. 194.

[46]*Ibid.*

[47]Tomkins, "Georgia O'Keeffe," p. 50.

[48]Georgia O'Keeffe, *Exhibition Catalogue,* An American Place, January 22–March 17, 1923, p. 3.

[49]H. H. Arnason, *History of Modern Art* (Englewood Cliffs, N.J.: Prentice-Hall, Inc., 1965), p. 69.

[50]*Ibid.*

Chapter Seven
The World of Nature

The most frequent type of criticism, pertaining to O'Keeffe's work is the discussion of the relationship of nature to her work, although such criticism has not been as controversial as the criticism concerned with the feminine experience, and questions of symbolism. To read these critics, one must first establish a definition of nature. Nature here, is considered as "the all-embracing universe about us, the tangible world of land and water, the intangible world of light, sky and air, the eternal forces of germination, growth and death which make up the cycles of life and season—with man and man-made things alone excluded."[1]

To better understand the critics' discussions concerning nature and O'Keeffe's work it is also necessary to understand the tradition of still-life paintings containing specific objects in nature, and the tradition of landscape painting in America. Some of O'Keeffe's paintings of various objects—rocks, bones, flowers, etc.—have been called still lifes. Many of her paintings are called landscapes.

The tradition of the still life as an art form first really flourished in the low countries of Europe in the seventeenth century. The development of the science of optics at the time led to an interest in optical clarity in painting. Seventeenth-century Dutch still lifes were usually painted with exquisite detail. The objects painted were from everyday life but represented larger themes, "the passage of time, the mutability of life," served as "an allegory of the human condition,"[2] with such images as a perfect flower juxtaposed to a wilted or blemished flower. Spanish still lifes done at a similar time, such as those by Luis Melendez, contained more surreal elements in the strange use of perspective and eerie empty spaces. By the eighteenth century, still-life paintings, such as those of Desportes and Oudry, were more important in their function as decoration on screens or furniture. "With Chardin, however, the art of still-life painting took on a new solemnity. More than any other painter he transformed the genre into the highest form of abstract poetry."[3] French nineteenth-century painters such as Manet, Monet, and Cézanne transformed the still life still further through explorations of objects bathed in light and color, or reducing objects to the essential geometric forms, such as the cylinder, square, or cube. In the twentieth century, because of the belief that there is no longer one absolute reality, there has been a great diversity of approach to the still life. Many twentieth-century artists from cubists to surrealists to abstract expressionists, have explored the possibilities of still life in creating new possible realities for everyday objects and scenes.

In America a major exploration of nature through landscape painting occurred in the 1830's. Prior to that time there was more emphasis on portraiture and the painting of historical topics. Artistic portrayal of the American landscape was to serve as religious and moral inspiration. The landscape, seen as solid and eternal, served also as a solace and escape from a world of ever-changing values brought about by scientific and technological discoveries. O'Keeffe's landscapes must be seen in the context of the growth and development of American landscape paintings.

The Hudson River School of painters, with work such as that by Asher Durand, Thomas Cole, and Albert Bierstadt, was born in the mid-nineteenth century. It has been seen as the first "American" painting not relying exclusively on European styles and subject matter. Land for Americans at this time was a valuable resource—physically, aesthetically and spiritually. The westward expansion of the United States had opened up new vistas, and artists as well as settlers traveled westward. The "cult of nature," emphasizing the spirit and force of the landscape, began to take on the stature of religion. Man in comparison to an awesome nature was usually portrayed as very small and dominated by the elements of nature. The Hudson River School painters in their reverence for nature may be seen as a part of the larger Romantic movement.

The philosophic groundwork for much of American Romanticism was laid to a large extent by the poetic and pantheistic writings of some of the transcendentalists such as Ralph Waldo Emerson. In his famous 1836 essay, *Nature,* Emerson set out some of the principles of New England transcendentalism and established the importance of a direct "religious" experience with nature and arrival at a sacred sense of wholeness with the universe, as the individual human soul became one with nature. "Standing on the bare ground—my head bathed by the blight air, and uplifted into infinite space—all mean egotism vanishes. I become a transparent eyeball; I am nothing; I see all; the currents of the Universal Being circulate through me; I am part or parcel of God."[4]

This spirit of transcendentalism was to be attributed many years later by some of O'Keeffe's critics to her life and work. Critic Barbara Rose has called O'Keeffe a latter day Emersonian transcendentalist.[5] Writer Eleanor Munro felt that O'Keeffe's values were very close to Emerson's exhortation in *Self-Reliance.* "There is a time in every man's education when he arrives at the conviction that imitation is suicide, that he must take himself for better or worse as his portion."[6] Further, Munro has noted that O'Keeffe and Stieglitz believed in the theory of correspondences espoused by the Romantic-Transcendentalists and later by the Symbolists and Expressionists: "the idea that nature presents the mind with a number of symbolic expressions of an inner reality; that these forms are related to one another; and that between them all and that inner essence a clear correspondence exists."[7] (O'Keeffe was first awakened to the idea of correspondences in Alon Bement's classroom.)

In its early years, transcendentalism was thus both foundation and complement to many of the landscape painters.

Of the younger generation painters of the Hudson River group, such as Thomas Cole, Asher Durand, and Thomas Doughty, Thomas Cole was perhaps the most passionate and dramatic and was influenced by Transcendental thinking of his day. His allegorical series, such as the *Voyage of Life* and *Course of an Empire* illustrate his belief in the religious power of nature and his portrayal of that nature. The romantic landscape tradition was carried on by a later generation consisting of painters such as Frederick Church, Albert Bierstadt, and Thomas Moran. Emphasis on landscape inspiration moved to the west as American exploration of the west reached its height. Artists such as Bierstadt made several trips to the west where he painted his majestic images of places such as Yosemite Valley and the Rocky Mountains. In his work, the mountains and clouds are portrayed as elemental forces that have a special life of their own. The several generations of landscape painters in the mid-nineteenth century established the richness of the American landscape with its expansive spaces and infinite variety for both the artist and the viewer.

American landscape painting expanded further in the mid-nineteenth century as painters explored a lovely, still, "American" light in what came to be called "luminism." Such painters included Fitz Hugh Lane, Martin Johnson Heade, and John Kensett, who produced magical paintings with an emphasis on the horizontal, on very realistic details and smooth, subtle variations of light and color. Quite often the upper half of the canvas was devoted to the sky, and much of the rest to water. An enduring calmness radiated from works such as Kensett's *Shrewsbury River,* 1859. This expansive horizontal treatment of the sky may be seen in some of O'Keeffe's landscapes such as her *Red Hills and Sky,* 1945 or in her "cloud" series.

During the post-Civil War years there was less interest in landscape, although George Inness carried on the tradition of a deep involvement with nature. Matthew Baigell briefly describes Inness's approach to nature in comparison to Cole and Church. "Cole used nature as a vessel for his emotions and Church let nature speak for itself, but Inness endeavored almost from the first actually to become a part of nature's fabric. . . On occasion, he identified himself with objects in nature. . . ."[8] Slightly later, American landscape impressionists such as John Twachtman, Theodore Robinson, and Childe Hassam adopted the techniques of the European impressionists.

Toward the end of the century many American painters journeyed to Europe and were highly influenced by European work. Expatriates, Whistler, Cassatt, and Sargent were among those spending much time in Europe. One painter who remained largely uninfluenced by European work and who continued to explore nature was Albert Pinkham Ryder. Ryder's mystical landscapes were important for the creation of a new, highly personal reality by the artist, rather than a relatively strict observational transcription of nature.

In the twentieth century, two very varied approaches to nature, important to consider in comparison to O'Keeffe's work, have been the American scene painters and the abstractionists. Major American scene painters were John S. Curry, Grant Wood, and Thomas Hart Benton. In their landscapes of the Midwest in particular, they attempted to capture with nostalgia America's heartland and thus escape contemporary reality. Benton described his, Wood's, and Curry's "revolt" "against the general cultural inconsequences of modern art" and their belief "that only by our own participation in the reality of American life . . . could we come to forms in which Americans would find an opportunity for genuine spectator participation."[9] As previously mentioned, O'Keeffe's work in New Mexico has been described as a kind of regionalism.

In a study in 1958, John Baur attempted to determine what the relationship between American abstract art and observed nature was. He used the term abstract to describe "any art not clearly based on recognizable visual reality."[10] To Baur's question, "Do you feel that nature has any serious relation to your own work?", most of the artists questioned such as O'Keeffe, William Baziotes, Leo Amino, Lawrence Calcagno, Perle Fine, Helen Frankenthaler, Joan Mitchell, and Robert Goodnough responded, "yes." Some artists stated they dealt with nature consciously, while others were involved in less direct ways. The conscious approach to nature involved the use of abstraction as a tool to rearrange, distill, and intensify.[11] Among those stating a very conscious approach to nature was O'Keeffe.

> *From experience of one kind or another shapes and colors came to me very clearly. Sometimes I start in a very realistic fashion and as I go on from one painting [to] another of the same thing, it becomes simplified till it can be nothing but abstract, but for me it is my reason for painting, I suppose.[12]*

A more indirect approach involved the identification of artists with natural rhythms and forces. Theodore Stamos wrote of his work, "The whole combined series evolved from thoughts of the solstice. As I worked, things which a painter knows about picture-making began automatically to take their rightful place in controlling the abstract arrangement, the distribution of form and color on the canvas, but always retaining one thing above all, 'the idea.'"[13] Although artists' styles varied greatly, Baur felt there was a desire on the part of the majority of the artists questioned to reach and express the essence of an object or idea connected with nature.

In general, nature for American twentieth-century artists has frequently been seen as a reflection of "self" rather than evidence of a higher divinity. The following statements from a variety of artists affirm the importance of nature for their work and illustrates their search for the primordial and infinite.

> *I paint to rest from the phenomena of the external world—to pronounce it—and to make notations of its essences with which to verify the inner eye.[14]*

Morris Graves

> *My concern is with the rhythms of nature . . . the way the ocean moves. . . . The ocean is what the expanse of the west is for me. . . . I work from the inside out, like nature.[15]*

Jackson Pollock

> *I am nature.[16]*

Jackson Pollock

> *White lines symbolize light as a unifying idea which flows through compartmented units of life, bringing a dynamic to men's minds ever expanding their energies toward a larger creativity.[17]*

Mark Tobey

> *Seems to me the true artist must go from time to time to the elemental big forms—sky, sea, mountain, plain,—and those things pertaining thereto, to sort of nature himself up, to recharge the battery. For these big forms have everything.[18]*

John Marin

I've been up on the roof watching the moon come up—the sky very dark—the moon large and lopsided—and very soft—a strange white light creeping across the far away to the dark sky— the cliffs all black—it was weird and strangely beautiful.[19]

Georgia O'Keeffe

Thus nature has been a primary inspiration to a large number of artists since the nineteenth century. The growth of the American tradition fostering land and light as a physical and spiritual resource has been an integral part, directly or indirectly of the background or education of many artists and critics in this century. With such a background and tradition behind them, be it conscious and/or unconscious, the critics have approached O'Keeffe's work throughout the century.

What then, have critics said concerning the relationship of nature to O'Keeffe's work: "One constant factor throughout O'Keeffe's career has been her love of the physical objects of nature. Concentrating on the object, she isolates it from the world of reality, and gives it a new significance."[20] "And not only nature, but nature's fertility is Georgia O'Keeffe's major point of reference."[21] "No matter how abstract her work, the smell and forms of the land are still there."[22] These three statements, all written in 1970 after seeing the 1970 Whitney Museum O'Keeffe retrospective exhibition, indicate the continuing importance of nature in O'Keeffe's work throughout her career. Critics have been concerned with the role of nature in O'Keeffe's work since the beginning of her career, but earlier criticism places more emphasis on the feminine imagery and symbolic aspects of her work. In the past two decades, articles have mainly dealt with O'Keeffe's retrospective shows, putting her work in a larger perspective.

Critics have described the role of nature in O'Keeffe's work in various ways. A frequently stated opinion has been O'Keeffe's expression of universal and elemental forms through her treatment of objects in nature in realistic, semiabstract, and abstract terms. Duncan Pollock wrote, "O'Keeffe has developed a vocabulary of forms that express the universal in nature. The sources of her images lie in the New Mexico country but they are transported outside the ordinary realm of time and place."[23] Bob Martin wrote, "Mountains are conceptualized into something beyond mere depiction; an old cow skull takes on a kind of collective universal meaning in the way the artist etches it sharply before our eyes, and yet transports it beyond the realm of everyday reality."[24] There is then a certain ambivalence of imagery in O'Keeffe's work—a presentation of various possible realities, from the realistic, concrete object to the universal. As Doris Bry wrote, "So the paintings of the mountains are the mountains, but go beyond the particular mountain; the flower paintings are and are not flowers."[25]

In a step beyond expression of the universal through nature forms, some critics (mainly earlier ones) have identified O'Keeffe's portrayal of nature with mystical representations. In 1936 Marsden Hartley described O'Keeffe's work, "From the first, the element of mystical sensation appeared—and it is not difficult to think of O'Keeffe as a mystic of her own sort—passionately seeking direct relationship to what is unquestioned, to her, the true force of nature from which source and this alone she is to draw forth her specific deliverance."[26] Earlier, Paul Rosenfeld wrote of O'Keeffe's paintings, "Pearly shapes chant ecstatically against somber backgrounds. Life seems to rise on wings, in the dumbness of utter bestowal into a climax of seraphic hues."[27]

Some critics have felt O'Keeffe created a microcosm in her forms, a microcosm where humans seem to be the butterflies.[28] "By enormously enlarging the flower she transformed it, gave it not only a new dimension but a new kind of existence. Magnification enabled her to reveal its structure with complete clarity. The flower became a world in itself, a microcosm. Magnification was another kind of abstraction of separating the object from ordinary reality, endowing it with a life of its own."[29] Some feel nature has become almost human for O'Keeffe. "Throughout her work there is a dual conception of nature: a nature as the painter herself; and nature as an unfailing companion with whom she converses in terms of wonderful precision, intimacy and shades of meaning."[30] O'Keeffe herself has said, "I wish people were all trees and I think I could enjoy them,"[31] although she does not hate people.

The search of Americans for a cultural identity and expression of an American identity in the twenties and thirties in particular, is seen in some of the critics' description of O'Keeffe's brand of regionalism through her nature images (See previous discussion in Chapter Three.)

Much of the more recent discussion by various critics concerning the role of nature in O'Keeffe's work deals with O'Keeffe's methods of portraying various images. Most critics mention the varied range of realistic to abstract imagery. For some, her more realistic paintings represent objectification. "When she objectifies rather than condenses nature, O'Keeffe often paints what is before her with tremendous realism. Many of her flowers . . . capture the exact transparent tissue and textures of the original blossom."[32] In her more abstract paintings critics often speak of further objectification and magnification of close-up and enlarged segments. As Goodrich wrote, "Magnification was another kind of abstraction, of separating the object from ordinary reality and endowing it with a life of its own."[33] This concern with magnification and close-up imagery reflected the growing popularity of the art of photography in the twentieth century. Further associated with her abstractions from nature has been the use of words such as reduce and condense. Of her bone paintings, Daniel Catton Rich wrote in 1941, "this new statement gains by reduction to essentials."[34] Later he wrote, "O'Keeffe has always believed it possible to condense, to make a part stand for the whole."[35] O'Keeffe's simplified and condensed forms have also been called "nature-inspired geometry."[36] O'Keeffe's work has been recently seen as an anticipation of the color field abstraction of those such as Kenneth Noland and Ellsworth Kelly. "In its uncompromising objectivity, O'Keeffe's intense vision seems more coordinate with art of the last decade than with that of her own decade."[37] It is interesting to note that O'Keeffe has expressed a particular interest in Kelly's work, which is also often based on natural shapes. "Sometimes I've thought one of his things was mine," she has said. "I've actually looked at one of Kelly's pictures and thought for a moment that I'd done it."[38]

Whether painting in realistic, semiabstract, or abstract terms, O'Keeffe has been consistent in her use of nature in her work. "Concepts which meant much to her in the past are not forgotten, but recreated in a new form."[39] O'Keeffe herself wrote in 1957 of her various versions of *From the Plains,* 1919. "It was painted from something I heard very often—a very special rhythm that would go on for hours and hours. That was why I painted it again a couple of years ago."[40] Throughout O'Keeffe's career critics have continued to respond with various interpretations and viewpoints to her powerful imagery and its relationship to nature.

There seems to be no doubt that the critics are correct in emphasizing the importance of nature for O'Keeffe's work. In response to a question by Katherine Kuh, "What do you feel has been the strongest influence on your work?" O'Keeffe replied, "Some people say nature," but did quality her statement in speaking of the influence of Arthur Dow. "But the way you see nature depends on what influenced your way of seeing."[41] Other statements by O'Keeffe throughout her career further illuminate the importance of nature for her work. She painted her large flower images so that "people would 'be surprised into taking time to look at it' [O'Keeffe's words] and would then perhaps see it as she did, in all its miraculous shape, color, and texture."[42] She wrote of her love for the New Mexican landscape, "The color up there—the blue green of the sage, and the mountains, and the wildflowers—is a different kind of color from anything I'd ever seen. . . It was the shape of the hills there that fascinated me. The reddish sand hills with dark mesas behind them. It seemed as though no matter how far you walked you could never get into those dark hills, although I walked great distances."[43]

There is little evidence that O'Keeffe has taken issue with most of her critics' writing concerning the relationship of nature to her work, although in general she seems to object to being placed in any box or "ism." Some of her statements do serve as complement to various critics' statements. O'Keeffe spoke of the popularity of American scene painting in the late twenties and thirties.

> *"People wanted to 'do' the American scene. I had gone back and forth across the country several times by then, and some of the current ideas about the American scene struck me as pretty ridiculous. . . . I knew America was very rich, very lush. Well, I started painting my skulls about this time. . . . I thought, the people who talk about the American scene don't know anything about it. So, in a way, that cow's skull was my joke on the American scene, and it gave me pleasure to make it in red, white, and blue."[44]*

Of her use of both realistic and abstract imagery she stated in 1970, "There must be changes. I paint what interests me and what I see. At times you can't find them in your head and you have to find them as they are in the world."[45] And in 1974 she said, "Sometimes I know where an image comes from, sometimes not. . . . Often, a picture just gets into my head without my having the least idea how it got there. But I'm much more down-to-earth than people give me credit for. At times, I'm ridiculously realistic."[46]

In general the critics' writings have reflected much of the philosophical or artistic thought of their day. Those earlier critics associated with the Stieglitz circle such as Mumford, Hartley, Seligmann, and Rosenfeld, continued to reflect much of Stieglitz's philosophy in their writing about O'Keeffe's work in relation to nature. The other critics, too, besides those associated with the Stieglitz circle, reflected much of the thinking of their time. Later critics have tended to use less emotionally charged language.

A continuing concern in twentieth-century thought has been the varying expressions of reality. The suggestions by some of O'Keeffe's critics of a new kind of reality in her nature images reflects the concept, that grew in this century, that there is no absolute reality. Scientific discoveries—the disintegration of the atom, Einstein's theory of relativity, Freud's theory of the unconscious, and quantum physics—destroyed the idea of a fixed image of the world around us. Like many of the critics writing of the relationship of nature to O'Keeffe's work, the philosophers James and Dewey emphasized "the openness of nature, the way in which 'truth' grows and changes in the experimental process of the world."[47] One is also reminded of William Carlos Williams' concept of the "reality beyond actuality." The opinion some critics expressed that O'Keeffe was portraying aspects of the essential, elemental, and basic rhythms of nature in a very individual way, is consistent with early twentieth-century thinkers' emphasis on the intuition and instincts of individuals as seen in the writings of a D. H. Lawrence or Henri Bergson. The general defense of the spirit, and sense of the importance of intuition is seen in those writings ascribing a mystical quality to O'Keeffe's portrayal of nature.

The tendency of most of the aforementioned critics to praise or at least accept the nature imagery of O'Keeffe may also be seen as a part of the growing twentieth-century conflict between the worlds of nature and urbanization. Such a conflict has increased as technology and the growth of cities has increased through the century. America first began to realistically face the strange world of a changing technology and urbanization following World War I as the country turned inward to a world of broken down values. The world of nature appeared in opposition to such technological development. O'Keeffe's continuing concern for nature has provided new ways of looking at the world. Some critics have felt that our rapidly increasing technology, when not properly utilized, has had harmful effects on our society. Indeed, the conflicts of nature versus the city, the human versus the mechanical, have been prevalent in American art for a large part of the century.[48] O'Keeffe's vision of nature and transformation of objects in her environment have served as a refreshing alternative for a fast-paced technological world.

More recent criticism relating O'Keeffe's work to that of Kelly, Noland, or other abstractionists reflects a growing historical perspective of such critics and their ability to deal with a work of art outside of the time it was created. At the same time, these critics' writings[49] have suggested the use of nature's basic rhythms as a continuing common point of reference for better understanding a line of development in American and European art despite difference in style. Some critics felt O'Keeffe's work could be seen as part of a tradition that began with the acceptance of landscape painting in America and the beginning of the Hudson River School. Other critics were more interested in trying to understand O'Keeffe's individual vision in relation to nature. Still other critics saw O'Keeffe's depiction of objects in nature as part of the development of still-life painting that has become increasingly varied and abstract as the twentieth century has progressed. O'Keeffe's *Single Alligator Pear*, 1922, her *Shell and Old Shingle VI*, 1926, and her *Black Rock with Blue III*, 1970 are only a few examples of her ability to portray the essence of an object. In each of the above paintings the objects appear solid and Zen-like, filled with a sense of serenity and oneness with the surrounding environment. Critics' expansion of traditional notions of still-life painting seems exemplary of a growing, open, historical perspective in regard to studying painters' portrayals of objects in nature.

Thus the critics' discussion of the relationship of nature to O'Keeffe's work reflects in many ways the thinking of their times, as well as a basic desire by man to understand some of the elemental rhythms and forms in nature. O'Keeffe has provided a new language for her viewers to explore nature, a language with which to express part of an infinite variety of possibilities with regard to nature. As O'Keeffe herself says, "The unexplainable thing in nature that makes me feel the world is big far beyond my understanding—to understand maybe by trying to put it into form. To find the feeling of infinity on the horizon line or just over the next hill."[50] Lloyd Goodrich perhaps best summarizes the relationship of nature to O'Keeffe's work. "Her art is an individual one, expressing personal emotions and perceptions in a style that combines strength and crystalline clarity. The sources of her imagery lie in the world of nature, but nature interpreted with great freedom, from precise realism to abstraction as pure as music."[51]

Despite the great variety of criticism about her work, O'Keeffe has continued to work and show little interest in how she is judged by others. "I have never cared about what others were doing in art, or what they thought of my own paintings. Why should I care? I found my inspirations and painted them."[52] Thus her tough and hearty individualism continued to prevail.

Notes

[1]John Baur, *Nature in Abstraction* (New York: Macmillan Co., 1958), p. 5.

[2]"The Object as Subject," *Exhibition Catalogue,* Wildenstein Gallery, April 4–May 3, 1975, p. 2.

[3]*Ibid.,* p. 3.

[4]Ralph Waldo Emerson, *Emerson: A Modern Anthology,* eds. Alfred Kazin and Daniel Aaron (Boston: Houghton Mifflin, 1958), p. 113.

[5]Barbara Rose, "O'Keeffe's Trail," *New York Review of Books,* March 31, 1977.

[6]Eleanor Munro, *The Originals: American Women Artists* (New York: Simon & Schuster, 1979), p. 489.

[7]*Ibid.,* pp. 489–490.

[8]*Ibid.,* p. 146.

[9]Thomas Hart Benton, *An Artist in America* (New York: Robert M. McBride and Co., 1937), p. 48.

[10]Baur, *Nature in Abstraction,* p. 5.

[11]*Ibid.,* p. 6.

[12]*Ibid.*

[13]*Ibid.,* p. 14.

[14]Morris Graves, in exhibition catalogue, *Morris Graves: Retrospective Exhibition,* California Palace of the Legion of Honor, San Francisco, May 21–June 29, 1948, p. 3.

[15]Jackson Pollock, quoted in B. H. Friedman, *Jackson Pollock: Energy Made Visible* (New York: McGraw-Hill, 1972), p. 228.

[16]Jackson Pollock, quoted in Francis V. O'Connor, *Jackson Pollock* (New York: The Museum of Modern Art, 1967), p. 26.

[17]Mark Tobey, quoted in Sidney Janis, *Abstract and Surrealist,* Art in America (New York: Reynal & Hitchcock, 1944), p. 98.

[18]John Marin, quoted in Dorothy Norman, ed., *The Selected Writings of John Marin* (New York: Pellegrini & Cudahy, 1949), p. 127.

[19]Georgia O'Keeffe, From a letter to Alfred Stieglitz from O'Keeffe dated August 26, 1937 reprinted in

catalogue of *14th Annual Exhibition of Paintings,* An American Place Gallery, New York, December 27, 1937–February 11, 1938, p. 8.

[20]Goodrich, *Georgia O'Keeffe,* p. 17.

[21]John Canaday, "Georgia O'Keeffe: The Patrician Stance as Esthetic Principle," *New York Times,* October 11, 1970, p. 25.

[22]Davis, "Return of the Native," p. 105.

[23]Duncan Pollock, "Artists of Taos and Santa Fe: From Zane Grey to the Tide of Modernism," *ARTnews,* January 1974, p. 21.

[24]Bob Martin, "Exhibit Brings New Look," *Tampa Times,* November 19, 1970, p. 14.

[25]Doris Bry, "Georgia O'Keeffe," p. 80.

[26]Marsden Hartley, "Georgia O'Keeffe, A Second Outline in Portraiture," *Exhibition Catalogue,* (New York: An American Place), p. 3.

[27]Paul Rosenfeld, *Port of New York,* p. 207.

[28]Katz, *Georgia O'Keeffe, Portfolio of Twelve Paintings,* p. 2.

[29]Goodrich, *Georgia O'Keeffe,* p. 18.

[30]Soby, "To the Ladies," pp. 14–15.

[31]Hartley, "Some Women Painters—Georgia O'Keeffe," p. 31.

[32]Rich, "Georgia O'Keeffe," pp. 3–4.

[33]Goodrich, *Georgia O'Keeffe,* p. 18.

[34]Daniel Catton Rich, "The New O'Keeffes," *Magazine of Art,* March 1941, p. 110.

[35]Rich, "Georgia O'Keeffe," *Exhibition Catalogue,* Worcester Museum, pp. 4–5.

[36]Geldzahler, *American Painting in the Twentieth Century,* p. 129.

[37]E. C. Goosen, *The Art of the Real: U.S.A., 1948–1968* (New York: Museum of Modern Art, 1968), p. 6.

[38]Tomkins, "Georgia O'Keeffe," p. 53.

[39]Goodrich, *Georgia O'Keeffe,* p. 27.

[40]Baur, *Nature in Abstraction,* p. 77.

[41]Kuh, *The Artist's Voice,* p. 189.

[42]Tomkins, "Georgia O'Keeffe," p. 48.

[43]*Ibid.,* p. 54.

[44]*Ibid.,* pp. 48–49.

[45]Davis, "Return of the Native," p. 105.

[46]Tomkins, "Georgia O'Keeffe," p. 48.

[47]Ellmann, *The Modern Tradition,* p. 384.

[48]Rose, *American Art Since 1900,* p. 51.

[49]Examples of such critics include: Goosen, "O'Keeffe," Goosen, "The Art of the Real," and Frank Getlein, "In the Light of Georgia O'Keeffe," *The New Republic,* November 7, 1960.

[50]Georgia O'Keeffe, *Georgia O'Keeffe.*

[51]Goodrich, *Georgia O'Keeffe,* p. 7.

[52]Leo Jones, "Georgia O'Keeffe at Eighty-Four," *The Atlantic,* December 1971, p. 117.

III. THE WORK

Colors and shapes make a more definite statement than words.[1]

I've never thought of having a great gift. I don't think I have a great gift. It isn't just talent. You have to have something else. You have to have a kind of nerve.[2]

Notes

[1]*Georgia O'Keeffe* (New York: Viking Press, 1976).

[2]Mary Lyn Kotz, "A Day With Georgia O'Keeffe," *ARTnews,* December 1977, p. 45.

Chapter Eight

The Paintings and Sculpture

Since 1916 when O'Keeffe's drawings and watercolors were first shown at Stieglitz's gallery, O'Keeffe has created a tremendous body of work both highly praised and criticized by her critics. Her artwork has been her chief concern since that first show almost sixty years ago. She has continued to paint prodigiously through the years, driving to various sites in the desert and camping overnight if necessary. She has also prepared her own canvases since she couldn't get the quality of canvas she wanted. As Anita Pollitzer said in 1950, "She is so in love with the thing she does that she subordinates all else in order to win time and freedom to paint. . . ."[1] O'Keeffe herself has said that because of her drive to paint, "I know I am unreasonable about people whom I can't take the time to know."[2] Further she has written a statement that indicates how much painting is an integral part of her life.

*One works I suppose because it is the most
interesting thing one knows to do.*

*The days one works are the best days. On the other
days one is hurrying through the other things one
imagines one has to do to keep one's life going.*

*You get the garden planted.
You get the roof fixed.
You take the dog to the vet.
You spend a day with a friend.
You learn to make a new kind of bread.
You hunt up photographs for someone who thinks he needs them.
You certainly have to do the shopping.*

*You may even enjoy doing such things.
You think they have to be done. You even think you
have to have some visitors or take a trip to keep
from getting queer living alone with just two chows.
But always you are hurrying through these so that
you can get at the painting again because that is
the high spot—in a way it is what you do all
the other things for.
Why it is that way I do not know.*

I have no theories to offer.
The painting is like a thread that runs through all
the reasons for all the other things that make one's life.[3]

O'Keeffe's paintings are like her children. As she said long ago of some of her work, "Wise men say it isn't art! But what of it, if it is children and love in paint?"[4] Even today in her nineties, despite failing eyesight, O'Keeffe continues her strong, independent existence in New Mexico, and her continued passion for her artwork. The following pages contain representative examples of the many O'Keeffe creations since 1916. Enter then, into her world.

O'Keeffe did many of her early watercolors and drawings while teaching in Texas. Some of the motifs of these early works have appeared at various times throughout O'Keeffe's career. One of the most frequently mentioned early pieces is her watercolor *Abstraction No. 11, The Two Blue Lines,* 1916 ($25'' \times 19''$). The simplicity of design, line and color with a balance of vertical and horizontal lines illustrate the influence of Arthur Dow and his emphasis on the Oriental concepts of design and harmony. The upward thrusting forms from a ground base suggest the organic budding of a plant reaching toward the sky. Although there is a definite base, the extended delicate tips of the two blue lines suggest an infinite space beyond the painting. O'Keeffe's use of a lighter shade of blue at various intervals along the upward thrusting forms adds further dimension to the composition.

F.S.C. Northrop used this watercolor as a frontispiece to his book, *The Meeting of East and West,* feeling that the composition represented the uniting of an intuitive aesthetic component and intellectual theoretical component. Northrop refers to Stieglitz's similar interpretation of the same composition, ". . . the one blue line represents the female aesthetic component in things. And the common base from which they spring expresses the fact that although each is distinct and irreducible to the other, both are united."[5]

One may or may not consider this painting a uniting of intellectual and intuitive methods of thought. But this work along with the other drawings and watercolors brought to Stieglitz in 1916 by Anita Pollitzer, marks the beginning of O'Keeffe's rebellion against the academic forms of her early training and her beginning to paint according to her own intuition. The painting provides an "early glimpse of the poetry wrought of a severe reduction of means through which O'Keeffe transfigured the real."[6] Edward Alden Jewell suggests that if one were to take just one of these beautiful blue lines, one can follow it into many of O'Keeffe's canvases and that these blue lines are "one aspect of the mystical rhythm that animates O'Keeffe's art."[7]

Painting No. 21 (Palo Duro Canyon), ($13'' \times 16''$), suggesting the contours of a rolling Texas landscape, is somewhat more realistic than some of the others done at this time. Like some of her charcoal drawings done during this period, this painting contains swelling budding forms that suggest the growing and maturing plants, here seen in ripe reds and yellows. When O'Keeffe taught in Canyon, Texas she and her sister Claudia often drove to the Palo Duro Canyon, about twenty miles away, to climb the meandering pathways that few people had ever traversed. They rarely met anyone there. The only life they encountered were lines of black cattle crossing the hilly terrain. But O'Keeffe revelled in the lonely and perilous splendor of that wild canyon. "Those perilous climbs were frightening but it was wonderful to me and not like anything I had known before. The fright of the day was still with me in the night and I would often dream that the foot of my bed rose straight up into the air—then just as it was about to fall I would wake up. Many drawings came from days like that, and later some oil paintings."[8] The curvilinear road-like forms are well balanced intersecting arcs that are repeated in a smaller format in the cluster of bud-like shapes in the lower part of the canvas. Together the varied arcs give a solid, continuous rhythm to the piece. The road-like forms appear later, in variation, in such paintings as *The Winter Road,* 1963 and *The Road Past the View,* 1964.

The lighter, yellow center area in contrast to the darker surrounding red and black forms suggests that sense of infinite space so common to O'Keeffe's work. One seems able to step inside the painting. The painting well-illustrates O'Keeffe's ability to synthesize abstract and realistic forms.

This painting must have meant a lot to both Stieglitz and O'Keeffe, for it appears in some of the photographs comprising Stieglitz's composite portrait of O'Keeffe. In the photograph O'Keeffe appears to be a part of the landscape and painting with the rounded form of her body reflected in the rounded forms of the painting.

O'Keeffe did a number of series of watercolors at this time that illustrate her spare but eloquent vocabulary of basic shapes and colors. A series, *Blue 1–4,* completed in 1916 shows an early interest in organic free-flowing forms that come alive through O'Keeffe's subtle blue and blue-green watercolor washes. A gentle tension, established by the wet and dry brush areas pulls the viewer closer and closer to examine the more complex washes of the curvilinear shapes. The series becomes increasingly abstract and simplified. *Blue #4* appears to be very similar to Chinese calligraphic strokes, indicating O'Keeffe's early affinity with Oriental art.

The following year, inspired by her late-afternoon walks in Texas, where she was fascinated by the evening star, O'Keeffe did a series of ten watercolors from the star. O'Keeffe has vividly described those walks.

> The evening star would be high in the sunset sky when it was still broad daylight. That evening star fascinated me. It was in some ways very exciting to me. My sister had a gun, and as we walked she would throw bottles into the air and shoot as many as she could before they hit the ground. I had nothing but to walk into nowhere and the wide sunset space with the star.[9]

The vibrant red, yellow, blue, and green washes O'Keeffe used confront the viewer head on, as the star did to O'Keeffe. Noteworthy are the curvilinear red shapes that remain open in the series, suggesting an ongoing infinite space. The paintings are at once realistic and abstract, distinct and indistinct as O'Keeffe captures the vitality and power of a blood red sunset on the open Texas plains. The target-like forms of *Evening Star III* were to inspire color field painter Kenneth Noland as he dealt with similar open forms in the sixties.

In another watercolor of the same year, *Light Coming on the Plains II* (12″ × 9″), O'Keeffe has solidified and magnified her curvilinear shapes to a large dome of radiating light and color. The viewer is pulled into the eerie blue-yellow light of the center area, captured by "that light coming on the plains." The large floating forms take away from the sense of a deep traditional pictorial space and bring one immediately into the world of modern painting.

These early watercolors illustrate O'Keeffe's version of the tradition of biomorphic abstraction as her free-flowing forms approximate lived experience rather than exist solely as an exercise in formal experimentation. In such paintings there is, as Sam Hunter well expressed, "a daring reduction of pictorial means to a simple scheme of symmetrically opposed color stains or a serpentine spiral of graduated rings. . . .O'Keeffe submits rational ego in favor of a more informal and 'open' kind of painting as Mark Rothko, and in a different fashion, Kenneth Noland have more recently done."[10]

With the encouragement of Stieglitz, O'Keeffe began to work again in oils, carrying some of the rhythms and forms of her earlier drawings and watercolors further.

The 1919 oil, *From the Plains* (27″ × 23″) suggests the sunset colors of a Texas plain, with an intense sense of light, space, and wind. Without the title, though, the painting could be viewed in only abstract terms. The combination of sharp, angular forms with the center, lighter, roughly delineated mass of shades of blues, purples, and red, is reminiscent of the combination of forms in some of her earlier charcoal drawings and watercolors. Most noticeable about this painting is the undulating wave of magenta gradations passing through the near center of the painting. The arc formation of color holds together the jagged forms in the upper part of the canvas with the more mottled forms below.

O'Keeffe wrote of her great pleasure in viewing the Texas plains. "And then of course, I liked everything about Texas . . . . I was just crazy about all of it. . . . The light would begin to appear and then it would disappear and there would be a kind of halo effect and then it would appear again. . . ."[11] *Orange and Red Streak,* also done in 1919, contains imagery similar to *From the Plains,* but with a palette of mustards, reds, and greens. These two paintings were actually painted several months after O'Keeffe left the Texas plains. But the sights and sounds of that Texas terrain stayed with her. She recalled in her book,

> For days we would see large herds of cattle with their clouds of dust being driven slowly across the plains toward the town. When the cattle arrived they were put in pens near the station. . . . The cattle in the pens longing for their calves day and night was a sound that has always haunted me. It had a regular rhythm beat like the old Penitente songs, repeating the same rhythms over and over all through the day and night. It was loud and raw under the stars in that wide empty country.[12]

Carrying on the same rhythms, O'Keeffe painted *From the Plains II* (48″ × 72″) in 1954 with angular yellow and mustard forms streaking across a field of orange and red. The later, more abstract 1954 painting with fewer and flatter areas of color does not contain the deep sense of space and mystery, evoked through lovely blues and purples as in the earlier painting. Yet O'Keeffe's continuing interests in particular nature forms and rhythms is remarkable. In 1957 she wrote about her feelings concerning her versions of *From the Plains*: "I think I would say that I have worked differently at different times. *From the Plains* was painted from something I heard very often—a very special rhythm that would go for hours and hours. That was why I painted it again a couple of years ago."[13]

In another painting of 1919, *Music—Pink and Blue I,* O'Keeffe has transformed the waves of the Texas plains into waves of music. The painting calls to all of the senses with its diaphanous folds in shades of rose, opening around a larger cavity of blue, which reminds one of the sky. "Her color with its prismatic brilliance and its complete freedom from canons of good task was prophetic of present-day color painting with the considerable difference that her color was not used in flat patterns or over all unmodulated color fields but to create three dimensional forms and space."[14]

O'Keeffe's evocation of an intense musical language with a fine sense of rhythm, form, and color, as in this painting is consistent with some critics ascribing symbolist characteristics to her work. The painting suggests the French symbolist theory of synaethesia, where expression of one sense might evoke another. The subtly delineated forms and colors seem to evoke the senses of sound and touch. There is a strong sense of rhythm and melody, particularly in the way Baudelaire described melody. "Melody is unity within color. Melody calls for a cadence; it is a whole, in which every effect contributes to the general effect."[15]

Some have described paintings such as this or *Gray Line with Black, Blue and Yellow* of 1923, or *Green-Gray Abstraction,* 1931, in sexual terms, relating the paintings' shapes to the vaginal form. However, it seems unfair to describe the paintings and artist's intentions in such narrow terms. The works may have sexual overtones to some, but other ways of looking at the painting are indeed possible. Part of the beauty of the work is in its ambiguity of interpretation for the viewer. Indeed, it is not necessary to speak of any specific subject matter.

Another abstraction using a darker, low-keyed palette, *Dark Abstraction,* 1924 (24⅞" × 20⅞"), indicates (even in these early years) the variety of O'Keeffe's approaches to painting, while still expressing an individual inner spirit in her work. The downward flowing forms in the upper part of the painting are similar to the diaphanous folds of the two previously described paintings. In this painting such are reminiscent of the flowing of a river or perhaps a crack in a rock. The gradated edges of the forms delineate them further, giving the forms depth. The subtlety of the modeling of the purples, magentas, and Prussian blues gives the painting a sense of mystery. The contrast of the lighter upper areas with the lower large, dark area provides a strange balance of delicacy and strength, indicating the variety of O'Keeffe's skills. As in almost all of O'Keeffe's paintings, there are no superfluous details. Everything is necessary as the intangible becomes tangible. As O'Keeffe wrote of her feeling about abstraction, "The abstraction is often the most definite form for the intangible thing in myself that I can only clarify in paint."[16]

In the early twenties O'Keeffe also abstracted from larger scenes of nature as in her painting *Spring,* 1922. The budding forms of her Texas paintings have become more delicate and less focused in the billowing young tree. The painting is divided sharply into two sections with the strong diagonal dividing the recognizable tree form from curvilinear abstract shapes that remind the viewer of ripening fruit forms. O'Keeffe most likely did this painting during one of her visits to Stieglitz's family home at Lake George. A new season, new life, new forms, and a new freedom are inherent in this piece.

The curvilinear lines of some of O'Keeffe's abstractions in the late teens and early twenties gave way to sharp diagonals and larger, well-defined planes in some abstractions done later in the twenties, such as her *Abstraction,* 1926. Predominant in such paintings is the slender, black line in contrast to the lighter-colored areas that varies in width as it appears to continue infinitely beyond the perimeters of the canvas.

Many of O'Keeffe's early abstractions are marked by an intense feeling of rhythm and movement and seem to reach what Mallarmé called a "musicality of the whole."[17] There is a sense of the "arabesque" as Baudelaire used it—the Arabesque " 'symbolizing philosophically the rhythms of the universe. . . .' It was not only a direct emblem of the painter's spirit, but also an abstract conception of space—the space in which imagination summarizes our 'sensations' of space."[18] As Bergson professed in his philosophy, space and time spans in these paintings do not seem to have fixed boundaries. Always there is to be a sense of the beyond, of the infinite, and a direct confrontation with the senses. These paintings and others of the early years, mark the beginning of O'Keeffe's continued bold statement of her intuition, and individual intuition, important to the artists and writers of the "innocent rebellion," during the early part of this century.

In 1924, O'Keeffe completed her first large flower painting. She also married Stieglitz in the same year. For the next several years she created a varied group of flower paintings as well as continued to do abstractions. It is many of these flower paintings that were the basis for the criticism written relating her work to sexual imagery. The flower paintings discussed here are representative of the types of visual statements O'Keeffe made using a flower as the basis of the content of the painting. One of the earlier flower paintings is *Black and Blue Petunias,* 1925. *Black and Blue Petunias* is quite straightforward in its imagery—the frontal view of two petunias in shades of black and blue with carefully executed green leaves in the upper left and bottom of the painting. The sharply contrasting background area of white forms surrounding the petunias lift the petunias to a heightened perspective and give the petunias a further life of their own—"a reality beyond the actuality." (William Carlos Williams' phrase.) The inner depth of the flowers are beautifully painted in rich velvety tones with an intense depth as the eye descends into the unknown world of the flowers' pistils and stamens. Indeed, the blue petunias might "cause blue to become an emotional experience in and for itself," as Duncan Phillips suggests.[19] One senses the structural rhythm of nature as the eye moves back and forth from the tips of the petals to the center of the flowers. The different coloring of the centers of each of the two flowers—the center white and violet bursting crown-like areas—give each flower a life of its own.

Among the flower paintings that evoked the most controversial critical responses were her images of the black iris, such as her *Black Iris,* 1926 (36″ × 30″), an enlarged and abstract version of the flower. Most striking about this painting is the magnification of the frontal flower image so that the painting quickly takes on abstract qualities. The extreme enlargement and sharp focus of the painting lead some to point to the influence of photography on O'Keeffe's work, although others claim she is the innovator of such magnified views. The more abstract flower images, such as *Black Iris,* received the most associations with sexual imagery and body forms by various critics. O'Keeffe, denying any specific sexual imagery has said, "I'll tell you how I happened to make the blown-up flowers. In the twenties, huge buildings seemed to be going up overnight in New York. At that time I saw a painting by Fantin-Latour, a still life with flowers I found very beautiful, but I realized were I to paint the flowers so small, no one would look at them because I was unknown. So I thought I'll make them big like the huge buildings going up. People will be startled; they'll have to look at them—and they did."[20] Further she has stated, "I am attempting to express what I saw in a flower which apparently others failed to see."[21] As one looks at the delicate parts of the flower and deep center area one feels that one is entering another world, a new world created by O'Keeffe's vision.

In 1936, O'Keeffe painted *Small Black Iris* in which there is further enlargement and magnification of the flower image than in the 1926 version. There is less detail in this 1936 version, and a more restricted palette of soft grays and muted browns. But again there is the careful symmetrical balance and precision of line and modeling. O'Keeffe painted other versions of the iris, as well, at various points throughout her career. While living in New York she searched diligently for a living black iris in flower shops for the two weeks it was available each spring. She even tried to find a black iris bulb to plant in her garden in New Mexico, but lost the one address she had to obtain the bulb. The last known iris painting was *Lavender Iris*, 1950, (40⅛″ × 30″) with the same frontal view as the 1926 *Black Iris*.

O'Keeffe also painted a number of images of calla lilies and morning glories. In a painting such as *Morning Glory with Black,* painted in the same year as *Black Iris*, O'Keeffe leads the viewer more closely into the private world of the flower. The interior of the flower is at once realistic and abstract as the flower becomes a graceful study of gentle curves, shapes, and colors. The morning glory is seen from two other perspectives in a later morning glory piece *Blue Morning Glories, New Mexico II*, 1935. The two flowers in this painting are to be examined from the interior and the outside rim, as if one were a hummingbird perched on the tip of a flower ready to descend into a special world of delicate blues, yellows, and pinks that mark the flowers. The blue background or sky is closely related to the blue of the morning glories. The flowers thus become one with their surrounding world through O'Keeffe's vision.

O'Keeffe's *Yellow Calla—Green Leaves*, 1927 illustrates another approach to the flower image. Almost more important than the lily in this painting are the green leaves and gray-green background. The lilies appear as solid and secure resting on their leafy stocks, which in turn provide an interesting contrast to the lighter background area. The sharply delineated lines of the leaves and the callas give the painting a stylized effect. One becomes almost more interested in the interplay of line and color than in the image of the lily. In the same year O'Keeffe painted a close-up of the callas, *Two Calla Lilies on Pink*, 1928, where she judiciously cropped the edges of the flowers to "fill a space in a beautiful way" as Arthur Dow had advocated. The enlarged lilies almost become landscapes as the contours of the magnified flowers become rolling hills.

A description of the lilies in a 1938 *Life* magazine indicates O'Keeffe's continued interest in the originally observed object. "O'Keeffe found these in a Lake George florist's window and painted them because she liked their tight formation. . . ."[22]

Five years earlier O'Keeffe had done several calla lily compositions such as *Calla Lily in Tall Glass, No. 1,* 1923, which appears to have more elements of the traditional still life with specifically arranged objects, painted quite realistically. But in this painting as in most of her others, there is something emotionally stirring in O'Keeffe's work.

"Her pictures look like portraits of herself, so intensely personal are they. Last year she concentrated on cannas, the walls glowed with them; this year it is lilies; again portraits of herself. No one has ever painted lilies quite like this; it is as if she had got at the essence of the flower; saw it almost as if it were suspended in a vacuum, untouched by the changing effects of light and atmosphere."[23]

In 1927 O'Keeffe also turned to the rose, expressing her personal and intimate experience with this flower as she had with the others. The intense close-up images became her "equivalents" for an intense experience. In her *White Rose with Larkspur No. 2*, 1927, the white rose is reborn, representing a world of delicate sensitivity, as it is gently embraced by the blue and purple tones of the protective larkspur. In the same year, in *Abstraction— White Rose III*, O'Keeffe abstracted the rose petals to curvilinear bands of white light, emanating from a mysterious center—a glistening pearl shape. The mystery of this and other enlarged and abstracted flower details recalls Thoreau's admonition that "Nature will bear the closest inspection; she invites us to lay our eyes level with her smallest leaf, and take an insect view of its plan,"[24] or Emerson's statement that "man never sees the same object twice; with his own enlargement the object acquires new aspects."[25]

As has been seen, O'Keeffe often dealt with the same subject in various versions. As she has stated, "I work on an idea for a long time. It's like getting acquainted with a person and I don't get acquainted easily . . . .Sometimes I start in a very realistic fashion, and as I go on from one painting to another of the same thing, it becomes simplified till it can be nothing but abstract."[26] *Jack-in-the-Pulpit, No. 5,* 1930 (48″ × 30″), is part of a remarkable O'Keeffe series where she does transform the initial image from a fairly realistic representation to an abstract or semiabstract version. The six paintings in the "jack-in-the-pulpit" series, all done in 1930, begin with a small, relatively realistic image of the plant. In the larger Number 2 canvas (40″ × 30″) the plant becomes a giant, with focus on radiating lines from the pulpit. Number 3 (40″ × 30″) is simpler in format, with the flower fitting into a background space to create an overall design. Number 4 again shows O'Keeffe's ability to magnify a form or image. The flower is alone with a magnified view of the flower-pulpit area. Number 5, the largest of the series (48″ × 30″), appears almost as a total abstraction. Yet the colors, the powerful purples and greens, and the strong curving forms of the other paintings in the series continue in this Number 5 painting. The flowing tendril-like forms that appear in many of O'Keeffe's paintings add a dynamic sense of rhythm and movement to the painting. Further, reduction and abstraction of the original image occurs in painting Number 6 of the series, where only the dark pistil occurs in a very simplified composition. The black shape of the pistil is set against a white "halo" which is, in turn, mirrored in rising halo-like forms which become darker toward the top of the painting. The black shape of the pistil with its white halo has a striking religious and mystical appearance.

Interesting to compare to this series is O'Keeffe's *Shell and Old Shingle* series of 1926 where she also progressed from realistic to abstract images in seven paintings. The paintings in this series are not as large in scale and do not contain the bold forms and strong colors of the "jack-in-the-pulpit" series. This series, the "jack-in-the-pulpit" series, and O'Keeffe's various versions of other particular flowers provide a visual example of the use of "accretive imagery" as practiced by poets of the time such as Williams and Pound.

Again turning to more realistic images than *Jack-in-the-Pulpit* Numbers 5 or 6, O'Keeffe created a painting such as *The White Calico Flower* (30″ × 36″) in 1931. Although the image of the flower is relatively realistic, the painting becomes somewhat stylized and unreal with the appearance of the white leaves. The diagonal placement of the flower on the canvas, rather than in the usual vertical growing position, contributes to the notion of a stylized world and new reality. The green fibrous forms behind the large flower provide contrast, balancing the more open and rounded forms of the petals and leaves. The center area of the flower, almost a miniature of the outer, larger area, suggests an even different world than that of the larger flower. O'Keeffe's concentration on the vital center of the flower is seen further in her 1935 sunflower paintings. Two such paintings, *Sunflower* and *Sunflower for Maggie,* show a single sunflower standing proudly in the open sky. The detailed, target-like centers painted in staccato, pointillist brushstrokes, can be seen as forerunners of larger abstract paintings of the sixties.

O'Keeffe continued to do flower paintings through the fifties, although most of such paintings were done in the twenties and thirties. In 1950 O'Keeffe painted *Poppies.* The vivid colors and kaleidoscopic centers of the poppies quickly draw the viewer into the flowers' vibrant world.

The flower paintings, as seen here, represent a variety of approaches by O'Keeffe to the basic flower image, from realistic to abstract. To none of the paintings does it seem fair and valid to attribute only a particular sexual symbolism as interpretation. If there is a sense of a feminine experience in the flower paintings, it may best be seen in the intensity and depth of the paintings, often due to the magnification of the image and use of new forms that may evoke an emotional and sensual response in the viewer. "One also suspects that if O'Keeffe's curving and undulating forms suggest analogies between the human body and landscape, these analogies are better explained by the sense of the unity of nature and the correspondences between all natural forms than they are by Freudian or Surrealist symbolism."[27] Indeed, according to Barbara Rose, Stieglitz and artists close to him such as O'Keeffe, Marin, and Dove "believed that the creative life was tied to the senses. Social progress they thought would issue from sensual liberation, without which there could be no aesthetic appreciation."[28]

Further, O'Keeffe's flower paintings must be seen within the context of flower painting throughout art history—the painting of flowers has a long history in Oriental art. In America during the nineteenth century, luminist painter Martin Johnson Heade enlarged flowers such as roses and orchids. In Europe during the twentieth century, artists such as Mondrian, Van Gogh, and Gauguin painted large, intense flower images with dream-like and symbolic implications. American male painters of O'Keeffe's own generation such as Charles Demuth, Joseph Stella, and Stefan Hirsch also painted flowers. Contemporary artists such as Jim Dine have also painted close-ups of flowers. None of the male work has been interpreted as sexual in form.

The flower paintings also illustrate a new approach to still-life painting with abstract forms and concentration on single flowers rather than on bouquets and arrangements. O'Keeffe's "still lifes" have been described by one writer: "O'Keeffe displays a sense of beauty in abstract forms in her still-lifes. . . She combines with this a feeling of growth and aliveness as she isolates, magnifies and simplifies flowers and plants. Forms seem to swell and enlarge themselves in an explosive manner—soft forms appear to pulsate and irregular outlines constantly meander and curve in dynamic patterns."[29]

O'Keeffe does indeed create a new reality beyond the observed world of nature. As Doris Bry wrote, ". . . the flower paintings are and are not flowers."[30] O'Keeffe continually reaches for the radiant gist of an object that William Carlos Williams describes as possible in the intensity of experience with an object. The importance of intuition, as stressed by writers such as Henri Bergson, is inherent in O'Keeffe's vision illustrated in these paintings. As Bergson felt, "it was through intuition and not analysis that one could transcend the facts of outward appearance."[31] Intuition by ". . . the sympathetic communication which it establishes between us and the rest of the living, by the expansion of our consciousness which it brings about, introduces us into life's own domain which is reciprocal interpenetration, endlessly continued creation."[32] O'Keeffe's intuitive vision is continued throughout her career as will be seen in her treatment of various objects, both natural and man-made.

During the same years that O'Keeffe worked on her flower paintings, she did many paintings based on the Lake George area where she and Stieglitz spent their summers during the twenties. Since O'Keeffe preferred the country to the city, she usually went there in April and stayed until late fall. The paintings done there mark a wide variety of technique and content theme as evidenced by the paintings selected for discussion here. One of the early paintings done near Lake George is *My Shanty—Lake George* 1922 (20″ × 27″). *My Shanty,* with its broad dark planes of color, evokes a sense of eeriness in the viewer. Duncan Phillips described it as "the stark expression of a sombre Celtic mood."[33] O'Keeffe, however, with her ironic humor, has given other information about this painting. She has stated that she was merely tired of people saying she could only handle light colors. According to O'Keeffe, she painted this "to 'show the boys' that she could paint a dark picture."[34] Actually the golden mustard tones of the surrounding plant life and grass area, along with the white cloud add enough light to the painting to alleviate a total somberness of mood. In the Stieglitz portrait of O'Keeffe there are several shots of O'Keeffe standing near a shanty near Lake George similar to the one in the painting. The flowing black she wears in several of the photographs (her usual dress consists of black or white) seems to be a part of the darkness of the wooden shanty.

The sharply refined edges of the shanty roof, door, window and walls are seen later in other barn paintings such as *Lake George Barns,* 1926 or the barns painted in Canada.

O'Keeffe has described the old barn at Lake George that inspired her.

> *There was a fine old barn at the Lake George farmhouse. You could see it from the kitchen window or from the window of Stieglitz's sitting room. With much effort I painted a picture of the front part of the barn. I had never painted anything like that before. After that I painted the side where all the paint was gone with the south wind. It was weathered grey—with one broken pane in the small window.*[35]

One of O'Keeffe's barn paintings sold at a 1925 auction at the highest price for a painting of American artists of that period. The price was four hundred dollars.

The somber tones and the distinct verticals and horizontals of *My Shanty* and the Lake George barns are a sharp contrast to the light pastel tones and curvilinearity of a number of the flower paintings done during the same time period, illustrating O'Keeffe's great versatility.

At Lake George O'Keeffe also did a number of paintings of leaves. In the leaf paintings, unlike *My Shanty,* O'Keeffe concentrates on a detail from nature rather than a landscape view. One might easily find such a cluster of leaves at one's feet as the leaves begin to fall in autumn. But it takes a vision such as O'Keeffe's to transform that cluster to an image such as one finds in these canvases. O'Keeffe did a number of canvases concentrating on the patterns of leaves such as *Large Dark Red Leaves on White,* 1925 and *Pattern of Leaves (Leaf Motif),* 1926. In such paintings O'Keeffe sometimes uses her own color scheme, that may differ from nature's scheme. Always there is a sense of severe and intense concentration and thought about the object to be painted. The layers of leaves, similar in form, yet diverse in coloration, set against the sharply contrasting white background in *Large Dark Red Leaves on White,* are a strong study in repetition and contrast. The painting is one of many that illustrate the influence of Dow and Fenellosa who taught the Japanese principle of notan or balancing out tonal contrasts and creating strong surface patterns.

In *Pattern of Leaves* the central tear in the brown maple leaf, like a burst of lightning, provides dynamic movement for the painting. Upon viewing the central area of the painting, one sees O'Keeffe's careful attention to line and color modulation. With the dynamic downward force of the tear in the leaf, the shapes of the split brown leaf and surrounding gray leaves can be seen in terms of abstract forms. E. C. Goosen spoke of the possible influence of these leaf paintings on a painter such as Jasper Johns. "To solve the problem of subject matter in relation to the flat canvas and perhaps taking a hint from O'Keeffe's leaf pictures of the twenties, he often selected targets, maps, topographical elements and flags."[36]

A landscape painted at Lake George is *Red Hills and the Sun, Lake George,* 1927 (27″ × 32″). Unlike the earlier landscape, *My Shanty,* there is a mystical, transcendental quality about this painting. The red hills and sun have a life of their own. The red hills are monumental in their brightness, the vibrant color extending beyond the real. Important are the strong, rhythmic lines of the sloping hills and radiating sun. This painting is actually somewhat bolder in statement than many of the other landscapes done near Lake George. Many such paintings are darker and quieter in tone, depicting night scenes, crows flying, or dark trees. The radiating light beyond the scarlet hills suggests, as in many O'Keeffe paintings, an ongoing space, the world beyond the real, a universal.

In 1929, O'Keeffe painted *Lake George Window* (40″ × 30″). Though realistic, the starkness of the rectangular forms in almost perfect symmetry and limited color scheme quickly give the painting an abstract quality. The only curvilinear form in the painting, the scroll design at the top of the window, adds a surreal crown to the work. The simplicity and austerity of the painting is further enhanced by the direct frontal view O'Keeffe has used. The window confronts the viewer like a large, looming face. The clear, precise architectural forms have inspired critics to label the piece precisionistic. The severe simplification of form can also be seen as precursory of later minimal art forms. Indeed, E.C. Goosen compares O'Keeffe's *Lake George Window* with Ellsworth Kelly's reconstruction of a window.[37]

The Lake George paintings, in general, illustrate O'Keeffe's continued love of nature, and her ability to give new significance to the forms around her whether through landscape scenes or concentration on a single object or form.

In a change from using nature as the usual source of her painting, O'Keeffe painted approximately fifteen city scenes in the twenties while living with Stieglitz at the Shelton Hotel in midtown Manhattan. Their thirtieth-floor apartment enabled O'Keeffe to easily view the East River and surrounding skyscrapers that were to appear in her paintings. Her *East River From the 30th Story of the Shelton Hotel, New York,* 1928 shows the strong architectural forms of the apartment buildings, industrial buildings, and office buildings that were part of the rapidly growing technology and commerce of New York at a time when there was no inkling of an approaching Depression. The strength of the painting lies in its system of well-balanced verticals and horizontals created by the buildings, the smokestacks, and the flow of the East River. This type of painting was somewhat unusual for O'Keeffe for she did not concentrate on a single or enlarged object, but rather had a wide-angle approach to her world from the thirtieth story of the Shelton.

O'Keeffe did a number of paintings of the East River from her apartment. Very realistic and factually rendered *River, New York,* 1928 (12″ × 32″). The painting, in grays, black, and some violets, is again a careful scheme of horizontal and vertical shapes, with the billowy puffs of smoke providing some relief to the straight-edged building forms. The painting is well-balanced with an almost-perfect symmetry, the vertical smoke stacks dividing the composition in two. Because of these flatter, more geometric forms, and very limited palette, this painting does not have the vitality of some of O'Keeffe's other paintings.

As indicated, the urban theme was a predominant one of the precisionists. It was ". . . during the twenties because of their avid interest in the city as a subject that the Precisionists seemed most nearly a group. 'The Men' as O'Keeffe refers to the painters and photographers of the Stieglitz circle—Marin, Weber, Steichen, Strand, and Stieglitz himself—while producing their own interpretive portraits of the metropolis, were amused that even she could want to depart from her familiar repertory of flowers, rocks and barns to paint the buildings of New York."[38] O'Keeffe's portrayal, in general, of the forms and patterns of city buildings, streets, and lights, appears to reflect the same kind of intense study of a given subject as in her other work, whether realistic or abstracted.

The portrayal of various city scenes by the precisionists was quite different from The Eight's versions of an uglier side of city life. The precisionist visions of the metropolis present a clean, hard-edged view of a utopian world. Little attention was paid to sociological issues of the day and to the oncoming Depression. More important was the expression of the individual artist.

O'Keeffe's paintings of the city do contain some of the simplified, severe geometric forms characteristic of the precisionist vision, but they also contain her own individual fantasy. One of her early urban paintings, *The Shelton with Sunspots,* 1926 (40⅝″ × 30⅝″), is filled with sunspots one might see by looking into the sun through a camera or after looking directly into the sun with the naked eye. Indeed, the inclusion of sunspots in photographs has become a popular technique in recent years. The upward-thrusting rectangular forms of the building are somewhat new to the paintings of O'Keeffe, although some of her abstractions such as *Black Spot, No. 3,* 1919 (24″ × 16″), contain such sharp-edged, angular forms. The building almost seems to be on fire and alive with the sunspots. Little attention is paid to the details of the building except for a few windows on the left. The total dynamic image of the sunspots on the receding rectangular planes is more important.

In 1929 O'Keeffe did a number of paintings of a New York City night. *New York Night,* 1929 (40⅛″ × 19⅛″) contains a somewhat impressionistic view of the city lights and towering buildings. Indeed, the contrast of the lights and darks becomes more important than the structure of the buildings. The rounded window of the central tower and its lighted top are points of particular interest in contrast to the dominating vertical and horizontal shapes of the painting. In general, as illustrated by this painting and *The Shelton with Sunspots,* O'Keeffe's city paintings do not emphasize volume and architectural structure as in a Sheeler or Demuth or other precisionist painting. In these city paintings, "O'Keeffe's approach is curiously impressionistic: the typical Precisionist sharp contours are present but the real emphasis is on the opulent surface decoration, a patterning in which volume is dissolved."[39] There is actually more of a sense of precise architectural structure and order in some of O'Keeffe's barn paintings and in some of her Ranchos Church paintings.

Beginning in 1929, with her first summer in New Mexico, O'Keeffe did many paintings of the New Mexican landscape, a subject quite different from her urban themes. In 1929 O'Keeffe attended a rodeo in Taos, New Mexico, and recorded her impressions in the colorful kaleidoscopic painting, *At the Rodeo.* The painting is actually an enlargement of a Mexican Indian ornament. The opulent colors—scarlets, blues, and rich greens and yellows—along with the quivering movement created by the floating disc forms have made some see the work as a forerunner of later op art paintings.

Another early painting involving the New Mexican terrain was *Black Cross, New Mexico*, 1929 (39″ × 30″). Like some of the flower paintings the black cross is a frontal magnification with the middle ground eliminated in order to emphasize the looming cross. The forbidding looking black cross overpowers the canvas. The purples and reds of the dwarfed hills below the blood-red streak in the sky suggests the setting of the sun. The severity of the awesome image mirrors the severity of the land and the Catholic Penitentes who have inhabited the region for years. Originally founded by the Franciscans in Spain, the Penitente order in Mexico and New Mexico became noted for its extremely harsh penitent rites of self-flagellation. O'Keeffe has captured well a sense of such a harsh lifestyle in her painting. Mahoriri Young has written, "daughter of an unbeliever, she has never had any formal religious belief, but she admits that the Catholic Church has an attraction for her."[40] O'Keeffe herself has said, "In New Mexico the crosses interest me because they represent what the Spanish felt about Catholicism—dark, somber—and I painted them that way."[41] The dark wooden cross is typical of Catholic Spain. The four gray dots on the cross are perhaps the nails of a past crucifixion. Thus the dramatic close-up view of the cross expresses a whole way of living—a life of austerity and severity in a powerful terrain. O'Keeffe actually did several paintings of this subject around 1929 and has said of such paintings, "Anyone who doesn't get the cross simply doesn't get this country."[42] *Black Cross, New Mexico* is the most powerful and bold of the cross paintings.

In 1929, O'Keeffe also began painting a series of the Ranchos Church in Taos. The church was first painted in a very objectified realistic manner with cool colors. The final picture is a detail of the curving adobe walls set against an intense blue sky and white cloud. Daniel Catton Rich has written of her ability to condense and eliminate, "She has always believed that a long poem could be said in a few intense words and that a painting could likewise be stripped down to its essential form and meaning."[43] One of the interim versions of the Ranchos Church is *Ranchos Church*, 1930 (24″ × 36″), which hangs in the Phillips Collection in Washington, D.C. The painting depicts the west-end, facing east, of the mission church of St. Francis of Assisi at Ranchos de Taos. Most striking about this painting is the beauty of the architectural forms of the adobe walls of the church and the light that shines upon these walls. The cloudless blue sky and smooth tans of the earthen walls provide a warm and idyllic atmosphere. As mentioned earlier, this Ranchos Church painting is perhaps a better example of precisionist techniques where the vitality of a painting "is in its insistent logic and discipline, through which the familiar object—a building, a complex machine or even a flower—is stripped to its ultimate structure and presented with astonishing lucidity."[44] The painting reveals O'Keeffe's precision in rendering the essential volume and strength of the adobe walls. On viewing the painting there is a sense of an infinite endurance of these walls and their surroundings. The light quality, as in other precisionist paintings "is brilliant, never vague or 'atmospheric.'"[45]

Very similar in content and interesting to compare to the above painting are *Ranchos Church No. 1*, 1929, owned by the Norton Gallery, *Ranchos Church*, 1930 (24″ × 36″), owned by the New York Metropolitan Museum, and *Ranchos Church*, 1930, owned by the Amon Carter Museum of Western Art. The structure of the adobe walls is almost the same in each painting. Different is the sky and general lighting. The low-lying clouds in the Norton Gallery painting at the intersection of the adobe walls on the left and right of the painting serve to soften the lines of the firm walls and balance the foreground that looms larger than in the other paintings. The Metropolitan's painting has grayer sky tones and somewhat fluffy clouds, while the Amon Carter Museum's painting has wispy clouds in a gray-blue sky. The Phillips' painting has the most brilliant lighting. In these various paintings of the church, one sees O'Keeffe's deep and intense concentration on one subject.

Dark Mesa and Pink Sky (16″ × 29⅞″), also painted in 1930, is an example of O'Keeffe's portrayal of the area surrounding her in New Mexico. O'Keeffe has continued to have a deep love for the New Mexican landscape since her first visit there. Of the desert and mountains in New Mexico O'Keeffe has said, "The desert is the last place you can see all around you. The light out here makes everything close, and it is never, never the same. Sometimes the light hits the mountain from behind and front at the same time, and gives them the look of Japanese prints, you know, distances in layers."[46] The layers of the desert and mesa become lovely sculptural forms with O'Keeffe's vision. There is a sense of timelessness and deep space and one views this painting with its expansive view. As Van Deren Coke has written, "The energizing effect of the Southwest has never lost its impact on O'Keeffe. In New Mexico she lays bare nature's enigmatic secrets, converting the cluttered ocular world into elemental and purified forms."[47] O'Keeffe has continued to paint many views of the New Mexican landscape throughout her career, appealing directly to the viewer's senses with the richness of her colors and the depth of her forms. In a painting such as *Red Hills with White Cloud* one sees the sculptural form of the land well articulated.

In 1946 O'Keeffe painted *The White Place in Shadow,* a place she loved to visit near Abiquiu. The formal qualities of the painting, emphasizing large rectilinear and planar shapes in contrast to the curvilinear and three-dimensional areas, recall the teaching of Arthur Dow and even some of his paintings, such as *Deep Down,* 1913. As in many of her paintings, O'Keeffe has carefully carried out the Japanese principle of notan with elements such as the small, dark green area of foliage in the lower section of the canvas that balances the foliage at the top of canyon. The surging "V" shape, or reverse triangle, balances the large triangular shapes of the massive stone on the left and right. O'Keeffe opens and expands the "V" shape to suggest an abstract infinity in later paintings such as *Red Hills and Sky,* 1945 or *A Black Bird with Snow-Covered Red Hills,* 1946.

O'Keeffe often went camping in the hills and mesas near Ghost Ranch, sometimes traveling as much as one hundred fifty miles to paint one of her favorite places she called the black place, and the grey hills, which she traveled over to reach the black place. In a painting such as *The Grey Hills,* 1942, O'Keeffe captured the lonely but majestic beauty of the crackled earth that so attracted her. The grey, black, ochre, and sienna tones of the barren hills became alive through O'Keeffe's vision and strength of expression.

O'Keeffe's landscapes, particularly those painted in New Mexico, are different from earlier accepted American landscape painting, such as the Hudson River School, and different from the American regionalist painters of the thirties. The sculptural forms in her paintings and her very individual interpretations of American scenery sets her work apart from other landscape images to some extent. Yet it must be seen as part of a continuing American tradition that values the American land as an important resource and as an ongoing inspiration for American painters.

Her paintings of the Southwest were somewhat interrupted by a trip to the Gaspé country in Canada in 1932 with Stieglitz's niece, Georgia Engelhard, which was her first trip outside the United States. During her sojourn there, O'Keeffe painted a number of the crosses and barns that dotted the Canadian countryside. Three paintings representative of her Canadian visit are: *Cross by the Sea,* 1931 (36″ × 24″), *Stables,* 1932 (12″ × 32″), and *White Canadian Barn,* 1932 (16″ × 29¾″). The cross in *Cross by the Sea* is a memorial to a young priest who died at sea. Unlike the overpowering cross in *Black Cross, New Mexico,* this cross is more fragile and not as strong as the ocean behind it. O'Keeffe has described her reaction to the Canadian crosses.

> *After my summers in New Mexico where I had heard the Penitente songs and painted the dark crosses as I felt them there, the Canadian crosses seemed very different. The Canadian crosses were singing in the sunlight. Sometimes there were pottery figures around them—always they had a feeling of gaiety.*
>
> *There was one pure stark cross in the center of a profusely blooming potato field overlooking the water where the river was very wide. Each end of the cross was carved and there was a plaque in memory of a father who had drowned trying to save someone else who was drowning at sea.*[48]

This "one pure stark cross" is the subject of *Cross by the Sea,* 1931. In the years since the painting was done, the modern art world has been besieged by such diverse and eclectic forces as minimalism, pop art, happenings, and conceptual art. Yet the painting, in its pristine spareness, continues to have much relevance and meaning for people today in both technique and iconography. The large wooden votive cross in the painting is a memorial to a drowning victim at sea. The tablet on the lower end of the cross reads:

ICI/SEST NOYE LE 4 JUIN 1875/LE REVD. E. V. COTE/PETRE MISS. DU MONT LOUIS/AGE ENVIRON DE 25 ANS/PRIEZ POUR LUI.

Here/drowned on June 4, 1875/the Rev. E. V. Cote/Miss. priest from Mont Louis/Approximately 25 years of age/Pray for him.

The cross, by its powerful central position in the canvas, strongly suggests the traditional symbolism this motif connotes. The cross, one of the oldest and perhaps most universal of all symbols, usually stands for Christ and His sacrifices on the cross. In a broader sense, it is the emblem of atonement and the symbol of salvation and redemption through Christianity. O'Keeffe depicts the Latin cross (instead of a Greek, tau, or St. Andrew's cross) which has a longer upright piece than crossbar. According to tradition, Christ was crucified on such a cross. The Latin cross is also associated with various saints such as St. Reparata and St. Margaret. Thus, O'Keeffe's painting is at once specific and universal. A spirit of universality and infinity is further enhanced by the placement of the cross near a large body of water with little foreground. Since there is almost no foreground, one confronts this cross and its symbolism head-on. The position of the cross on the canvas, dividing it into four quadrants, gives a sense of order, while O'Keeffe's palette, confined to blues of various hues and intensities, grays, whites, and greens, gives the painting, and in turn the viewer, a sense of serenity.

Although the subject matter is traditional, O'Keeffe's approach to the composition is modern. The clean, precise lines of the cross, the edges of the plaque, the fence, and the horizon are akin to the work of the precisionists of the early part of the twentieth century, who emphasized line as well as and flat, even color. Although the verticals and horizontals in O'Keeffe's painting are strong and all of the geometric forms are carefully rendered, the underlying structure of the cross is not lost. There is also little evidence of an expressive brush stroke in the painting, another characteristic of some of the precisionists' paintings. The barns O'Keeffe painted on the same trip, such as *White Canadian Barn II,* 1932, are again examples of some of the precisionists' techniques, where the sturdy rectangular planes, formed by the doors, windows, and walls, give a sense of enduring stability to the painting.

When one focuses on the geometric forms of *Cross by the Sea,* the painting becomes quite abstract, anticipating some of the minimalist and color field painting of the sixties. Of comparative interest to *Cross by the Sea* is the treatment of a similar subject matter by Barnett Newman in *Stations of the Cross,* his series of large canvases created in the late fifties and sixties. Reduced to almost total abstraction, the recurrent image in *Stations of the Cross* is of two long, vertical bands of various widths. Newman's "colors" are confined to black, white, and the blond of the field of raw canvas. Like O'Keeffe, Newman grappled successfully with the problem of representing a deep and everlasting spirit.

Cross by the Sea also illustrates O'Keeffe's sense of rhythm. The carved pendants on the ends of the cross are repeated in a similar format in the four corners of the posts of the picket fence. The rhythmic waves of the sea lap gently toward the shore. The repetition of the whitecaps is accentuated by the white of the picket fence, the inscription on the plaque, and the slender line of grayish white on the upper vertical of the cross. The blues of the sea and sky merge majestically as the sky provides a subtly modeled color field for the cross.

O'Keeffe did one other cross painting while in Canada entitled *Cross with Red Heart,* 1932. This painting contains a cross with a brightly decorated floral design in the middle. O'Keeffe has written of her first sighting this cross:

> As we drove around a high hedge near the Laurentian Hills we saw a tall cross with a red heart carved and painted in the center of it surrounded by twelve sharply carved pieces of wood about a foot long. Each end of the cross had a three-lobed shape carved on it—a copper rooster weathervane on top of it—gay spring flowers at the foot of it—wild clouds racing over—a white picket fence around it.[49]

She also described the cross as "gay and witty" and representative of French Catholicism. "On the Gaspé the cross was Catholicism as the French saw it—gay and witty. I made two paintings of crosses when I was there in 1932. I would have been willing to stay on in Canada, if it hadn't been so terribly cold."[50] *Cross with Red Heart* and *Cross by the Sea* capture the spirit of the Gaspé land and seascapes, and a way of life indicated by the symbolism of the mariners' crosses.

O'Keeffe and her niece cut short their visit to the Gaspé because as O'Keeffe wrote, "we couldn't paint when we were hungry and tired all of the time."[51]

The depiction of the Canadian crosses may be viewed as an extension of O'Keeffe's concern with the cross as subject matter. She first confronted this issue in 1929 as seen in several paintings of the Catholic Penitente cross, which she executed while in New Mexico. In *Black Cross, New Mexico,* as in *Cross with Red Heart* and *Cross by the Sea,* one sees O'Keeffe's sensitivity to a particular way of life in a particular area, and her ability to express that way of life in condensed and poignant forms.

White Canadian Barn II is a good example of the use of some precisionist techniques. O'Keeffe herself, although always denying a relationship to any artistic movement, does admit that her Canadian Barn paintings might be called precise. "I'm not a joiner and I'm not a precisionist of anything else. It's curious that the show didn't stress what really might have been called precise in my work—the Canadian Barn."[52] O'Keeffe describes herself painting the barns. "Alfred [Stieglitz] had a niece, a most amusing girl with whom I sometimes traveled—once to the Gaspé. My barns were painted there. The southern side of the St. Lawrence River was lined with hideous houses and beautiful barns. The barns looked old, as if they belonged to the land, while the houses looked like bad accidents. That was a wonderful trip to the Gaspé."[53] O'Keeffe also says of the painting, "It is nothing but a simple statement about a simple thing. I can say nothing about it with words that I have not said with paint."[54]

As in many of the precisionist paintings, the underlying structure of the object through the careful rendering of geometric forms is not lost. The sturdy rectangular planes formed by the doors, windows, walls, roof, etc., give a sense of enduring stability to the painting. There is little evidence of an expressive brush in the painting, another characteristic of some of the precisionist paintings. The tiny spires of the roof provide a contrast and relief from the solid planes. *White Barn, No. 1,* 1932, is almost identical in content to *White Canadian Barn, No. 2,* but does not contain these spires.

O'Keeffe's *Stables,* also painted in 1932, contains the same pristine forms of the barn paintings. The doors and windows have been further reduced to simple geometric forms with no evidence of window panes. The pure blue sky of *White Canadian Barn II* that sharply contrasts with the roof, has been replaced by a wall and ceiling of fluffy clouds that soften the sharply defined lines of the stable.

A number of years later O'Keeffe, reflecting on her Canadian trip and on life along the St. Lawrence River, in contrast to life in Cebolla, a small village thirty miles north of her house in New Mexico, painted *Cebolla Church.* The county where Cebolla is located was considered one of the poorest areas in the United States, and life was difficult for its inhabitants. Through her painting of a typical church in Cebolla, O'Keeffe hoped to portray the difficulty of life for the people of Cebolla in contrast to the life of the Canadian farmer. The church stands isolated and stark, as symbolic of life in Cebolla. This is one of the few paintings that O'Keeffe has referred to as having a message—"I thought how different the life of the Canadian farmer was from life in Cebolla. So I painted the Cebolla church which is so typical of that difficult life. I have always thought it one of my very good paintings, though its message is not as pleasant as many of the others."[55] The bright blue sky, however, somehow gives the viewer a sense of optimism that there is strength and a will to survive in this community.

O'Keeffe usually spent the summers following her trip to Canada in New Mexico. During the thirties and forties she painted her famous bone paintings of skull and pelvis bones collected on the desert. These bone paintings in particular were often associated with death, symbolism, and surrealism. The paintings discussed in the following paragraphs are only a few of the many O'Keeffe painted with similar subject matter. O'Keeffe began to paint the bones she found in the desert in 1931, feeling they represented the life and beauty of the desert she loved. The early bone paintings usually were of animal skulls with horns and antlers, realistically portrayed. Sometimes the bones were arranged in a kind of formal still life, in ordinary settings, such as *Horns and Feather,* 1937. Most of the works, though, show a strange juxtaposition of objects such as the bleached dead skulls and flowers in bloom. One of the early bone paintings is *White Skull with White Roses,* 1931 (36″ × 24″). The skull and flowers are removed from their normal environment and appear to float in front of a ribbon of black. Despite the somber modulations in grays, black, and white, the painting in no way appears depressing or morbid. A strange new life is created from the combination of objects, usually associated with the polarities of life and death. The carefully executed calico roses are very similar to *The White Calico Flower,* 1931. These and other flowers, as well as the skulls, appear frequently in later paintings such as *Ram's Head—White Hollyhock Hills, New Mexico,* 1935 (36″ × 36″) and *Summer Days,* 1936 (36″ × 30″).

In some of the later skull paintings such as *From the Far Away Nearby,* 1937 (36″ × 40⅛″), the skulls are painted outside in various juxtapositions to the sky and hills. In *From the Far Away Nearby* a giant antlered skull looms over the dwarfed hills. Despite the subtle, soft colors of blues, pinks, grays, and browns, the painting is a powerful statement about nature, its life cycles, and desert life in particular, in O'Keeffe's visionary language. Some of the power of the painting lies in the beautiful design of the antlers in their graceful upward sweep. A close-up view of the painting reveals forms that are almost alive in themselves, carefully modeled and delineated against the softness of the pale pink and blue sky. The reversed arc forms of the mountains below provide a counter balance to the upward thrust of the antlers. This painting, too, contains some of O'Keeffe's most exact and beautiful details in the actual skull, of all of the skull paintings. The sleepy eye, the indented forehead, the pronounced set of teeth, etc., give a profound sense of life to the skull.

In another 1937 painting, *Mule's Skull with Pink Poinsettias,* O'Keeffe again juxtaposes the symbols of life and death, the flowers and skull. The poinsettias, usually associated with the new life of the Christmas season, float in a celestial light that shines directly on the mule skull. In O'Keeffe's light, the skull gleams, appearing almost metallic and more living than dead.

In 1943, O'Keeffe began a new series of bone paintings from pelvis bones. The pelvis bones were frequently to be found near her house. The paintings are of these pelvis bones picked up on the desert, with emphasis on the shapes created by the holes in the bones. The earlier pelvis paintings usually showed the blue sky showing through the holes, often creating an abstract composition. Unlike the frontal view of most of the skulls, the pelvis bones are seen from various viewpoints. Some of the early pelvis paintings include *Pelvis I,* 1944 (36″ × 30″) and *Pelvis III,* 1944 (48″ × 40″). One is hardly aware that the original image was a pelvis bone and background sky. In both paintings the oval blue shapes become alive through the recesses of the bone. The subtly delineated grays of the bone provide a porthole through which to view the infinite blue of the sky. Perhaps most important in these and other pelvis paintings, some of which are more abstract, is what O'Keeffe left out. The rest of the pelvis and the land and skyscape are not important. "Nothing remains of realism except what is necessary to express the depth and substance of feeling."[56] O'Keeffe herself has written of her pelvis paintings,

> *A pelvis bone has always been useful to any animal that has it—quite as useful as a head I suppose. For years in the country the pelvis bones lay about the house indoors and out—always underfoot—seen and not seen as such things can be—seen in many different ways. I do not remember picking up the first one but I remember from when I first noticed them always knowing I would one day be painting them. A particularly beautiful one that I found on the mountain where I went fishing this summer started me working on them.*

I was the sort of child that ate around the raisin on the cookie and ate around the hole in the doughnut saving either the raisin or the hole for the last and best so probably—not having changed much—when I started painting the pelvis bones I was most interested in the holes in the bones—what I saw through them—particularly the blue from holding them up in the sun against the sky as one is apt to do when one seems to have more sky than earth in one's world.

They were most wonderful against the Blue—that Blue that will always be there as it is now after all man's destruction is finished.[57]

Gradually, O'Keeffe changed her palette to portray the pelvis and negative space of the sky in reds and yellows. Further, O'Keeffe has said of these pelvis paintings,

At first these paintings were all blue and white—finally I tried red and yellow. I probably did between fifteen and twenty of them. They made a pretty exhibition. I'm one of the few artists, maybe the only one today, who is willing to talk about my work as pretty. I don't mind it being pretty. I think it's a shame to discard this work; maybe if we work on it hard enough we can make it fashionable again.[58]

In some of the pelvis paintings such as *Pelvis with Moon,* 1943 and *Pelvis with Shadows and the Moon,* 1943, one sees the complete pelvis and the bones float across the canvas in a dream-like image and do contain a sense of the surreal. The pelvis sometimes appears to be a giant bird winging its way through the wide desert skies. Later pelvis paintings become more abstract with increased magnification of the bones and their holes. In all of the pelvis paintings O'Keeffe's treatment of two colors is of particular interest. Frank Getlein has written of the pelvis painting, *Red with Yellow,* 1945; ". . . all around that oval (the pelvic aperture) the light and color modulate in and out of intensity from dark to light; each side of the line as closely related to the other at every point; each inch of red takes its intensity from the corresponding inch of yellow and the whole thing constitutes an unbelievable subtle and graduated run of color and light around an edge between a dead bone and infinity."[59]

As previously discussed, critics have identified these bone paintings with particular symbols and with surrealism. If these paintings are to be considered at all symbolic, it is in O'Keeffe's creation of a new artistic language, such as the French symbolists advocated. She juxtaposes strange elements, yet remains faithful to the world of nature and does not advocate use of the subconscious as did the surrealists. Although some of her paintings have a dream-like quality, they do not seem to be a part of the surrealist program. As Martin Friedman has written, "The symbolism in O'Keeffe's painting has more in common with the impersonal asceticism of Oriental art and the spiritualized visions of Odilon Redon than with Surrealism."[60] Ultimately in these and other paintings there is perhaps no direct translation into words, especially in reference to particular symbols, although often in her art there is a feeling of awe for nature which she has eloquently described as "sort of sparkling and alive and quiet all at the same time."[61]

Beginning in 1946, O'Keeffe began to paint more abstract images than the skull paintings, using her patio in Abiquiu, New Mexico, as the basis of her images. From 1946 to 1960, she did about twenty paintings with the patio motif, although she continued to paint other subjects as well, such as *Red Tree, Yellow Sky,* 1952 (30″ × 48″), *Poppies,* 1950 (36″ × 30″), and *Ladder to the Moon,* 1958 (40″ × 30″). The patio images with their vastly simplified, flattened forms (usually squares, rectangles, or diagonals) are among O'Keeffe's most simplified, condensed works. The shapes in the paintings deal with various elements in O'Keeffe's patio—the adobe wall, the door, stepping stones—

the ground, and the sky. O'Keeffe's patio is quite simple to begin with, and its elements become further simplified in her paintings. Beth Coffelt has described her house in Abiquiu. "Her house is there on a bluff overlooking the river valley and is a complex of dusty pink adobe buildings around a central patio with hidden secret gardens and small vistas of coolness, simplicity like Zen gardens."[62] O'Keeffe herself describes her patio, "The patio is quite wonderful in itself. You're in a square box; you see the sky over you, the ground beneath. In the patio is a well with a large round top. It's wonderful at night—with the stars framed by the walls."[63] Referring to her patio paintings, O'Keeffe speaks of her fascination with the door in particular, and claims her paintings are not really abstract.

> *Those little squares in the door paintings are tiles in front of the door; they're really there, so you see the painting is not abstract. It's quite realistic. I'm always trying to paint that door—I never quite get it. It's a curse—the way I feel I must continually go on with that door. Once I had the idea of making the door larger and the picture smaller, but then the wall, the whole surface of that wonderful wall, would have been lost.[64]*

An example of one of the early patio pictures is *In the Patio I*, 1946 (30″ × 24″). Concentration is on the window in the adobe wall and on the shadow therein. The adobe walls are large flattened forms with two arrow-like forms breaking up the central wall, perhaps representing a shadow or indentation in the wall. The distinct geometric shapes and earth tones of the painting are reminiscent of a Navaho Indian blanket. In *Black Patio Door*, 1955, the geometric shapes of the wall and the door are further simplified and magnified. The large flat areas of color and the vertical "stripe" on the right edge of the canvas can be seen as somewhat similar to some of Barnett Newman's work of the same period, where his forceful vertical "zips" appear in a large, expansive space. O'Keeffe has actually spoken of her interest in Barnett Newman's work.[65]

Patio with Cloud, 1956 (36″ × 30″) shows O'Keeffe's interest in her door with the door as a central, looming, dark rectangle set against a large flattened plane (the wall) with the rectangular "stepping stones" below. The only form without a sharp, straight edge is the wispy cloud in the upper left hand corner that balances the hard edges. One of the most striking of the patio paintings is *White Patio with Red Door*, 1960 (48″ × 84″). Not only is this painting larger in scale, but it also represents a dual vision of O'Keeffe. "A canvas like *White Patio with Red Door* has the uncompromising severity of the Constructivists. But look further. Even in abstraction O'Keeffe retains respect for the object. The large white plane is more than a white plane. It exists at the same time as an adobe wall. The twelve small rectangles serve not only to repeat, rhythmically, the shape of the red door but are also stepping stones set in the earth. Above the white plane a rose plane takes on the quality of the sky. Door and sky, moreover, are subtly modulated, suggesting space within or beyond. It is this double play of vision which sets her apart from such completely intellectualized painters as Mondrian or Albers."[66] The painting is further distinguished by the lack of specific boundaries. The white area appears endless on three sides of the piece and the pink border appears to extend continuously upward. O'Keeffe has painted the door in an alluring, ambiguous manner. The door may not only open to an interior but it may also open to a distant infinite vista. Within this abstraction, which is larger in scale than most of O'Keeffe's work up to this time, is a sense of mysticism that O'Keeffe evokes in her creation of another worldliness.

These patio paintings are the most geometric and hard-edged of O'Keeffe's later work. The subtle interplay between inner and outer spaces suggests more philosophical undertones than some of O'Keeffe's earlier, more concrete images such as her barns, city buildings, or flowers. The flattened forms, two-dimensional design, and some elimination of expressive brush strokes again recall Oriental techniques and the teaching of Arthur Dow. The expansive space of the later patio paintings is to dominate most of O'Keeffe's work in the sixties.

In the fifties, O'Keeffe began to travel somewhat, journeying to Mexico and Peru, and in 1953 she made her first trip to Europe. In 1959 she spent three and one-half months traveling around the world and in 1961 she took a trip down the Colorado River on a rubber raft. Based on her views from the air, O'Keeffe painted a number of aerial river views. She spoke to Katherine Kuh of her flying experiences and aerial views.

> *For instance those paintings in my present show—they are all rivers seen from the air. I've been flying a lot lately—I went around the world—and I noticed a surprising number of deserts and wonderful rivers. The rivers actually seem to come up and hit you in the eye. There's nothing abstract about those pictures; they are what I saw—and very realistic to me. I must say I changed the color to suit myself, but after all you can see any color you want when you look out the window.*[67]

O'Keeffe pursued the river image in charcoal as well as oil. *Drawing No. X,* 1959 (18⅝″ × 24⅝″) could actually be interpreted in terms of other subject matter than the river. As one critic wrote of the drawing, "The drawing works on a level quite free of specific limitation of subject—and yet it still includes that element of realism which prevents it being seen as primarily an abstraction."[68] The contrasting charcoal shades and the contrast between the large, rounded form and jagged tributary form give the sense of a balanced but dynamic composition.

In the same year O'Keeffe painted *It was Red and Pink,* 1959 (30″ × 40″). The sense of an aerial view is not as emphasized here as in some of the later paintings of river forms. Part of the beauty of the painting lies in its ambiguity and the interplay between the red and pink color areas. One is unsure whether the river forms might be the red or the pink area. Ultimately it does not matter what the exact interpretation of the content image might be. More important is the juxtaposition of forms and color combinations that communicate the essence of a changing, flowing, colored form as a river.

It was Blue and Green, 1960 (30″ × 40″) is one of O'Keeffe's most beautiful river paintings. The swirling shapes of blue and green have the dynamic rhythm of a flowing river, but are beautiful shapes in themselves. The narrower snake-like forms recall some of the antler designs in O'Keeffe's skull paintings. Both the colors used and flowing forms also remind one of some of O'Keeffe's earlier abstractions such as *Gray Line with Black, Blue, and Yellow,* 1923. The river forms are in sharp contrast to the bare, geometric forms of the patio paintings, but contain the same essence of the original subject matter. In these river paintings O'Keeffe often retained the river forms but experimented with a variety of colors. In *It was Yellow and Pink III,* 1960, the river has become a golden ochre, flowing gracefully in banks of red and pink. Like some of the patio paintings there are no distinct boundaries to the painting. The river flows off the canvas and appears to continue endlessly.

O'Keeffe's organic river forms were continued in a more slender, stylized manner in several paintings she did of the road that swept past her home toward Española and Santa

Fe. Fascinated by the ups and downs of the road, O'Keeffe photographed it and acciden-tally made the road seem to stand upright. The shape amused O'Keeffe and she did a number of paintings and drawings based on the road configuration in the mid-sixties. Two such paintings were her *The Winter Road,* 1963 (22″ × 18″) and *Road Past the View II,* 1964 (24″ × 30″). In *The Winter Road* there are no landscape props—no trees, mesas, or sky. Important is the shape of the brown road, with no beginning and no end. Set in a flat, open field of white, the curved undulating form is like the carefully defined form of a Japanese calligrapher. One can only sense calmness and serenity upon viewing the well-delineated form, set in a field of vast whiteness. A similar form is repeated in blue, in *Road Past the View II* in the lower part of the canvas. In this painting O'Keeffe has included suggestions of the New Mexican hills and mesas in loud tones of purple, blue, and mauve.

Some of the forms in O'Keeffe's "river" and "road" paintings are reminiscent of the forms in her 1915–1916 paintings and drawings, illustrating the consistency and strength of her vision.

Also based on O'Keeffe's flying experiences, are her sky and cloud paintings, completed in the sixties. Among them is a series of four paintings entitled *Sky Above Clouds.* The basic image consists of looking through a bank of clouds to the blue atmosphere below. Three of the paintings were done in 1963, the fourth in 1965. In the first and smallest (36″ × 48″), the clouds are separate and billowy with O'Keeffe's brush strokes appearing quite evident. In the second (48″ × 84″), the brush stroke becomes more refined with smaller, more defined clouds. The horizon is pushed back. In the third painting (48″ × 84″), the horizon is even dimmer. The clouds are closer together with their edges more precisely defined. The fourth *Sky Above Clouds* is the largest canvas O'Keeffe has ever painted, eight by twenty-four feet. It is remarkable that she stretched the canvas herself. Through the clouds, which are now painted in quite a stylized manner, one sees the sky below. Gradually the clouds disappear near the distant horizon. One critic has compared the diminishing size of O'Keeffe's clouds with the "op art device of bending a surface into distant space through progressive diminution in size of rhythmically repetitious units."[69] Indeed, there is a quiet, continuous rhythm created by the repeated cloud forms. Perhaps most striking about the painting is the lovely rose and blue sky in the background that seems to extend endlessly in all directions. Again O'Keeffe has created a sense of dynamic and infinite space. On viewing O'Keeffe's cloud paintings one may recall that Stieglitz, many years before, had done many photographic studies of clouds in his *Equivalents* which were for him a triumph in expressing some of life's experiences. Stieglitz said of his *Equivalents,* "My photographs are a picture of the chaos in the world, and of my relationship to that chaos. My prints show the world's constant upsetting of man's equilibrium and his eternal battle to re-establish it."[70] O'Keeffe's clouds are "equivalents" to her own private response to her experience of flying above the clouds. The "wideness and wonder" of her world is strongly expressed in these paintings. Most likely O'Keeffe was not directly influenced by Stieglitz's prints while painting her cloud series, but her paintings do establish a sense of serenity and universal order, which is consistent with Stieglitz's philosophical view concerning his work, as quoted here.

Returning to subject matter based on items she collected, in the early seventies O'Keef-fe painted various versions of rocks she had found. As O'Keeffe has said, "Wherever I go, I have an eye out for rocks. Outside my hotel in Pham Penh I picked up a stone and carried it back around the world in my purse. . . . Stones, bones, clouds—experience gives me shapes—but sometimes the shapes I paint end up having no resemblance to the actual experience."[71] Two of the rock portraits are *Black Rock with Blue III,* 1970 (20″ × 17″) and *Black Rock with Blue Sky and White Clouds,* 1972 (36″ × 30″). Both paintings contain the central, purified form of a rock that the artist obviously cherishes in her careful rendering of its shape. In the 1970 painting, the rock, of dark brown and black hues, seems very much a part of the white ground and what is perhaps blue sky. The small shadow at the base of the rock gives it a sense of place and depth. Otherwise the rock might become a floating form. The relative simplicity of the three large color areas are indicative of O'Keeffe's reduction of nature's forms to their essential core. The radiant gist of the rock becomes evident in this atmosphere. One critic wrote that this painting was "a triumphant fusion of subtle color, clear light and fundamental form. It demonstrates that age has increased the power of O'Keeffe."[72]

The rock in the 1972 painting is more definitely outlined, and more realistically placed on what appears to be a tree stump. The rock jumps out at the viewer from the blue background and shines with a strange irridescent light. The dark black shadow beneath the rock appears eerie in comparison to the luminescent face of the rock. The stark, flat blue sky stands as a strong comparison to the more somber and subtly modeled tones of the rock and stump. The rounded forms of the shadow and surface of the stump, though, counter balance the sharp black outline of the rock against the blue. The placement of the rock on its pedestal, with its surface carefully painted, does indicate O'Keeffe's concern for this particular object. These rock paintings have been considered as examples of new approaches to still-life painting in the twentieth century. As one writer has stated, there is a growing awareness in the twentieth century, ". . . of the duality of tangible reality and illusory image . . . With self-renewing energy the artist reworks again and again the form of still-life painting, and filled though it is with the commonplace, the banal, the detritus of everyday life, he distills from its silent realm a certain poetry."[73]

O'Keeffe had actually done some similar portraits of rocks nearly thirty years earlier. In 1944 she did a color pastel of two rocks, *Untitled 3* (27½″ × 21½″). The rocks appear in the anatomical shape of a heart. Another pastel of a rock, also done in 1944 is actually titled *My Heart* (27½″ × 21½″). The 1970's portraits of various rocks appear to be more refined and streamlined. Of the two examples discussed here, *Black Rock with Blue III* appears to be so serene and solid that the viewer immediately feels a sense of well-being. A slightly different version of this painting, *Black Rock with Blue, No. V,* 1971, is one of the few paintings that hangs in O'Keeffe's studio. Of the latter painting O'Keeffe has said, "I felt that I'd done what I wanted to do in it. I don't always get what I try for, you know."[74]

O'Keeffe continued the beautiful shapes of the rocks in the clay pots she created with the assistance of Juan Hamilton, when her eyes began to fail her. The very smooth texture of the rocks appeared in the pots as well. After four years of working with clay, O'Keeffe returned to painting. Still inspired by her immediate environment, O'Keeffe painted a series inspired by sightseeing in Washington, D.C. with Juan Hamilton. The abstractions done in her nineties, such as *Blue Circle and Line,* 1977, strongly resemble some of her abstract works of 1916–1919. O'Keeffe continues her work schedule of rising before daylight each day, watching the sun rise over the giant mesas, doing exercises, eating breakfast and then painting or doing other necessary chores. Always involved in some type of project, O'Keeffe completed a large-scale piece, *Abstraction,* at age ninety-four. The eleven-foot spiral sculpture of painted cast aluminum is a testament to her undying creativity and an expansion of the use of spiral forms throughout her career.

Stieglitz, near the end of his life, once described O'Keeffe as "absolute, clean cut like a crystal . . . . I don't believe she ever did anything which is contrary to her own inner feelings."[75] And so it seems she will continue to work.

Notes

[1]Anita Pollitzer, "That's Georgia," *Saturday Review,* November 4, 1950, p. 41.

[2]*Ibid.*

[3]Lee Nordness, ed., *Art : U.S.A.: Now* (New York: Viking Press, 1963), pp. 35–36.

[4]Read, "Woman Artist Whose Art is Sincerely Feminine," p. 4.

[5]Alfred Stieglitz, quoted in Northrop, *The Meeting of East and West,* p. 163.

[6]Douglas Crimp, "Georgia is a State of Mind," *ARTnews,* October 1970, p. 70.

[7]Jewell, "O'Keeffe: 30 Years," p. 6x.

[8]Georgia O'Keeffe, *Georgia O'Keeffe.*

[9]*Ibid.*

[10]Sam Hunter, *American Art of the Twentieth Century* (New York: Harry N. Abrams, Inc., 1972), pp. 105–106.

[11]Tomkins, "Georgia O'Keeffe," p. 42.

[12]Georgia O'Keeffe, *Georgia O'Keeffe.*

[13]Baur, *Nature in Abstraction,* p. 76.

[14]Lloyd Goodrich, *Georgia O'Keeffe,* p. 14.

[15]Ashton, *A Reading of Modern Art,* p. 11.

[16]Georgia O'Keeffe, *Georgia O'Keeffe.*

[17]Ashton, *A Reading of Modern Art,* p. 6.

[18]*Ibid.,* p. 11.

[19]Duncan Phillips, *A Collection in the Making* (Cambridge, Mass.: Riverside Press, 1926), p. 66.

[20]Geldzahler, *American Painting in the Twentieth Century*, pp. 131–132.

[21]Daniel C. Rich, *Georgia O'Keeffe, Exhibition Catalogue* (Chicago: Art Institute of Chicago, 1943), p. 22.

[22]*Life*, February 14, 1938, p. 30.

[23]Read, "Georgia O'Keeffe—Woman Artist Whose Art is Sincerely Feminine," p. 4.

[24]Henry David Thoreau, in Barbara Rose, "O'Keeffe's Trail," *New York Review of Books*, March 31, 1977, p. 31.

[25]*Ibid.*

[26]Goodrich, *Georgia O'Keeffe*, p. 19.

[27]Barbara Rose, "O'Keeffe's Trail," p. 32.

[28]Rose, *American Art Since 1900: A Critical History*, p. 50.

[29]*The Museum* (Winter–Spring 1961): 25.

[30]Bry, "Georgia O'Keeffe," p. 80.

[31]Haskell, *Arthur Dove*, p. 32.

[32]Henri Bergson, *Creative Evolution* (New York: Modern Library, 1944), p. 53.

[33]Phillips, *A Collection in the Making*, p. 66.

[34]Whitney Museum Files (New York: Whitney Museum of American Art).

[35]Georgia O'Keeffe, *Georgia O'Keeffe*.

[36]*Ibid.*, p. 8.

[37]*Ibid.*

[38]Friedman, *The Precisionist View*, p. 28.

[39]*Ibid.*, p. 29.

[40]Mahoriri Young, *Early American Moderns*, p. 35.

[41]Kuh, *The Artist's Voice*, p. 202.

[42]Beth Coffelt, "A Visit with Georgia O'Keeffe," *San Francisco Examiner Chronicle*, April 11, 1971, p. 20.

[43]Daniel Catton Rich, *Georgia O'Keeffe, 1943 Exhibition Catalogue*, p. 30.

[44]Friedman, *The Precisionist View*, p. 13.

[45]*Ibid.*, p. 12.

[46]Coffelt, "A Visit with Georgia O'Keeffe," p. 20.

47Van Deren Coke, "Why Artists Came to New Mexico: Nature Presents a New Face to Each Moment," *ARTnews,* January 1974, p. 24.

48Georgia O'Keeffe, *Georgia O'Keeffe.*

49*Ibid.*

50Katherine Kuh, *The Artist's Voice* (New York: Harper & Row, 1962), p. 202.

51Georgia O'Keeffe, *Georgia O'Keeffe.*

52*Ibid.*

53*Ibid.*

54Janis, *Abstract and Surreal Art in America,* p. 42.

55Georgia O'Keeffe, *Georgia O'Keeffe.*

56Neilson, *Seven Women: Great Painters* (Radnor, PA.: Chilton Book Co., Frances and Winthrop, 1969) p. 158.

57Goodrich, *Georgia O'Keeffe,* p. 25.

58Kuh, *The Artist's Voice,* p. 194.

59Frank Getlein, "In the Light of Georgia O'Keeffe," *New Republic,* November 7, 1960, p. 27.

60Friedman, *The Precisionist View,* p. 26.

61Rich, *Georgia O'Keeffe, 1943 Exhibition Catalogue,* p. 40.

62Beth Coffelt, "A Visit with Georgia O'Keeffe," p. 23.

63Kuh, *The Artist's Voice,* p. 190.

64*Ibid.*

65Barbara Rose, "Georgia O'Keeffe: The Paintings of the Sixties," *Artforum,* November 1970, p. 43.

66Rich, "Georgia O'Keeffe, Forty Years of Her Art," p. 2.

67Katherine Kuh, *The Artist's Voice,* pp. 199–200.

68Christopher Andreae, "You Don't Paint What You See," *Christian Science Monitor,* August 15, 1973, p. 4.

69Allen Frankenstein, "The Shape of O'Keeffe's America," *This World,* April 17, 1966, p. 15.

70Norman, *Alfred Stieglitz,* p. 161.

71Seiberling, "Horizons of a Pioneer," p. 46.

72Miriam Dugan Cross, *Oakland Tribune,* March 14, 1971, p. 26.

[73]"The Object as Subject," *Exhibition Catalogue,* p. 2.

[74]Tomkins, "Georgia O'Keeffe," p. 60.

[75]*Newsweek,* October 10, 1960, p. 52.

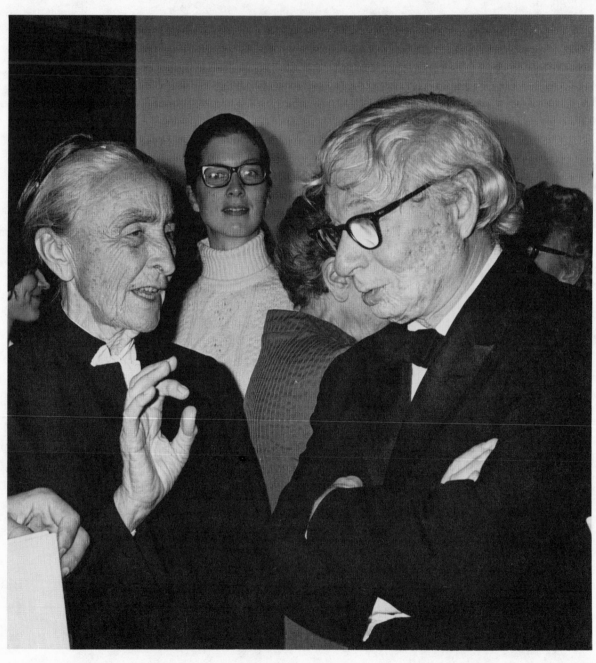

Georgia O'Keeffe and Louis Kahn. October 31, 1971. Photograph by Karl Dimler taken at M. Carey Thomas Award Ceremonies, Bryn Mawr College Visual Resources Department.

124

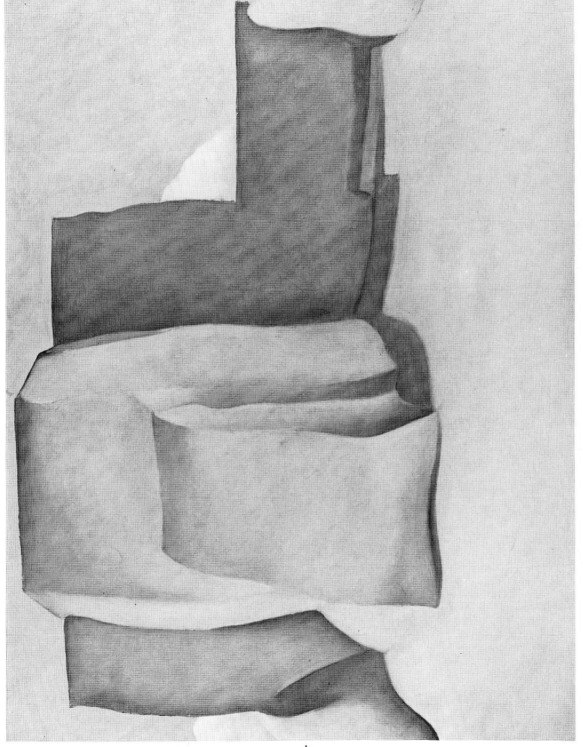

A

Ranchos Church No. 1. 1929 (18¾×24). Norton Gallery and School of Art, West Palm Beach, Florida.

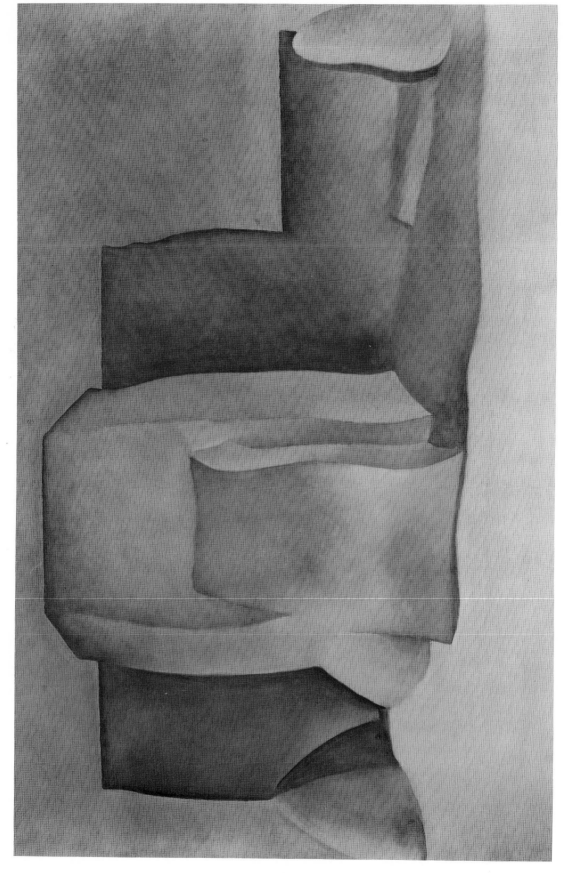

Ranchos Church. 1930 (24×36). The Phillips Collection, Washington, D.C.

B

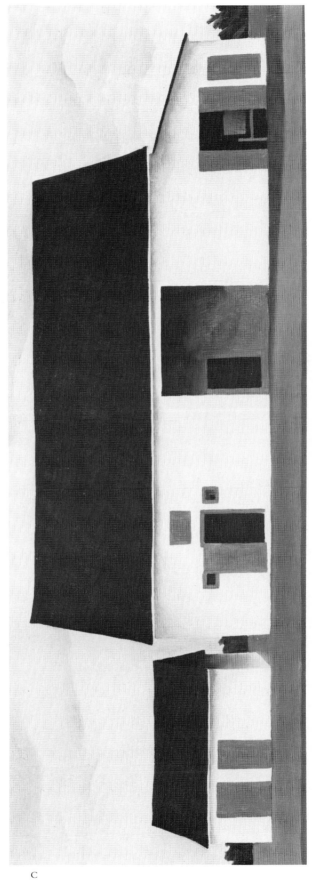

C

Stables. 1932 (12×32). The Detroit Institute of Arts. Gift of Robert H. Tannahill.

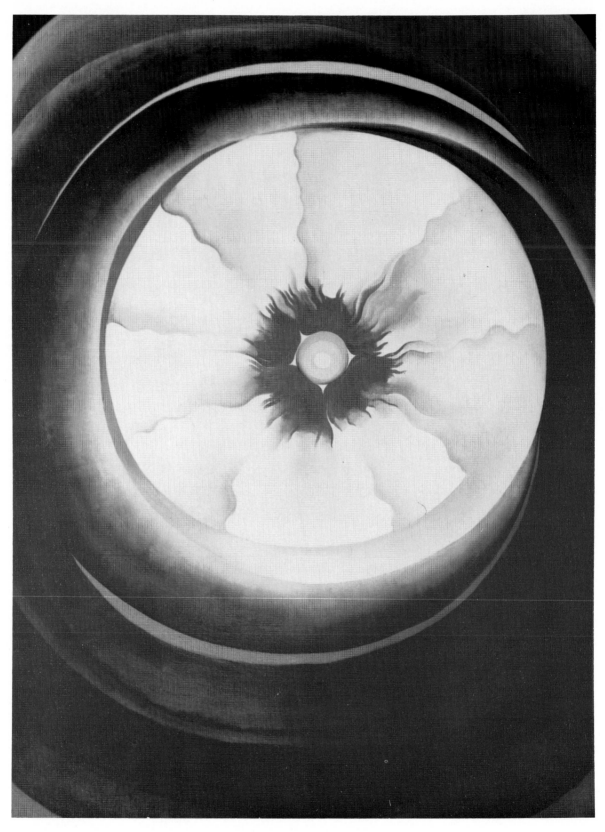

At the Rodeo, New Mexico. 1929 (40×30). Private Collection. Courtesy of Andrew Crispo Gallery, New York.

D

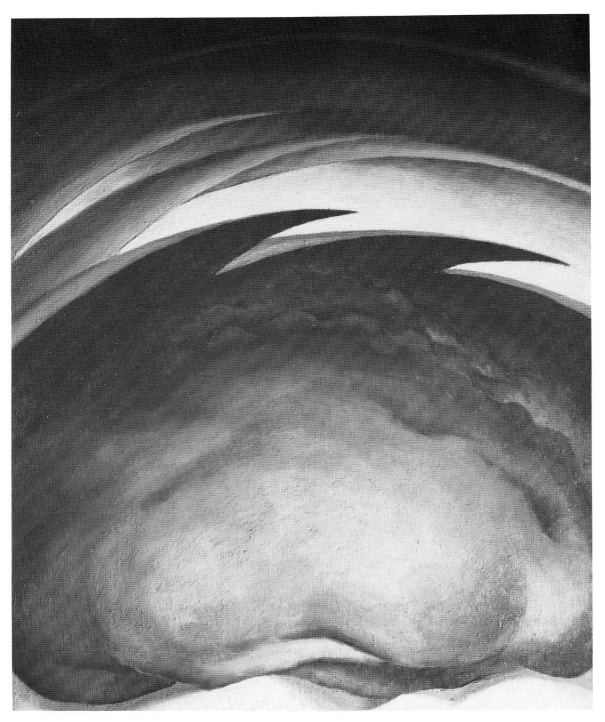

From the Plains. 1919 (27⅝×23⅝). Private Collection. Courtesy of Andrew Crispo Gallery, New York.

From the Plains II. 1954 (48×72). Photograph courtesy of Kennedy Galleries, Inc., New York.

F

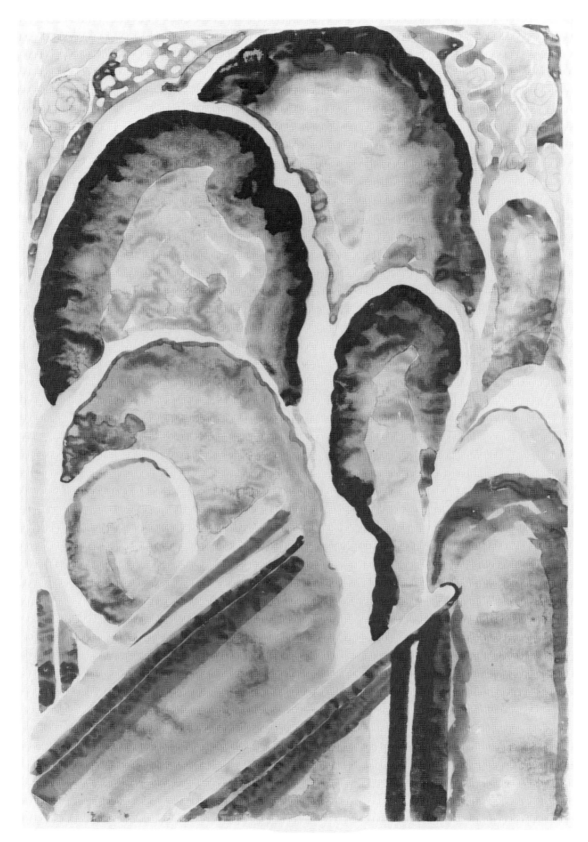

Blue #1. 1916, watercolor (15⅞×11). The Brooklyn Museum. Bequest of Miss Mary T. Cockcroft.

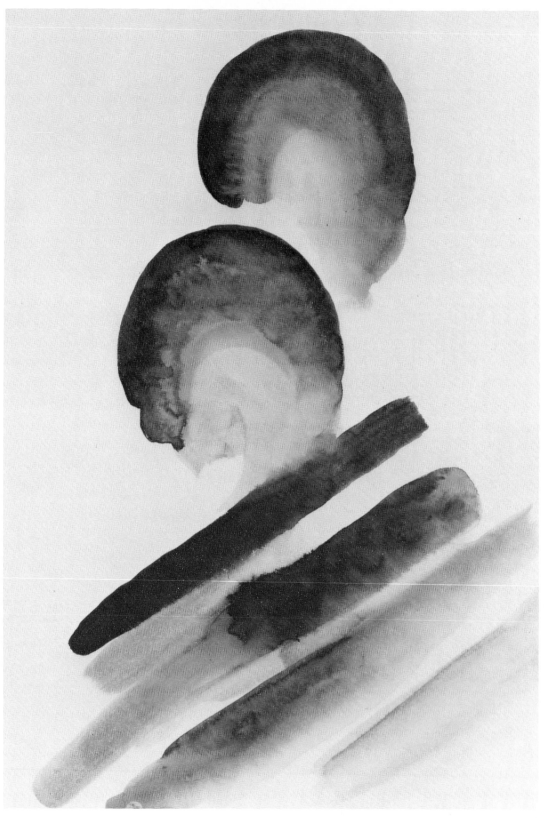

Blue #2. 1916, watercolor (15⅞×10¹⁵⁄₁₆). The Brooklyn Museum. Bequest of Miss Mary T. Cockcroft.

H

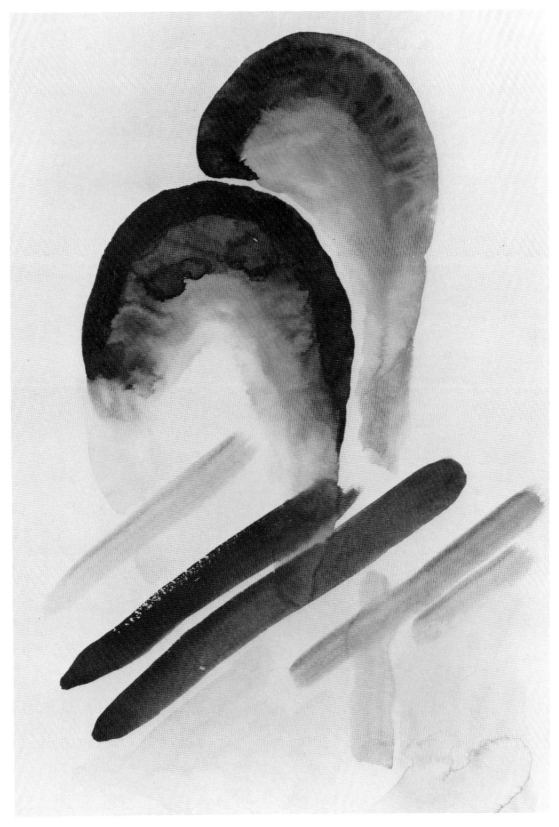

Blue #3. 1916, watercolor (15⅞×10¹⁵⁄₁₆). The Brooklyn Museum. Dick S. Ramsay Fund.

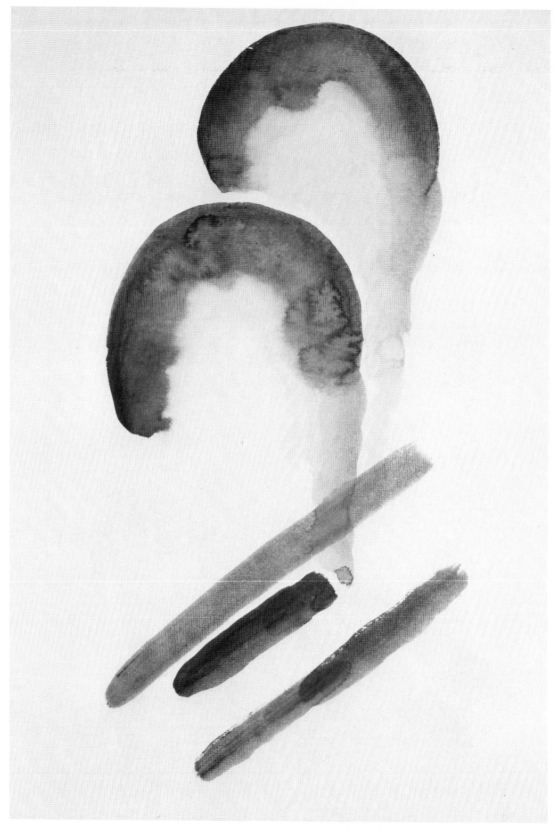

Blue #4. 1916, watercolor ($16 \times 10^{15}/_{16}$). The Brooklyn Museum. Dick S. Ramsay Fund.

J

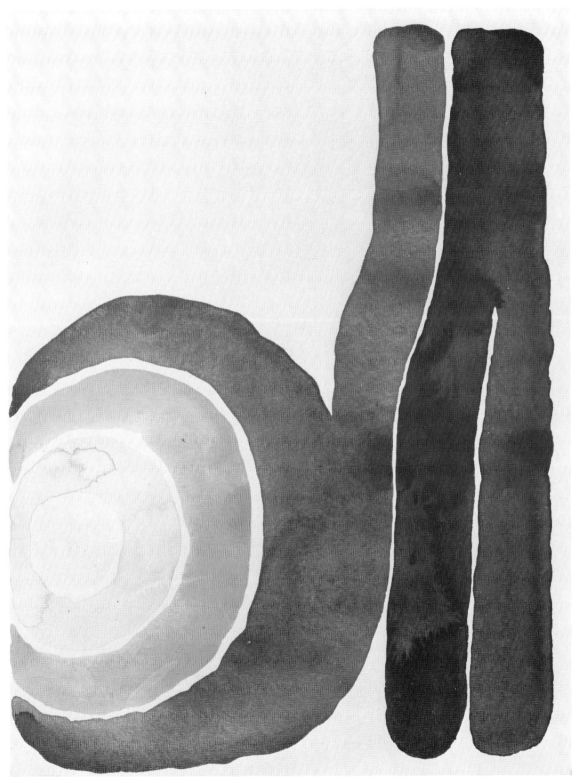

K

Evening Star III. 1917, watercolor (9×11⅞). Collection, The Museum of Modern Art, New York. Mr. and Mrs. Donald B. Straus Fund.

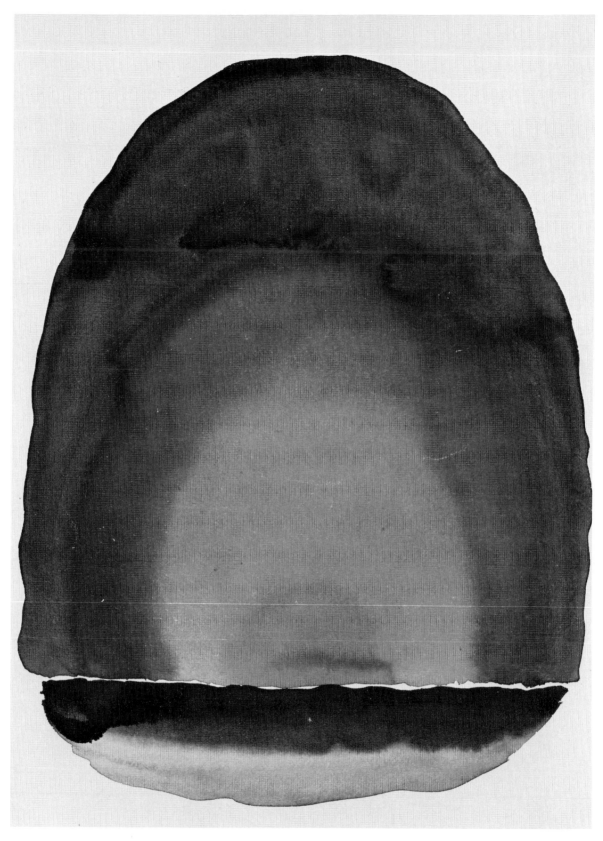

Light Coming on the Plains II. 1917, watercolor (11⅞×8⅞). Courtesy Amon Carter Museum, Fort Worth, Texas.

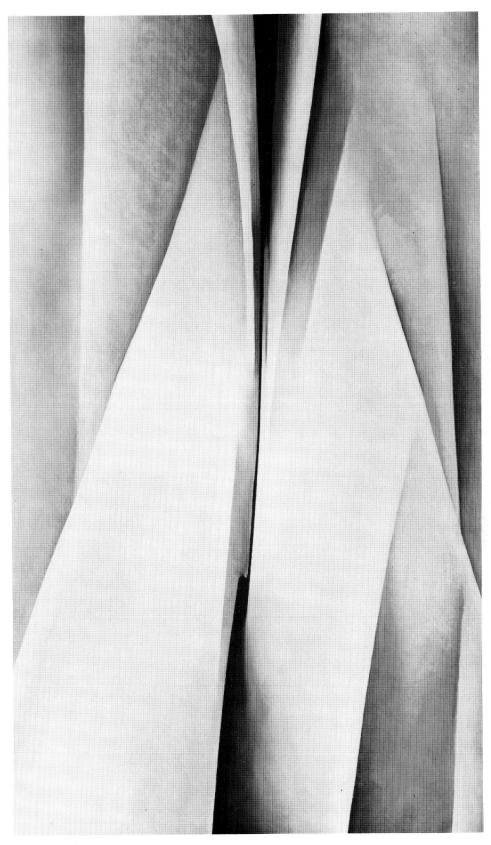

Abstraction. 1926 (30×18). Collection of Whitney Museum of American Art, New York.

M

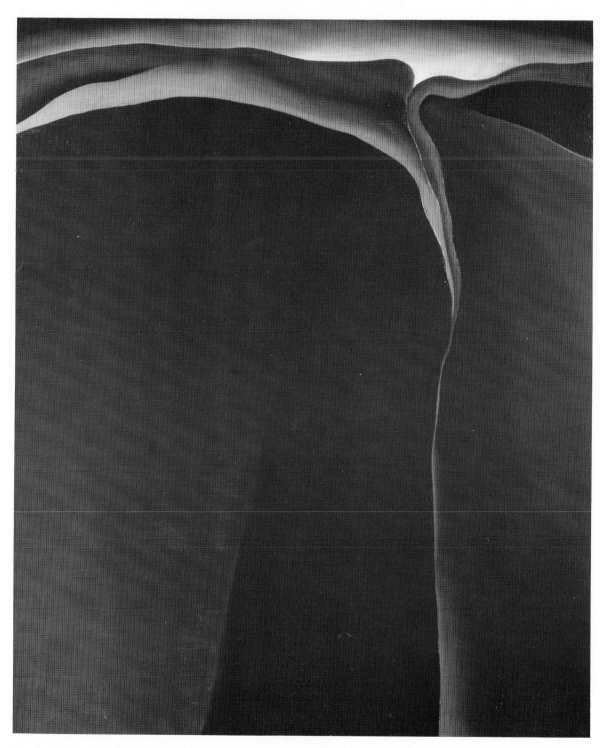

Dark Abstraction. 1924 (24⅞×20⅞). The St. Louis Art Museum. Gift of Charles E. and Mary Merrill.

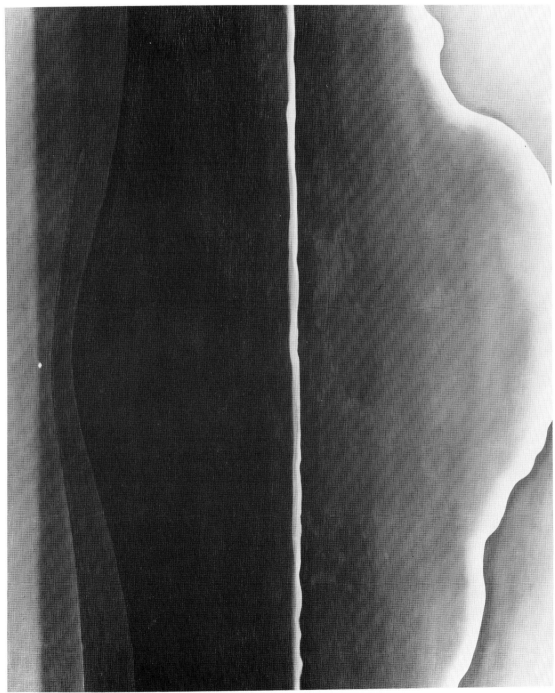

Wave, Night. 1928 (30×36). The Addison Gallery of American Art, Phillips Academy, Andover, Massachusetts. Gift of Mr. Charles L. Stillman.

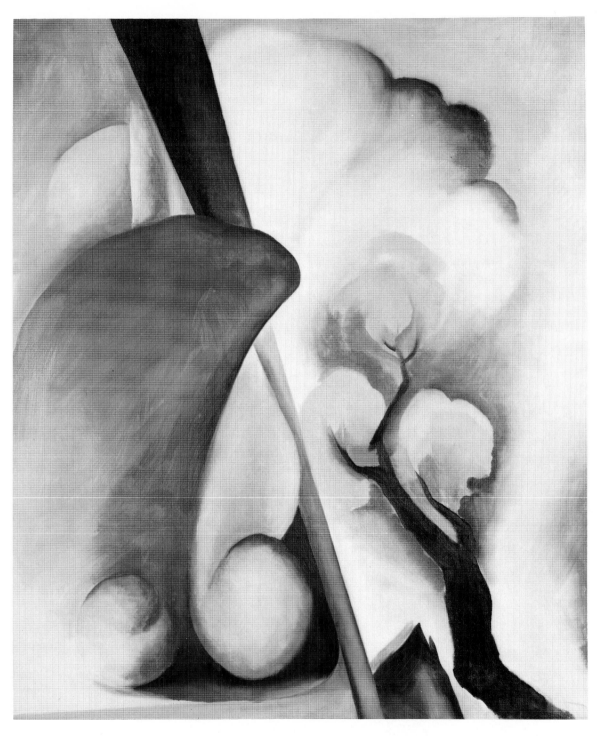

Spring. 1922 (35½×30⅜). Vassar College Art Gallery, Poughkeepsie, New York. Bequest of Mrs. Arthur Schwab (Edna Bryner '07).

P

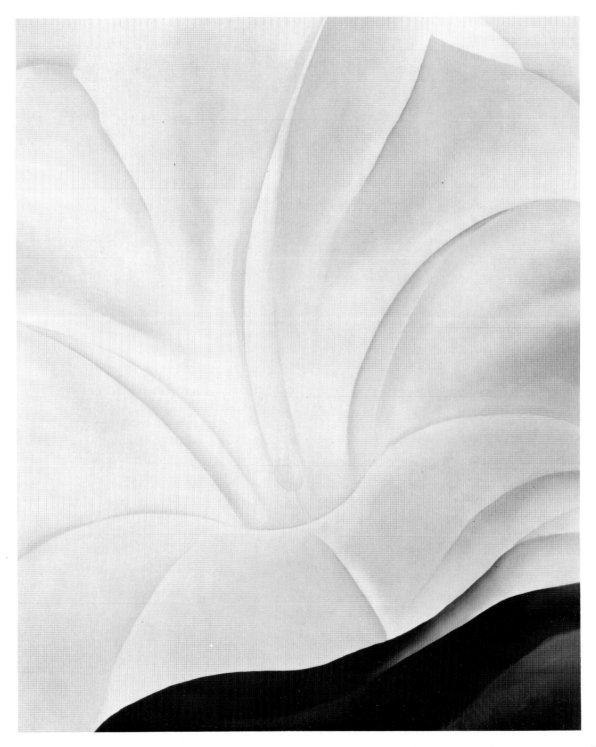

Morning Glory with Black. 1926 (13¹³/₁₆×39⅝). The Cleveland Museum of Art. Bequest of Leonard C. Hanna, Jr.

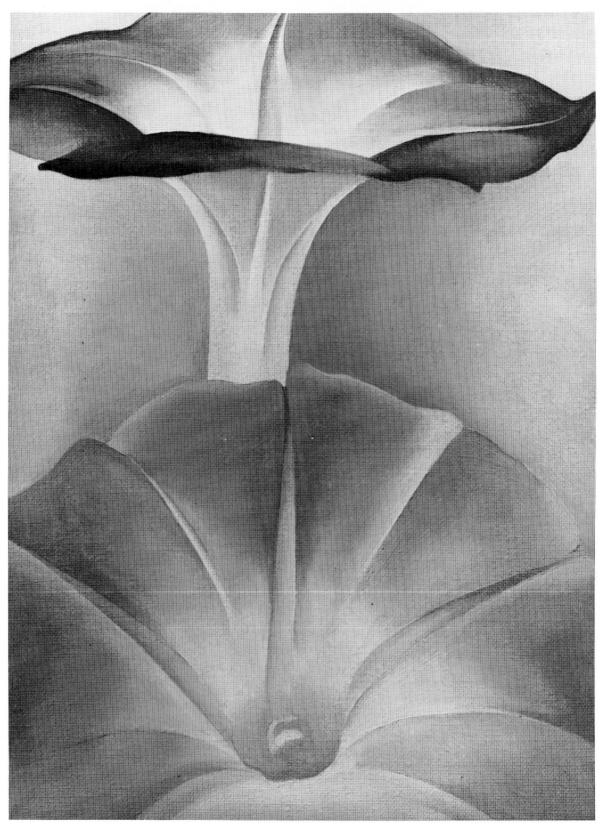

Blue Morning Glories, New Mexico II. 1935 (12¼×9). Private Collection. Photograph courtesy James H. Maroney, New York.

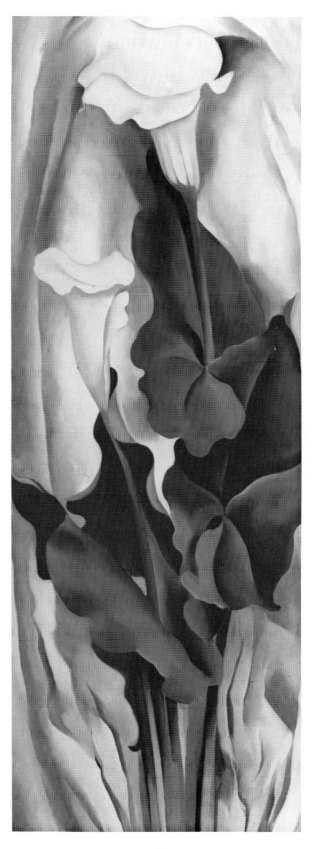

Yellow Calla—Green Leaves. 1927 (42×14). Collection of Steve Martin. Photograph courtesy James H. Maroney, New York.

s

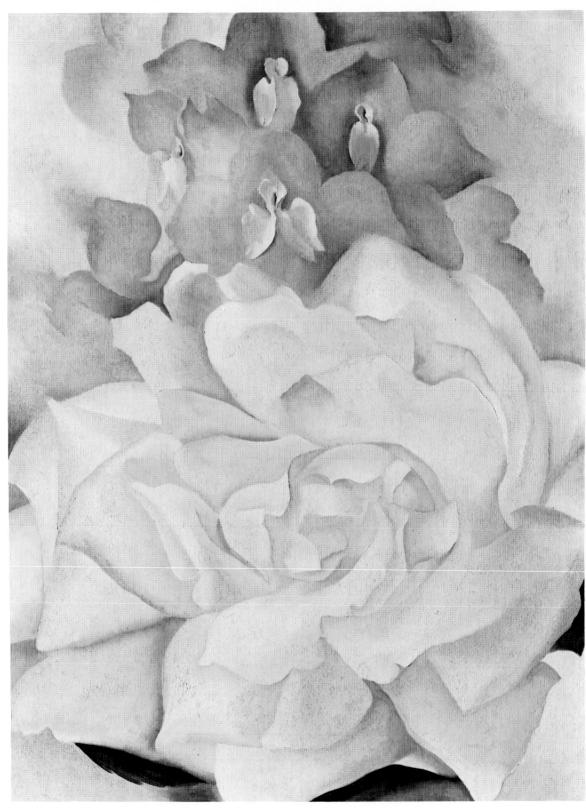

White Rose with Larkspur #2. 1927 (40×30). Courtesy, Museum of Fine Arts, Boston. Henry H. and Zoe Oliver Sherman Fund.

T

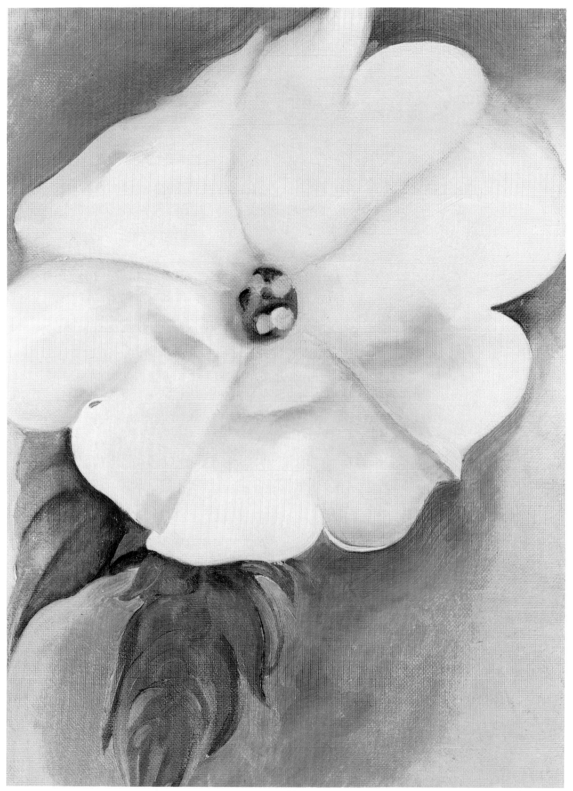

White Flower. Undated (8×11). Photograph courtesy of Kennedy Galleries, Inc., New York.

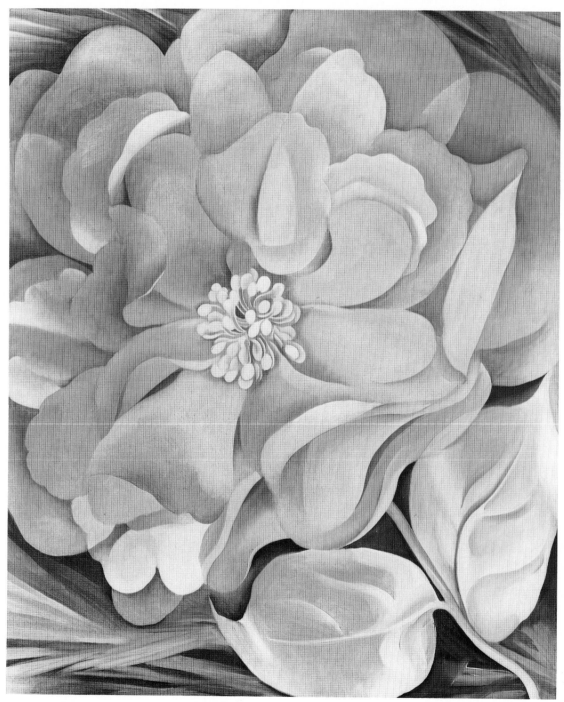

The White Calico Flower. 1931 (30×36). Collection of Whitney Museum of American Art, New York.

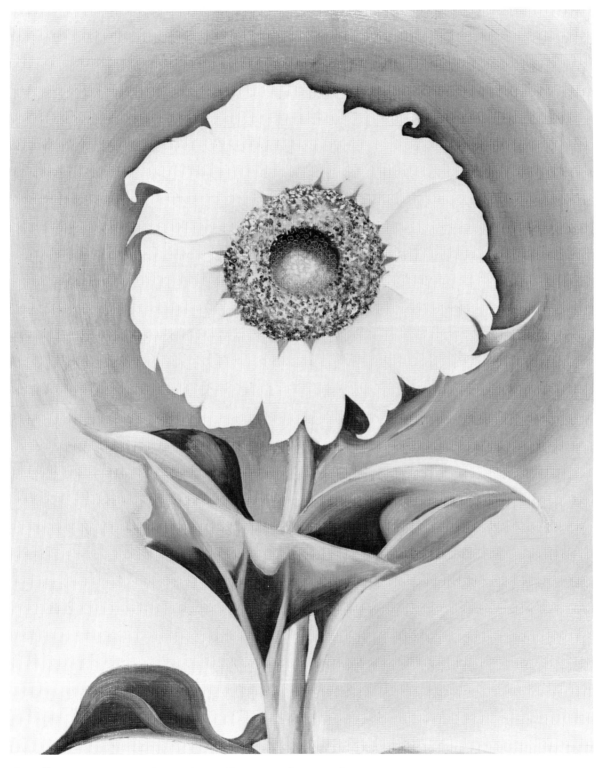

Sunflower. 1935 (15½×19½). Collection of Dr. Helen W. Boigon.

w

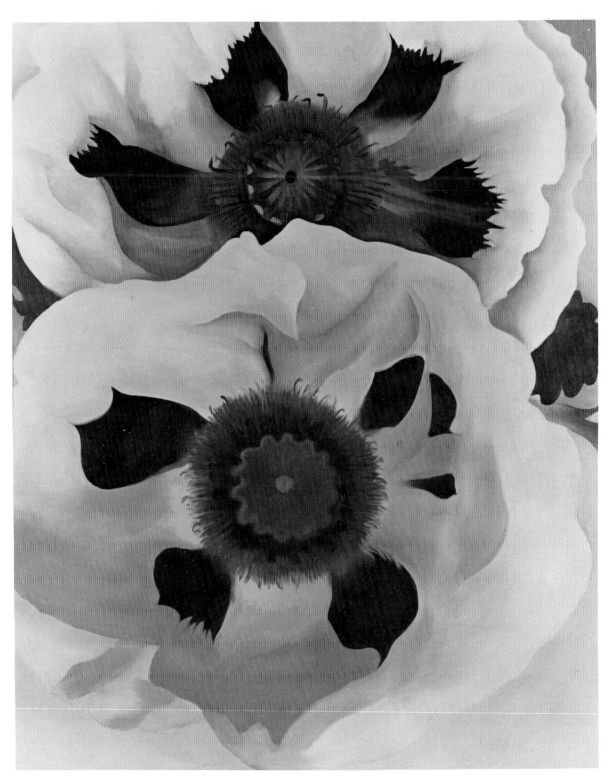

Poppies. 1950 (36×30). Milwaukee Art Museum Collection. Gift of Mrs. Harry Lynde Bradley.

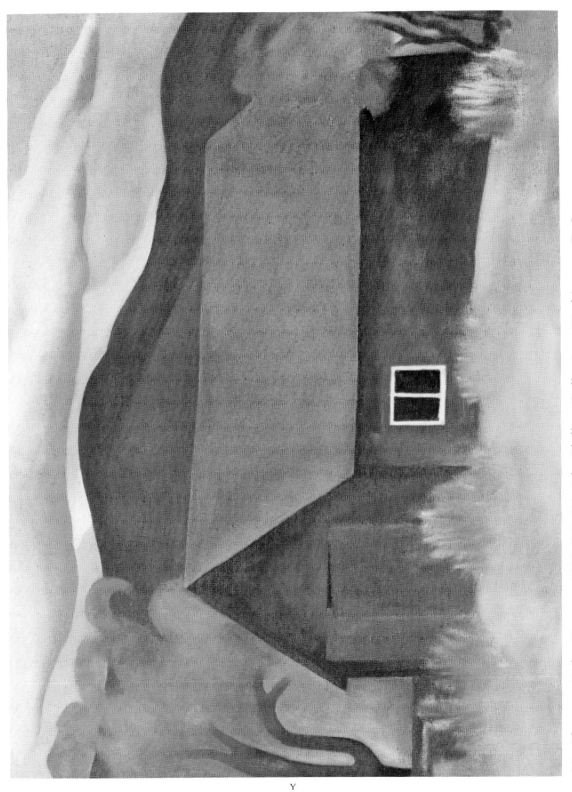

My Shanty—Lake George. 1922 (20×27). The Phillips Collection, Washington, D.C.

Y

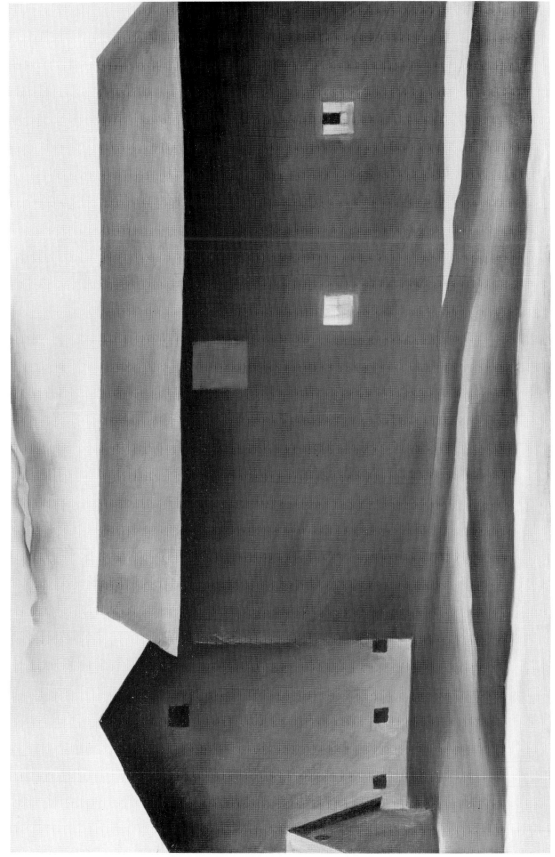

Lake George Barns. 1926 (21⅛×32). Collection Walker Art Center, Minneapolis. Gift of the T. B. Walker Foundation.

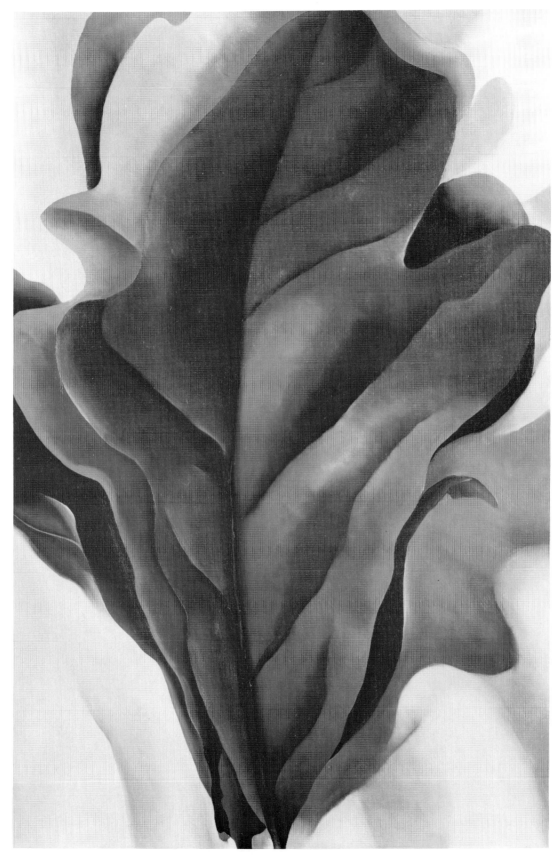

Large Dark Red Leaves on White. 1925 (32×21). The Phillips Collection, Washington, D.C.

AA

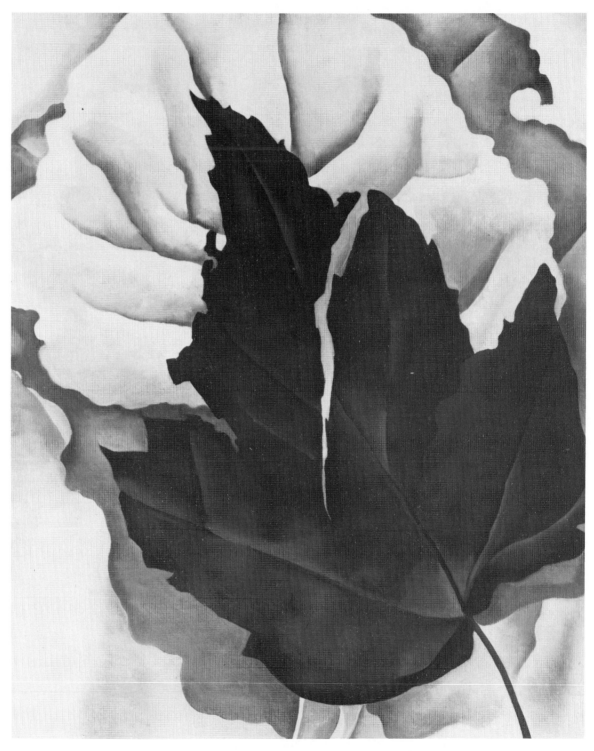

Pattern of Leaves (Leaf Motif). 1926 (22×18). The Phillips Collection, Washington, D.C.

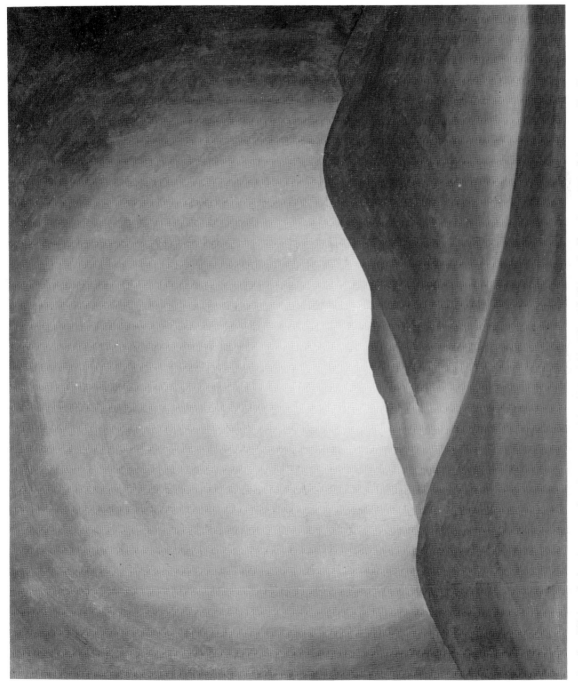

Red Hills and the Sun, Lake George. 1927 (27×32). The Phillips Collection, Washington, D.C.

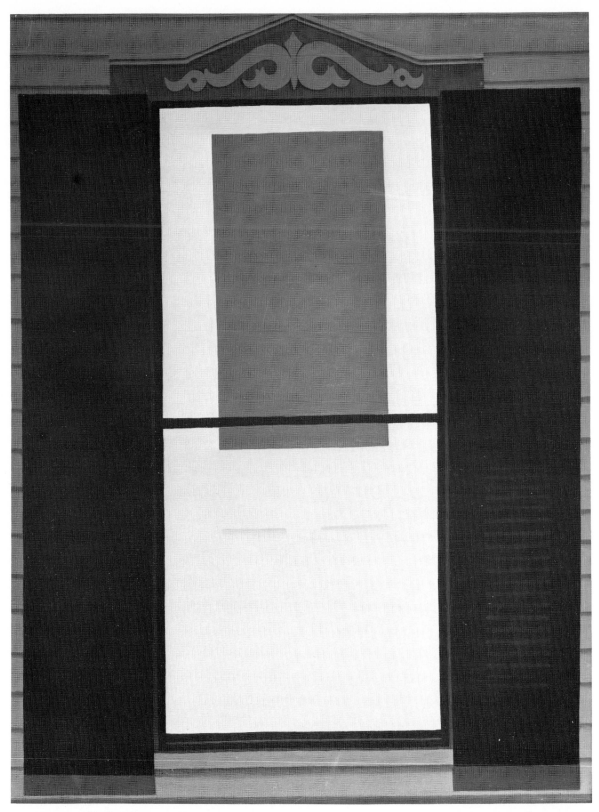

Lake George Window. 1929 (40×30). Collection, The Museum of Modern Art, New York. Acquired through the Richard D. Brixey Bequest.

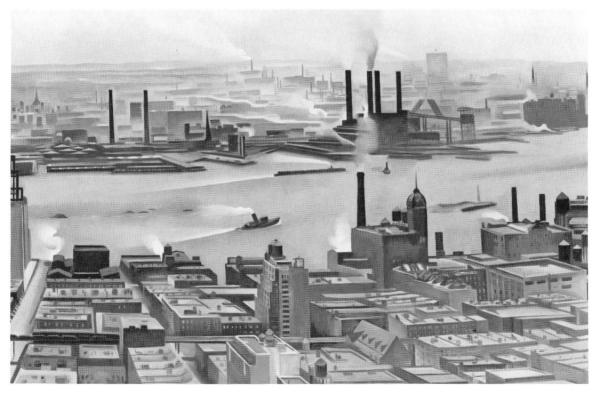

East River from the 30th Story of the Shelton Hotel, New York. 1928 (30×48). From the Collection of the New Britain Museum of American Art, New Britain, Connecticut. Steven Lawrence Fund.

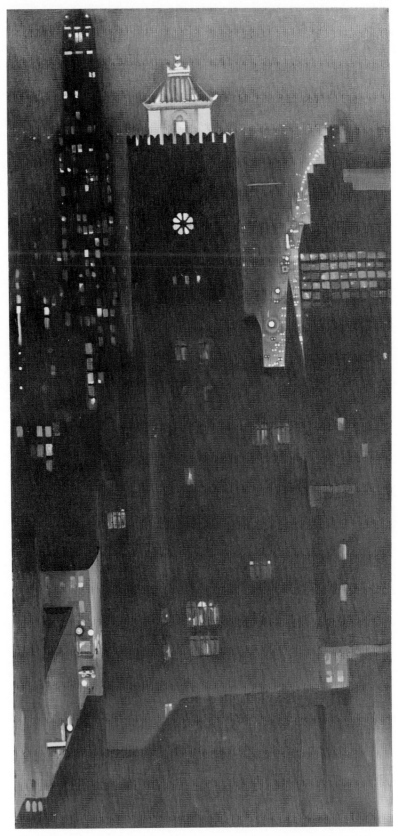

New York, Night. 1929 (40⅛×19⅛). Collection of the Nebraska Art Association. Courtesy of the Sheldon Memorial Art Gallery. Thomas C. Woods Memorial Collection.

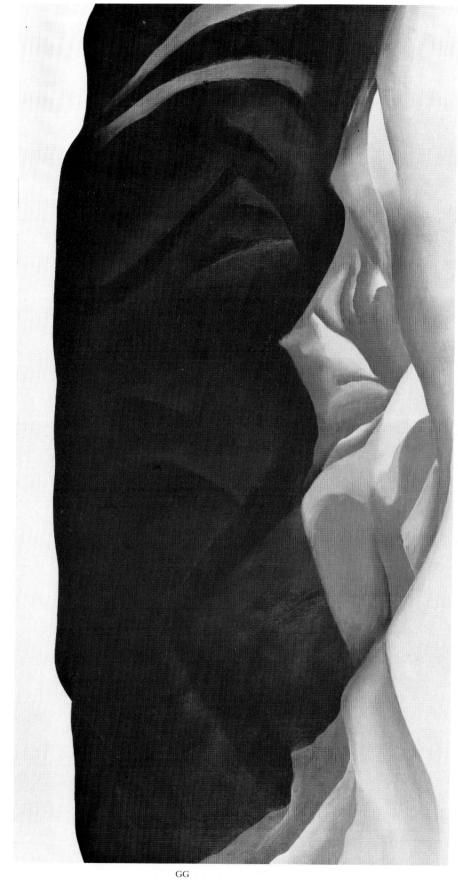

Dark Mesa and Pink Sky. 1930 (16×29⅞). Courtesy Amon Carter Museum, Fort Worth, Texas.

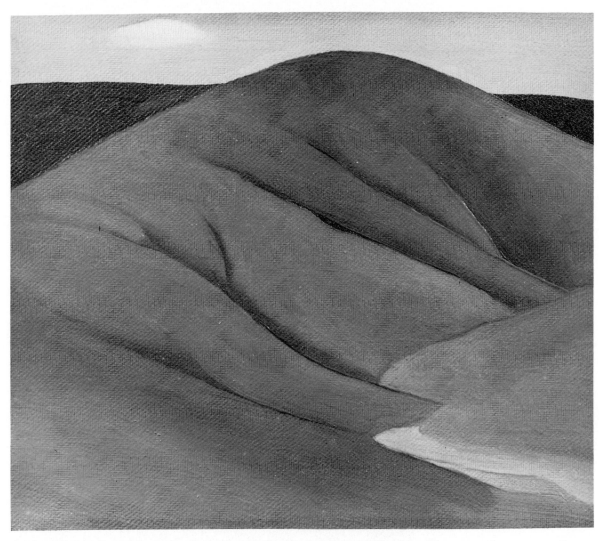

Red Hills with White Cloud. undated (6×7). Private Collection. Photograph courtesy James
H. Maroney, New York.

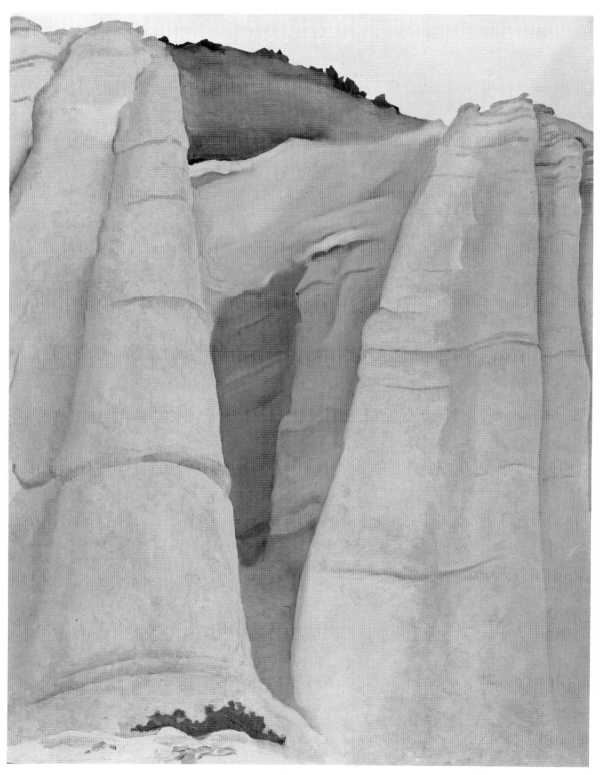

The White Place in Shadow. 1940 (30×24). The Phillips Collection, Washington, D.C.

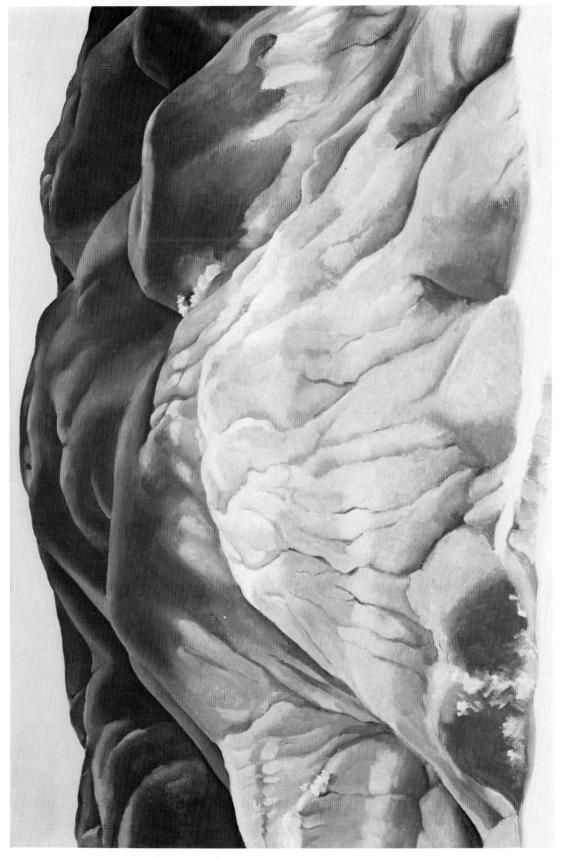

The Grey Hills. 1942 (20×30). Indianapolis Museum of Art. Gift of Mr. and Mrs. James W. Fesler.

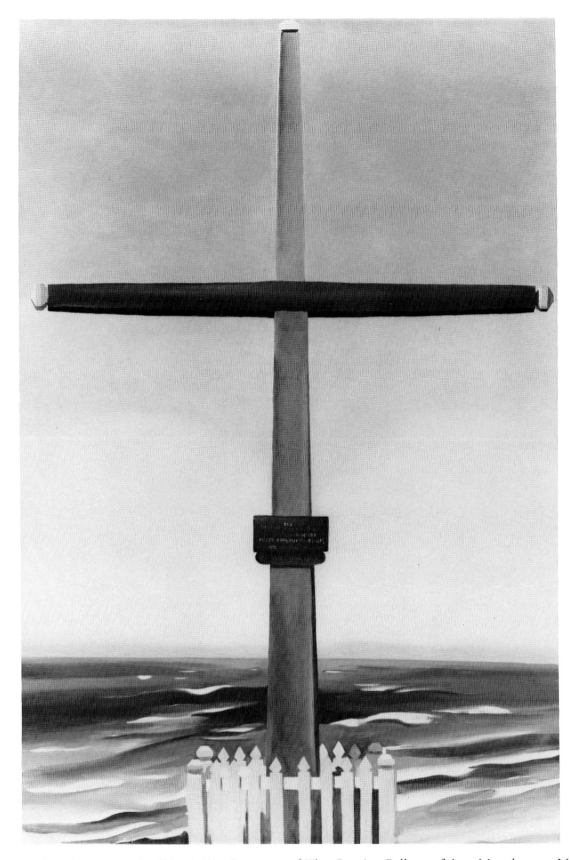

Cross by the Sea. 1931 (20×36⅛). Courtesy of The Currier Gallery of Art, Manchester, New Hampshire.

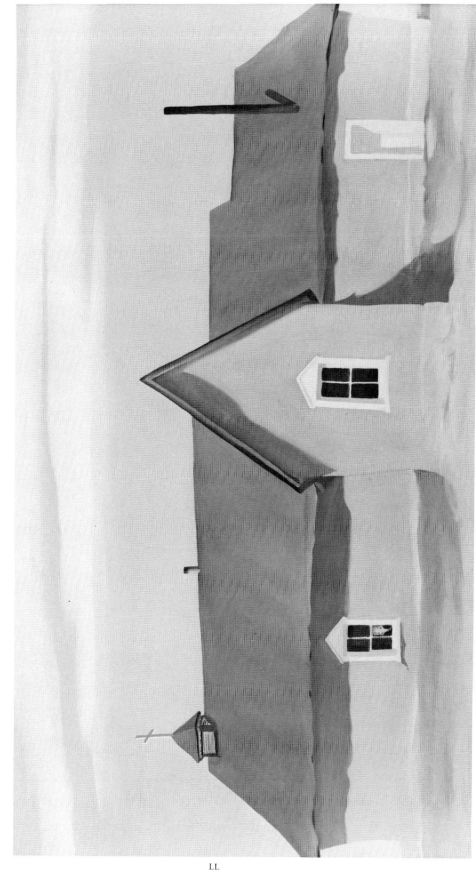

Cebolla Church. 1945 (20×36⅛). North Carolina Museum of Art. Gift of the North Carolina Art Society (Robert F. Phifer Funds) in honor of Dr. Joseph C. Sloane.

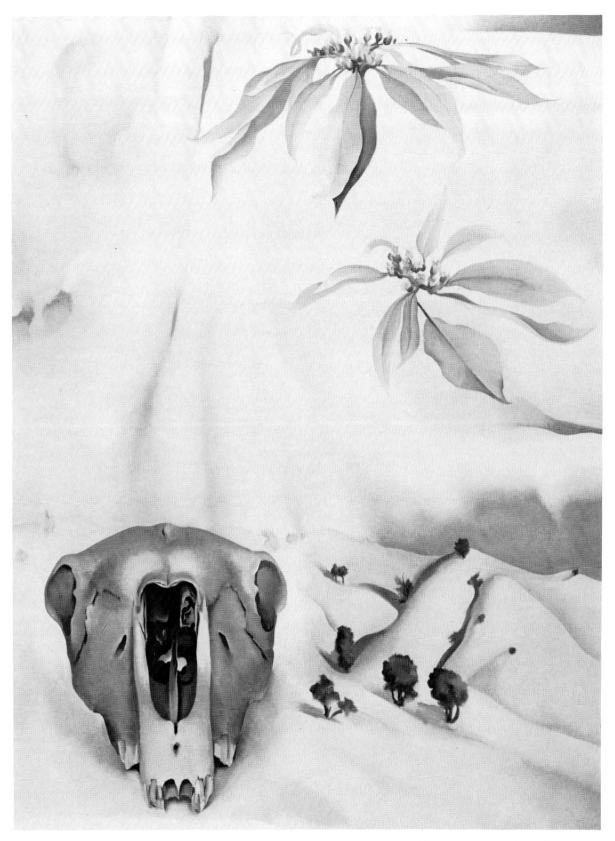

Mule's Skull with Pink Poinsettias. 1937 (30×40). Private Collection. Courtesy of Andrew Crispo Gallery, New York.

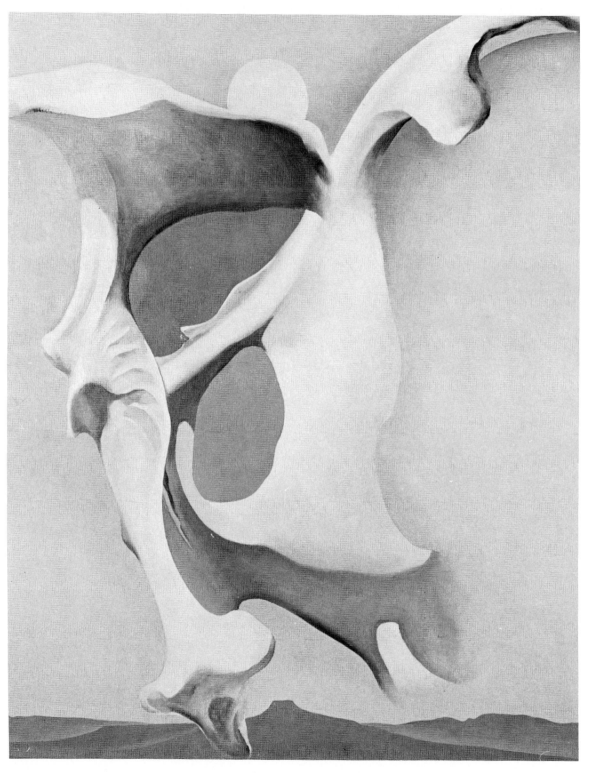

Pelvis with Moon. 1943 (30×24). Norton Gallery and School of Art, West Palm Beach, Florida.

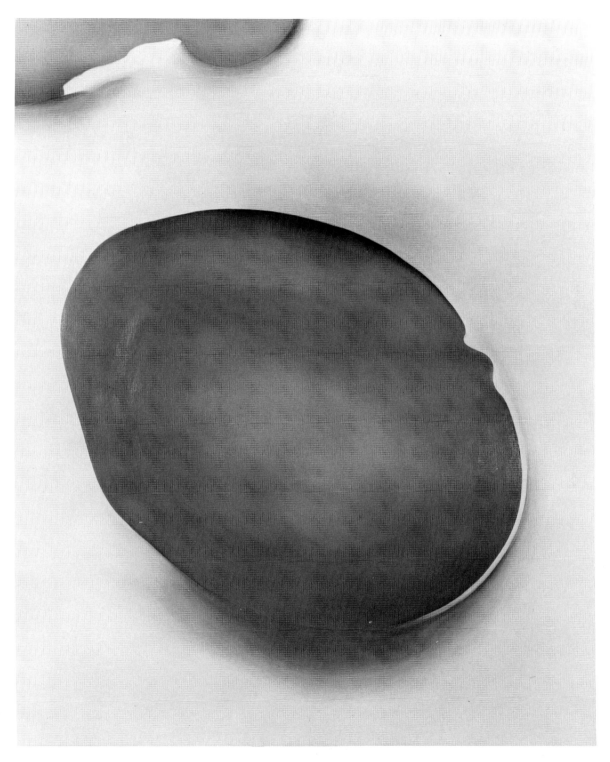

Pelvis with Blue (Pelvis I). 1944 (36×30). Milwaukee Art Museum Collection. Gift of Mrs. Harry Lynde Bradley.

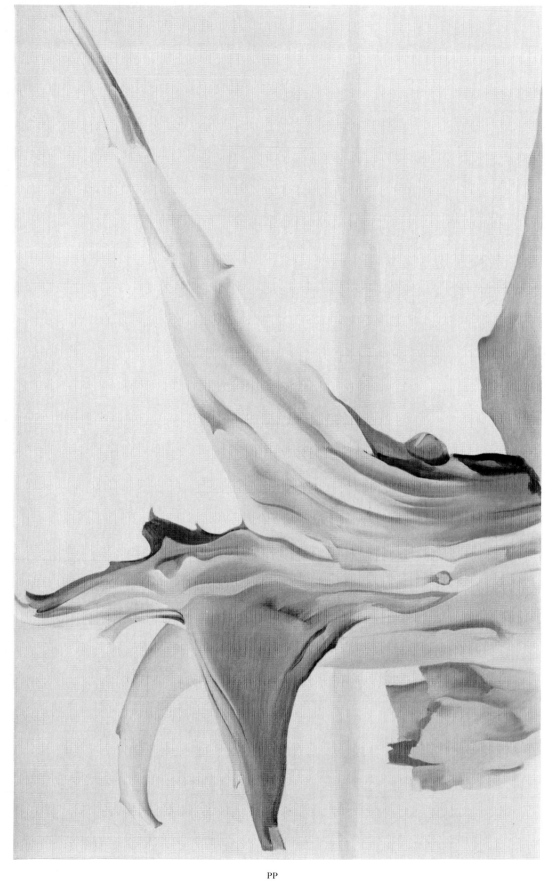

Red Tree, Yellow Sky. 1952 (30×48). The Lane Collection. Courtesy of Museum of Fine Arts, Boston.

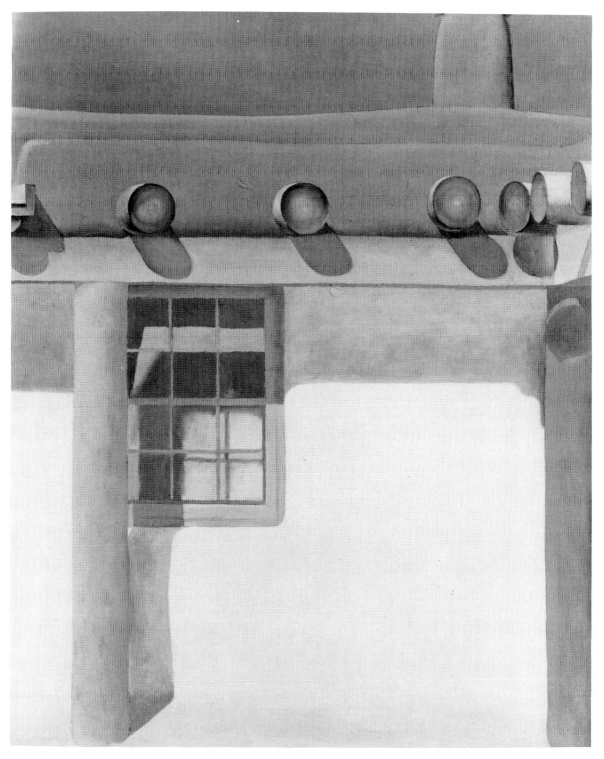

From the Patio II. 1940 (24×19). Photograph courtesy of Kennedy Galleries, Inc., New York.

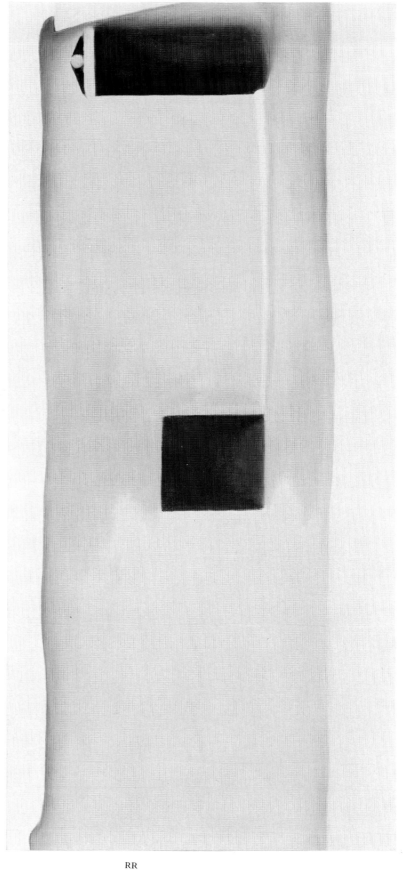

In the Patio IV. 1948 (14×30). The Lane Collection. Courtesy of Museum of Fine Arts, Boston.

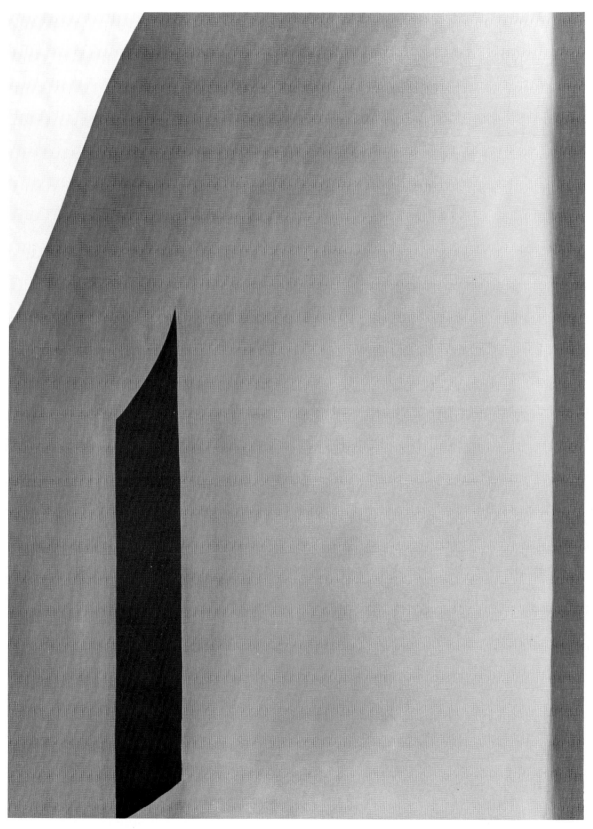

Black Patio Door. 1955 (40⅛×30). Courtesy Amon Carter Museum, Fort Worth, Texas.

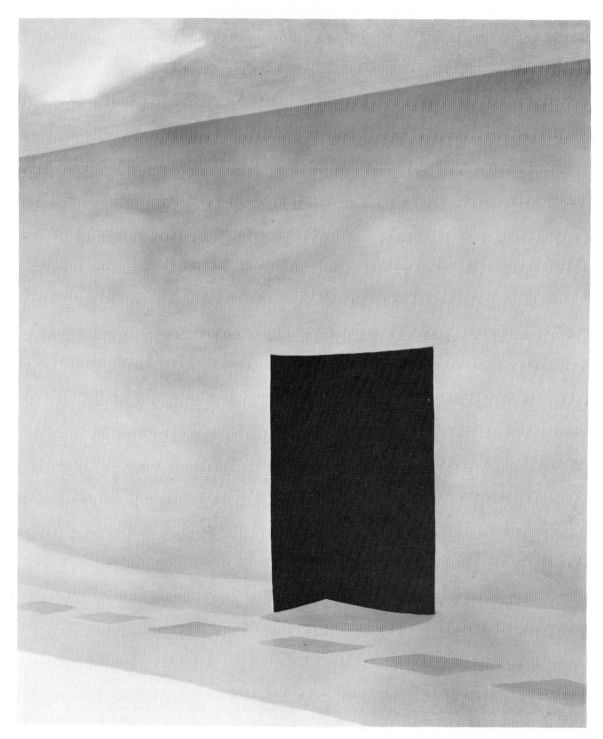

Patio with Cloud. 1956 (36×30). Milwaukee Art Museum Collection. Gift of Mrs. Edward R. Wehr.

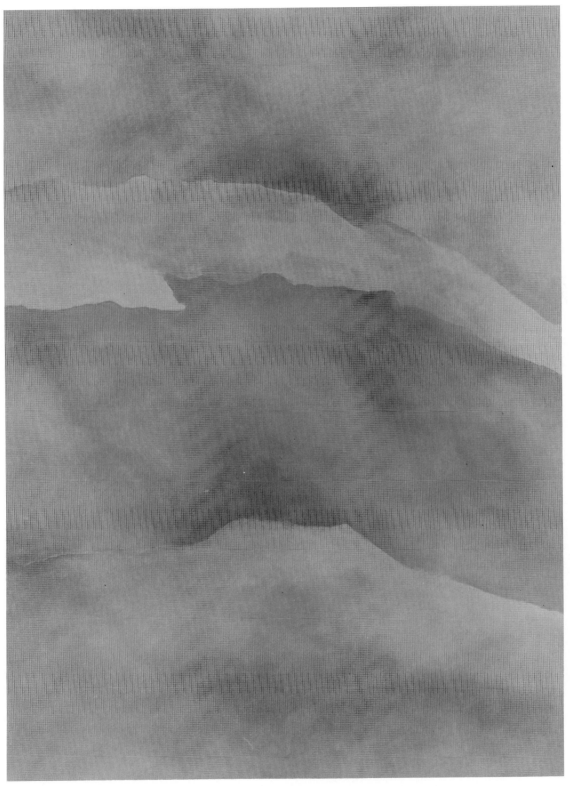

It Was Red and Pink. 1959 (30×40). Milwaukee Art Museum Collection. Gift of Mrs. Harry Lynde Bradley.

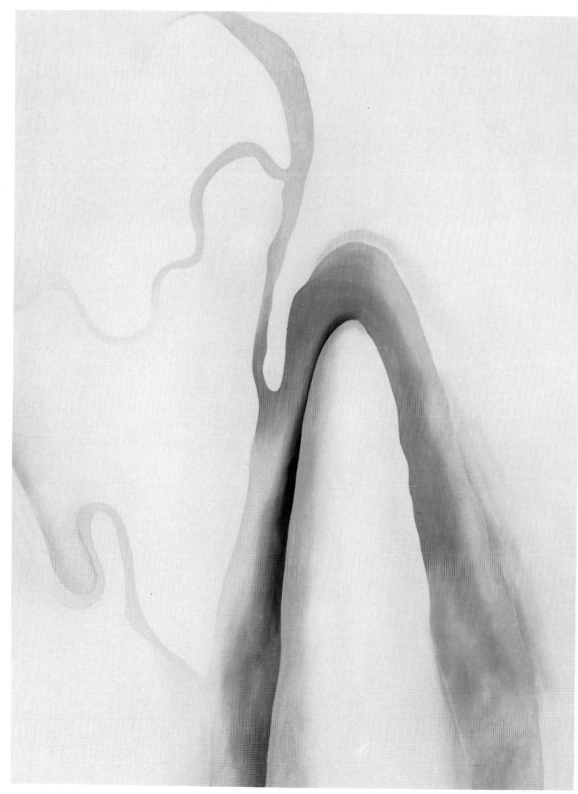

It Was Blue and Green. 1960 (30×40). Collection of Whitney Museum of American Art. Lawrence H. Bloedel Bequest.

Epilogue

The work O'Keeffe has completed into her nineties is remarkable in both volume and quality. Despite the changes in subject matter and accompanying stylistic emphasis over the years—the flowers, New York City buildings, the barns, the river forms, rocks, abstractions, etc.—there is a basic consistency in O'Keeffe's work, in her vision in general. Always she has sought the living essential of things, getting to the roots of nature and life. She seems to have accomplished what John Marin and other members of the Stieglitz circle saw as the eternal job of the artist: ". . . in all forms, his symbol everlasting to make a complete living organ which lives of its own right, gotten by his rebounds."[1] Always, too, O'Keeffe is true to her inner thoughts and intuition. Through the century O'Keeffe's work has been associated with various artistic movements such as cubism, surrealism, expressionistic or minimal art. Although her works may exhibit aspects of various established styles, her vision has remained intensely personal. As E. M. Benson wrote very early, "I never saw an O'Keeffe that reminded me of anything but O'Keeffe."[2] In general, O'Keeffe's work through the years has tended toward greater formal simplicity. Forms in more recent work become more flatly painted with less interaction between one another, i.e., the patio and cloud paintings.

Most important is perhaps the depth of feeling and quality of craftsmanship that is inherent in almost every O'Keeffe piece. The new reality that O'Keeffe creates in each work is a reflection of the acknowledgment of a changing reality in the beginning of this century. Sidney Janis has described such realities which ". . . transcend commonplace representation: the secret life of the objects, the dynamics of an expanding universe, unseen mechanisms of nature: pictorial law; all but inscrutable phenomena of mind and emotions; light and form, essence and sensibility."[3] As Lee Nordness has observed, the actual observed

> . . . physical facts of nature become less and less important to us in themselves. . . . It is the tension between forms, the effects of movement on shapes and qualities, the active spaces which surround solid masses, which seem to be the most tangible things which many artists need to work. There are of course striking parallels in the social and economic situation of our times. The great problems of our period are not material ones; they are problems of basic relationships . . . this new awareness of space, while it is inevitably tremendously exhilarating, also produces a new sense of fear. It represents the unknown and contributes to the anxiety and the loneliness of modern man. In itself space may be benign and all-embracing, but the way in which man is exploiting his newly acquired ability to enter it and explore it, is perilous. It results in a feeling that it is first of all necessary and inevitable for the artist to express whatever inner vitality he possesses and that a new aesthetic must be created to formulate new conceptions of space, light movement, and infinity.[4]

O'Keeffe has created her own individual aesthetic and remarkable sense of space which often throughout her career appears to be infinite in her paintings. She has also created a

125

new world of nature's forms through her powerful personal expression. Almost always one senses that inner vitality that is important for survival in our present age.

O'Keeffe's work has remained its own "ism," O'Keeffe being leader and follower. Although there are no real direct disciples of O'Keeffe, some artists have professed being influenced by her work, and some critics have felt that much of O'Keeffe's work fits well into a generation of abstract expressionists. "A great many of O'Keeffe's paintings from the 1915–1918 years, if blown up to the heroic size of the Abstract Expressionist could pass easily for slightly nature-oriented examples of this later period. In the broad color pictures the hues go down smoothly, anonymously, soaking the surface; the colors are rich and deep like the Rothkos of the early 'fifties; others are stained in a brilliance and manner reminiscent of Morris Louis. The frontality, the openness, the symmetrical simplicity all belong as much to the later period as to her own."[5] Among the artists admitting a strong influence in O'Keeffe's work are Paul Feeley and Kenneth Noland, as mentioned earlier.

The very spirit of O'Keeffe has undoubtedly influenced other women artists, encouraging them to push onward in their endeavors. O'Keeffe was placed at the center, in Christ's position, in Mary Beth Edelson's *Last Supper,* a large poster based on Da Vinci's painting of living American women artists in 1972. And O'Keeffe was the only living woman to be included in Judy Chicago's *The Dinner Party,* a large triangular banquet table paying tribute to thirty-nine women throughout history, through ornate embroidery and ceramic place settings representing each woman. The fact that O'Keeffe is a woman who has succeeded as an artist, helps pave the way for important roles for women in American art today and in the future. As early as 1945 O'Keeffe stated, "I believe in women making their living. It will be nice when women have equal opportunities and status with men so that it is taken as a matter of course."[6] O'Keeffe has not, however, usually participated actively in the woman's movement, preferring to be viewed simply as an "artist."

The success of O'Keeffe, though, has encouraged the exploration of new forms and for the establishment of a greater variety of places for women to show their work. During the seventies, when there was a push by women artists to have their work seen, cooperative galleries (such as A.I.R., beginning with twenty women) opened in New York. In California, Judy Chicago and Miriam Shapiro opened their "Womanhouse," a building taken over by female art students who filled each room with the then popular feminist iconography, such as associations with mothering, the female body, etc. As the seventies progressed the need for separate spaces to show one's work became less emphasized. More women's art was mainstreamed and women in general were given wider exposure in the art world. Some feel women artists have made great advances through the century. Others feel there have been only minimal advances. "When you get down to real money, to bread—the real issue it's still a hard scene. . . . In general the art world values aggressive art because it conveys power . . . it stifles respect for any work that is more delicate, 'more feminine'. . . . If a female Chardin were alive today—and Chardin, I think had a real feminine component to his sensibility—she wouldn't be able to make a good living."[7] Further, women artists still have to face the conflict of career versus family, and what they'll have to give up to be an artist. A young artist, Alexis Smith has stated, "The most serious obstacle women artists face is the one they have always faced—what I call internal problems. . . . For a woman to be an artist, she has to stay single or live with other artists. Male artists still get to have wives to take care of them. We don't."[8] O'Keeffe herself gave up the thought of having any children, which she did consider, and has lived throughout her career with the support of other artists. The paintings and sculpture she has created throughout the century are a testament to her success as a woman artist, and as an artist, as she would prefer to be viewed.

One might ask if O'Keeffe has been influenced or affected by the profound technological changes in this century. Although O'Keeffe has not been strongly influenced by changes in technology through the century, she has not been unaware of such changes. In general, she is very forward-thinking and stresses the need to follow one's dreams. On being asked in 1960 her feeling about man orbiting the earth for the first time, she replied, "Well, you see, we really haven't found enough dreams. We haven't dreamed enough. When you fly under even normal circumstances, you see such marvelous things, such incredible colors that you actually begin to believe in your dreams."[9] Since the fifties O'Keeffe has done a fair amount of traveling by air and, as was seen, utilized her aerial experiences in some of her paintings. Basically, though, the strength of O'Keeffe's personal vision and statements, visual and verbal, was fed and fostered by the milieu surrounding her in the late teens, twenties, and thirties. One cannot forget that she began her work in a particular milieu and time, as discussed in Part One. The avant-garde thinking of that period and her relationship with Stieglitz and his circle were most influential for O'Keeffe and her painting. The strength of O'Keeffe's own convictions and the support she initially received from her surrounding milieu in those early days has enabled her to survive in a century of constant change.

The enduring spirit of Georgia O'Keeffe continues to remain alive in her paintings and in her independent lifestyle in New Mexico. Since the time of her first show in 1916, she has continued to work prodigiously. As indicated here, the support she received from Alfred Stieglitz and from the rebellious temper of her time in the beginning years of her career were of utmost importance. The thinking of various writers and philosophers of the early twentieth century, the historical position of women, events such as the Armory Show, personalities such as Arthur Dow, Alfred Stieglitz, and his surrounding circle were all part of a supportive milieu, important for O'Keeffe's development. Without such intellectual, emotional, and financial support in these beginning years she might easily have remained an unknown teacher and painter in the plains of Texas. This support reached fruition in combination with O'Keeffe's individual spirit and drive and has enabled her to create a remarkable body of work.

As seen, the criticism in response to O'Keeffe's work through the years has been varied. The critics' responses have ranged from the highly emotional, often poetic language dealing with the so-called sexual or feminine imagery, to the more objective criticism of recent years, attempting to set O'Keeffe's work in a retrospective, historical perspective. The attempts made to associate O'Keeffe's painting with very specific symbols or to narrowly classify her paintings in a particular artistic movement seem unfair to her work. The critics dealing with the intensity of O'Keeffe's visual language, her treatment of various objects in nature, and her creation of a new reality seem to remain the most faithful to her work. And O'Keeffe, again and again, has stated that she only paints what she sees. "It's just what I do seems to move people today in a way that I don't understand at all."[10]

The New Mexican land and light have continued to inspire O'Keeffe well into her nineties. She has acknowledged that some of the secret of her continuing productivity has been the retention of her privacy and willingness to say "no." "I first learned to say no when I stopped dancing. I liked to dance very much. But if I danced all night, I couldn't paint for three days."[11] She continues to be ambitious, tough, driven, and disciplined, as well as vibrant in her life and work. Her individual vision has expanded and progressed in an unwavering fashion through the years. Her continuing creations throughout the century mark the possibility for an artist, whether man or woman, with an ongoing courage of conviction, to remain true to his or her individual instincts through years of change. To enter the world of O'Keeffe's paintings and sculpture is to enter a world of everlasting spirit.

> When I think of death, I only regret that I will not be able to see this beautiful country anymore . . . unless the Indians are right and my spirit will walk here after I'm gone.[12]

Notes

[1] Neilson, *Seven Women: Great Painters,* p. 154.

[2] E. M. Benson, "John Marin and Pertaining Thereto," in *John Marin* (New York: Museum of Modern Art, 1936), p. 24.

[3] Sidney Janis, *Abstract and Surrealist Art in America* (New York: Reynal & Hitchcock, 1944), p. 53.

[4] Lee Nordness, *Art: U.S.A.: Now* (New York: Viking Press, 1963), pp. 12–14.

[5] Goosen, "O'Keeffe," p. 224.

[6] Taylor, "Miss O'Keeffe, Noted Artist is a Feminist," p. 29.

[7] Nell Blaine, quoted in Avis Berman, "A Decade of Progress, but Could a Female Chardin Make a Living?" *ARTnews,* October 1980, p. 73.

[8] Alexis Smith, quoted in Avis Berman, *Ibid.,* p. 79.

[9] Kuh, *The Artist's Voice,* p. 202.

[10] Tomkins, "Georgia O'Keeffe," p. 66.

[11] Kotz, "Georgia O'Keeffe at 90," p. 44.

[12] Georgia O'Keeffe, quoted in Henry Seldis, "Georgia O'Keeffe at 78: Tough Minded Romantic," *Los Angeles Times West Magazine,* January 22, 1967, p. 22.

Bibliography

Adato, Perry Miller. "On Georgia O'Keeffe." *The Kaleidoscope,* January 1978.

> Discussion of research on making of WNET film on O'Keeffe, as part of "The Originals: Women in Art" series.

"Age of Experiment." *Time,* February 13, 1956, pp. 66–67.

> Description of O'Keeffe's experiments in abstraction.

Agee, William C. *The 1930's Painting and Sculpture in America.* New York: Whitney Museum of American Art, 1968.

> Contains information concerned with the turbulent forces of the thirties in America and abroad and its direct and indirect effects upon the major artists and artistic movements of the time. O'Keeffe is among those considered.

The Alfred Stieglitz Collection. Washington, D.C.: National Gallery of Art, Department of Graphic Arts, 1949.

> Catalogue of 1,400 Stieglitz prints given to the museum by O'Keeffe following Stieglitz's death. Largest collection of his work.

"Alfred Stieglitz Made Georgia O'Keeffe Famous." *Look,* September 27, 1960.

> Photographic essay with short paragraph concerning Stieglitz's influence on O'Keeffe.

Allen, Frederick Lewis. *Only Yesterday.* New York: Harper & Row, 1931.

> Study of life in the twenties in the United States. Emphasis on social and cultural history.

Allen, Frederick Lewis. *Since Yesterday: The Nineteen Thirties in America.* New York: Harper and Brothers Publishers, 1940.

> An in-depth account of the important historical, political, and social events and changes that occurred during the thirties.

Alloway, Lawrence. "Notes on Georgia O'Keeffe's Imagery." *Womenart,* Spring–Summer 1977, pp. 18–19.

Discussion of O'Keeffe's flower paintings and the sexual interpretations of the images. Links images with literary themes of the period. "What O'Keeffe did was to bring a literary theme into painting with a single emphasis."

Alloway, Lawrence. *Topics in American Art Since 1945.* New York: W. W. Norton & Co., 1975.

Series of essays on major American artists and art movements since 1945.

"American Abstraction 1903–23 at Downtown Gallery." *ARTnews,* April 1962.

Short paragraph praising the works of Demuth and O'Keeffe.

Amram, P. W. "O'Keeffe Case: New Questions About Stolen Art." *Museum News,* January 1958, pp. 47–49.

Account of case involving Barry Snyder, who legally purchased paintings reported to have been stolen from O'Keeffe thirty years before.

Anderson, Don. "O'Keeffe's Paintings Look Inside Her Mind." *Chicago Today,* January 17, 1971, p. 23.

Description of sky and clouds that provide a sense of overwhelming height, distance, and serene limitless space.

Anderson Galleries. *Exhibition Catalogue,* March 3–16, 1924.

Statements by critics such as McBride of *The Herald* and Royal Cortissoz of *Sun Tribune,* concerning the work of Alfred Stieglitz, Georgia O'Keeffe, and other members of the Stieglitz circle.

Andreae, Christopher. "You Don't Paint What You See." *Christian Science Monitor,* August 15, 1973, p. 4.

Gives interpretation of drawings with a brief statement by O'Keeffe.

"Architectural Digest Visits: Georgia O'Keeffe." Photographs by Mary Nichols. *Architectural Digest,* July 1981, pp. 77–85.

Lovely color photographic essay of O'Keeffe in her New Mexican home.

Arkin, Diane Lynn. "Georgia O'Keeffe: Her Work 1915–30." M.A. thesis, University of Chicago, 1976.

Study of development of O'Keeffe's early work after rebelling against her academic training.

Arnason, H. H. *History of Modern Art.* Englewood Cliffs, N.J.: Prentice-Hall Inc., 1965.

Survey of twentieth-century American and European art. Contains short section on Early American moderns.

Arnold, Armin. *D. H. Lawrence and America.* London: Linden Press, 1958.

> Discussion of Lawrence's writings and their impact on America, as well as account of his years in the United States.

"The Art of Being O'Keeffe." *The New York Times Magazine,* November 13, 1977, pp. 44–45.

> Brief article celebrating O'Keeffe's life and work as she reaches ninety.

Asbury, Edith Evans. "Georgia O'Keeffe is Involved in 2 Suits Linked to Agent Fees on Her Paintings." *The New York Times,* November 20, 1978, p. B10.

> Description of controversy and law suits involving Juan Hamilton and Doris Bry, O'Keeffe's former agent.

Asbury, Edith Evans. "Silent Desert Still Charms Georgia Near 81." *The New York Times,* 1970, undated article in Whitney Museum files.

> Description of O'Keeffe's lifestyle in the New Mexican desert.

Ashton, Dore. *The New York School.* New York: Viking Press, 1973.

> Study of the abstract expressionists and New York School, and their contribution to American art.

Ashton, Dore. *A Reading of Modern Art.* New York: Harper & Row, Icon Editions, 1971.

> Series of essays dealing with various aspects of twentieth-century art (i.e., cubism, surrealism, etc.).

"Austere Stripper." *Time,* May 27, 1946, pp. 74–75.

> Article contains personal comment by O'Keeffe about music and her work. It also contains a review of the show at the Museum of Modern Art and comments about her work by James Johnson Sweeney.

Bachmann, Donna, and Piland, Sherry. *Women Artists: An Historical, Contemporary, and Feminist Bibliography.* Metuchen, N.J. and London: The Scarecrow Press, 1978.

> Short, individual bibliographies of women artists and short accompanying biographical sketches. Includes O'Keeffe.

Baigell, Matthew. *Dictionary of American Art.* New York: Harper & Row, 1979.

> Biographical sketches of major contemporary American artists. Includes O'Keeffe.

Baigell, Matthew. *A History of American Painting.* New York: Praeger Inc., 1971.

> Survey of American painting from the colonial period to 1970. Good section on Early American moderns.

Baker, Elizabeth. "Sexual Art Politics." *ARTnews,* January 1971, pp. 47–48, 60–62.

> Discussion about women artists' problem being recognized.

Ballatore, Sandy. "Sculpture by the Bay." *Images and Issues,* November–December 1982, pp. 40–42.

> Discussion of large-scale sculpture in 1982 sculpture show at the San Francisco Museum of Modern Art in which O'Keeffe's cast and painted aluminum *Abstraction* appeared. Photograph of O'Keeffe and piece.

Baudelaire, Charles. "Philosophic Art," in *The Painter of Modern Life,* translated and edited by Jonathan Mayne. London: Phaidon Press, 1964.

> Baudelaire's symbolist philosophy of art. Discusses the importance of an evocative magic being inherent in the work.

Baur, John. *Nature in Abstraction: The Relationship of Abstract Painting and Sculpture in Twentieth Century American Art.* New York: Whitney Museum of American Art, 1958.

> Study of how modern artists have used nature. O'Keeffe is among those considered. An in-depth look at abstract expressionism; includes short biographies by Roslind Irvine.

Baur, John, ed. *New Art in America.* New York: New York Graphic Society & Praeger, Inc., 1957.

> Art during the twenties, thirties and forties, with personal comments by O'Keeffe concerning her art and the part her environment has played in her work. Section on O'Keeffe is by James Thrall Soby.

Baur, John. *Revolution and Tradition in Modern Art.* Cambridge: Harvard University Press, 1951.

> Discussion of trends in realism and abstractionism in twentieth-century art.

Bement, Alon. *Figure Construction.* New York: Gregg Publishing Co., 1921.

> Text by Bement, O'Keeffe's teacher at the University of Virginia. A less rigid approach than traditional academic figure drawing.

Benchley, Peter. "Georgia O'Keeffe—At 82 Still a Master in the Art World." *The Reporter Dispatch,* October 15, 1970, p. 29.

> Discusses the influence of nature upon O'Keeffe's work and her approach to it as well as O'Keeffe as a woman and her association with Stieglitz.

Benson, E. M. "John Marin and Pertaining Thereto." in *John Marin.* New York: Museum of Modern Art, 1936.

Benson reveals Marin's personal beliefs and dogmas and his unwillingness to identify himself with any school or doctrine of painting, foreign or domestic.

Benton, Thomas Hart. *An Artist in America.* New York: Robert M. McBride and Co., 1937.

A regionalist's discussion of the role of the artist in American society. Emphasis on American scene painting.

Berman, Avis. "A Decade of Progress, But Could A Female Chardin Make a Living Today?" *ARTnews,* October 1980, pp. 73–79.

Survey of contemporary women artists discussing the position of women in the art world.

Berman, B. Vladimir. "She Painted the Lily and Got $25,000 and Fame for Doing It." *New York Evening Graphic Magazine Section,* May 12, 1928.

Account of Stieglitz asking an outrageously high price for six small calla lily paintings by O'Keeffe, and a French collector paying the $25,000.

Bergson, Henri. *Creative Evolution.* New York: Modern Library, 1944.

Bergson's philosophy. Emphasis on importance of intuition versus the intellectual.

Bluemner, Oscar. "A Painter's Comment." *Exhibition Catalogue.* New York: An American Place, January 27–March 11, 1935, pp. 2–3.

Focuses on O'Keeffe's ability to go beyond the human form as motif while being able to present the form in every flower, hill, etc. Discusses O'Keeffe's ability to hold her own in a time when "the feminine principle often retreated behind the scenes."

Boswell, Peyton. *Modern American Painting.* New York: Dodd, Mead and Co., 1940.

Description of American art up to the forties. Some discussion of O'Keeffe's early works. Emphasis on a "national" kind of art.

Braggiotti, Mary. "Her Worlds Are Many." *New York Post,* May 16, 1946.

An insightful biographical article containing information about O'Keeffe as an individual, her life-style, and the importance of her paintings as a vehicle for self-expression.

Brett, Dorothy. *Lawrence and Brett: A Friendship.* Philadelphia: J. B. Lippincott Co., 1933.

Account of Brett's friendship with D. H. Lawrence.

Broder, Patricia Janis. *Taos: A Painter's Dream*. Boston: Little, Brown & Co. and the New York Graphic Society, 1980.

Impact of Taos and its environment on various painters.

Brook, Alexander. "February Exhibitions: Georgia O'Keeffe." *The Arts,* February 1923.

Review of O'Keeffe's early work.

Brooks, Van Wyck. *American's Coming of Age*. New York: B. W. Huebsch Co., 1915.

Discussion of changes in American thought and society at the turn of the century.

Broude, Norma, and Garrard, Mary, ed. *Feminism and Art History*. New York: Harper & Row, 1982.

Reinterpretation of various movements in art history with emphasis on female contributions.

Brown, Milton. *American Painting from the Armory Show to the Depression*. Princeton, N.J.: Princeton University Press, 1955.

Study of changes in American painting that resulted from the Armory Show. Includes discussion of artists, critics and collectors. Covers both conservative and avant-garde viewpoints.

Brown, Milton. *The Story of the Armory Show*. New York: Joseph Hirschhorn Foundation, 1963.

Study of the impact of the Armory Show—its organizers, buyers and collectors at the show, as well as the significance of the show to the artists and the public at large.

Brown, Hunter, Jacobus, Rosenblum, and Sokol. *American Art*. Englewood Cliffs, N.J.: Prentice-Hall and New York: Harry N. Abrams, 1979.

Survey of American painting, sculpture, architecture, decorative arts, and photography from the colonial period to the seventies. O'Keeffe, Stieglitz, and the Stieglitz circle are included.

Bruno, Guido, "The Passing of 291." *Pearson's Magazine,* Vol. 38, No. 9, 1918.

Description of the closing of Stieglitz's gallery 291 and the impact it had on the advancement of modern art.

Bry, Doris. *Alfred Stieglitz: Photographer*. Boston: Museum of Fine Arts, 1965.

Illustrated catalogue of Stieglitz's photographs with essay by Bry. Includes chronology. Plates are the actual size of the original photographs. First publication of entire collection of Stieglitz owned by the Boston Fine Arts Museum.

Bry, Doris. "Georgia O'Keeffe." *Journal of American Association of University Women,* 34 (January 1952): 79–80.

Bry, as O'Keeffe's agent, then wrote a complimentary and insightful article. Emphasis on O'Keeffe's ability to say "more with less."

Buchan, Elinor. "Sunflower, New Mexico." *Book-of-the-Month-Club News,* Midsummer 1950.

Brief description of O'Keeffe's flower paintings. Reproduction of sunflower painting available to club members.

Budnik, Dan. "Georgia O'Keeffe at 88 Finds Contentment—and a New Art—in the New Mexican Desert." *People,* November 20, 1975, pp. 64–67.

Description of O'Keeffe's life on the desert and her newfound pottery skills learned from her new assistant, Juan Hamilton.

Bulliet, C. J. *Apples and Madonnas.* Chicago: Covici, Friede, Inc., 1930.

Study of "emotional expression in modern art." O'Keeffe is included—"Georgia O'Keeffe has done the best work, perhaps, of any American male or female, in the pure abstract."

Bunoust, Madeleine. *Quelques Femmes Peintres.* Paris, 1936.

Study of role of women artists in the nineteenth and early twentieth centuries.

Caffin, Charles. *The Story of American Painting.* New York: Frederick A. Stokes Co., 1907.

Survey of American painting, with early description of changes in the art world beginning at the turn of the century. Caffin voices concern about some changes: ". . . a great deal of American painting is characterized . . . by irreproachable table manners rather than salient self-expression."

Canaday, John. "Georgia O'Keeffe: The Patrician Stance as Esthetic Principle." *The New York Times,* October 11, 1970, p. 23.

Discusses nature's fertility as a point of reference for O'Keeffe as well as later artists whose styles are somewhat akin to O'Keeffe's.

Canaday, John. "O'Keeffe Exhibition: An Optical Treat." *The New York Times,* October 8, 1970, p. 60.

Review of O'Keeffe's retrospective at the Whitney in 1970. Show viewed as refreshing and original.

"Career Women Are to be Feted." *New York Sun,* March 20, 1935, p. 5.

> Women selected by New York League of Business and Professional Women for recognition. Contains quotes by many highly successful women including O'Keeffe. Sheds light upon the obstacles that women are confronted with in a primarily male-dominated society.

Carter, Frederick. *D. H. Lawrence and the Body Mystical.* London: Denis Archer, 1932.

> Discussion of Lawrence's writings dealing with women and mysticism.

Catalogue of the Alfred Stieglitz Collection for Fisk University. Nashville: Fisk University, 1949.

> Catalogue of works donated to Fisk University from Stieglitz's collection following his death.

Cheney, Sheldon. *The Story of Modern Art.* New York: Viking Press, 1950, p. 618–619.

> A general survey of twentieth-century art. Description of O'Keeffe's style from 1935–1940. Cheney tends to be conservative in his opinions.

Chicago, Judy. *The Dinner Party.* New York: Doubleday and Co., 1979.

> Account of process of putting together the large work, made up of ceramic place settings and needlework, that commemorated contributions of women throughout history. Georgia O'Keeffe is among those honored with a complete place setting.

Coates, Robert M. "Abstraction-flowers." *New Yorker,* July 6, 1926, p. 146–154.

> Gives background concerning O'Keeffe's family, her personality, and interest in flowers.

Coates, Robert M. "Art Galleries; New Paintings at Downtown Gallery." *New Yorker,* April 16, 1955.

> Review of O'Keeffe's work of the early fifties.

Coffelt, Beth. "A Visit with Georgia O'Keeffe." *San Francisco Examiner Chronicle,* April 11, 1971, pp. 18–23.

> Includes McBride's description of the beautiful New Mexican countryside that is O'Keeffe's home and why it is so important to O'Keeffe. Also includes some of critic Henry McBride's responses to O'Keeffe's work.

Coffey, Robert Dale. *The Skull Painting of Georgia O'Keeffe.* M.A. thesis, Arizona State University, 1974.

> Descriptive and critical study of skull paintings. Discussion of their relationship to surrealism.

Cohen, Susan F. "An Analysis of Selected Works by Georgia O'Keeffe and a Production of Drawings by the Researcher Relating to the Work of the Artist Studied." Ph.D. dissertation, New York University, 1974.

> Stylistic study of O'Keeffe's work. Emphasis on formal elements in O'Keeffe's work and how they evolved throughout her career. Cohen's line drawings are interesting complements to O'Keeffe's work.

Coke, Van Deren. "Taos and Sante Fe." *Art in America.* October 1963, pp. 44–47.

> Biographical and critical information concerning artists who have lived and worked in the Taos and Sante Fe areas.

Coke, Van Deren. "Why Artists Came to New Mexico: Nature Presents a New Face to Each Moment." *ARTnews,* January 1974, pp. 22–25.

> Discussion of how artists have come to New Mexico hoping the uncluttered, magnificent surroundings might inspire them and free-up their creative energies. For many artists, such as O'Keeffe, it did just that, but for others New Mexico did not possess the magic. Color photograph of O'Keeffe on cover of issue.

Columbia Teachers College, New York City, Art Department files on Georgia O'Keeffe.

> Contain letters and transcripts relating to O'Keeffe's years of study at Columbia Teachers College.

Cooke, Regina, ed. *Taos Arts,* March 11, 1965, p. 1.

> State honors presented to O'Keeffe in 1939–1940, 1945, and 1965 for her achievements as a painter. Brief biography included.

Corn, Wanda. "The New New York." *Art in America,* July–August 1973, pp. 59–65.

> Discussion of new iconography that inspired artists and writers in the increasing modernity of New York City after 1900.

Cortissoz, Royal. *American Artists.* New York: Charles Scribner's Sons, 1923.

> Description of American traditions in art. Modernism seen as an attack on traditional art and upon the order of the world in general.

Cortissoz, Royal. *Exhibition Catalogue.* New York: An American Place, February 5, 1935.

> Description of new pieces by O'Keeffe—emphasizing her use of line and tone, as well as statements by O'Keeffe.

Cortissoz, Royal. "Review of Georgia O'Keeffe Exhibition of an American Place." *Herald Tribune,* January 12, 1936.

Discussion of O'Keeffe as deviating into the "cul-de-sac of surrealism" in a work such as *Ram's Head—White Hollyhock Hills, New Mexico*. O'Keeffe seen as finding new motives in still life.

Cowley, Malcom, ed. *After the American Tradition: American Writers 1910–1930*. Carbondale: Southern Illinois University Press, 1964.

Gives an in-depth look at a period in time when great social changes were occurring, and tells of their effects on the writers and the work they produced.

Cowley, Malcolm. *Exile's Return*. New York: Viking Press, 1934.

View of American life in the twenties through the literature of the twenties.

Craven, Thomas. *Modern Art: The Men, The Movement, The Meaning*. New York: Simon & Schuster, 1935.

Author writes of his dislike for most Modern tendencies and for Stieglitz and his circle. But he does admit to O'Keeffe's genius in the way she approaches and executes her work.

Crimp, Douglas. "Georgia is a State of Mind." *ARTnews,* October 1970, pp. 48–51, 84–85.

Viewing O'Keeffe, Crimp discusses the artist as a prophet receiving new relevance.

Cross, Miriam Dugan. *Oakland Tribune,* March 14, 1971, pp. 26–27.

Critical description of O'Keeffe's flowers.

Crowinshield, Frank. "A Series of American Artists—in Color: No. 1 Georgia O'Keeffe." *Vanity Fair,* April 1982, pp. 40–41.

O'Keeffe's work chosen for its avant-garde qualities to be profiled in an essay with color illustration.

Cuadrado, John A. "Art: Exalting the Flower." *Architectural Digest,* May 1983, pp. 108–112.

Study of a variety of approaches to flower painting, including Emil Nolde, Andy Warhol, Lowell Nesbitt and Georgia O'Keeffe. O'Keeffe's flowers are termed "monumental images." Her *Black Iris* is pictured in color.

Cummings, Paul. *Dictionary of Contemporary Artists*. New York: St. Martin's Press, 1971.

Brief biographical sketch of O'Keeffe included in survey of contemporary artists.

"Dark Abstractions." *Arts,* November 1955.

> Description of O'Keeffe's painting *Dark Abstraction.*

Davis, Douglas. *Art and the Future.* New York: Praeger, Inc. 1973.

> Exploration of the role and impact of technology on the twentieth-century artist. Speculations on changes in art for the future.

Davis, Douglas. "O'Keeffe Country." *Newsweek,* November 22, 1976.

> Description of O'Keeffe's New Mexican world and its importance for her work as she enters her ninetieth year.

Davis, Douglas. "Return of the Native." *Newsweek,* October 12, 1970, pp. 105–106.

> Describes O'Keeffe's fluctuation between realism and abstraction. It also contains O'Keeffe's responses to critics.

Deegan, Dorothy Yost. *The Stereotype of the Single Woman in American Novels: A Social Study with Implication for the Education of Women.* New York: Kings Crown Press, 1951.

> Describes derogatory social attention toward women as expressed through stereotypes in fiction.

Degler, Carl. *Out of the Past—The Forces That Shaped Modern America.* New York: Harper Colophon Books, 1959.

> Cultural history of America from the arrival of Columbus to 1959. Interesting anecdotes and details to illustrate major events and trends.

Dell, Floyd. *Women as World Builders.* Chicago: Forbes and Co., 1913.

> Early work advocating women's liberation from the home.

Devree, Howard. *The New York Times,* November 4, 1937.

> Describes O'Keeffe as a unique American artist with the ability to produce clear, vibrant forms.

Dewey, John. *Art as Experience.* New York: G. P. Putnam's Sons, 1934; Capricorn Books, 1958.

> Dewey's philosophic explication of a heightened intense experience as equivalent to the process and product of art.

Dikstra, Bram. *The Hieroglyphics of a New Speech.* Princeton: Princeton University Press, 1961.

Examination of the relationship of William Carlos Williams' work to the visual artists of the Stieglitz circle and others.

Dikstra, Bram, ed. *A Recognizable Image: William Carlos Williams on Art and Artists.* New York: New Directions, 1978.

Williams' comments in essays, addresses, and lectures on American art and artists. Emphasis on first half of century. Insight into Williams' relationship with visual artists of his time.

Doty, R. "Articulation of American Abstraction." *Arts,* November 1973, pp. 47–49.

Discussion of twentieth-century painting trends in abstraction, including O'Keeffe.

Dow, Arthur Wesley. *Composition,* 20th ed. New York: Doubleday, Doran and Co., 1938.

One of Dow's textbooks, emphasizing Japanese principles of design that so influenced O'Keeffe. Concentration on structure rather than imitation.

Dow, Arthur Wesley. *Theory and Practice of Teaching Art,* 2nd ed. New York: Teachers College, Columbia University Press, 1912.

Text by teacher of O'Keeffe at Columbia Teachers College. Emphasizes Japanese principles of design.

Dunham, Judith. "Georgia O'Keeffe, Painter of Essences." *Artweek,* October 1, 1977.

Review of O'Keeffe's book. "The volume is one of the best books I have ever seen on a single artist's work. . . "

Eddy, Arthur Jerome. *Cubists and Post Impressionism.* Chicago: A. C. McClurg & Co., 1914.

Discussion of cubist and post-impressionist experiments. Included section on "Color Music," and also listed exhibits at 291. The book impressed O'Keeffe.

Edelheit, Martha. "Georgia O'Keeffe: A Reminiscence." *Women Artists Newsletter,* Vol. 3. No. 6, December 1977.

Description of visit with O'Keeffe and exploration of her landscape.

Eldredge, Charles. "The Arrival of European Modernism." *Art in America,* July–August 1973, pp. 34–41.

Discussion of impact of cubism, expressionism, Fauvism, etc. on American art and culture, particularly in the years following the Armory Show.

Eldredge, Charles Child. "Georgia O'Keeffe: The Development of an American Modern." Ph.D. dissertation, University of Minnesota, 1971.

>General study of O'Keeffe's life and work with some discussion of the critical mythology relating to her feminine imagery.

"Elected Member of the American Academy of Arts and Letters." *Arts,* January 1963.

>Press release describing O'Keeffe's being honored by election to the American Academy of Arts and Letters.

Ellmann, Richard, and Feidelson, Charles, ed. *The Modern Tradition.* New York: Oxford University Press, 1965.

>Study of impact of modernism in literature and the arts on society at large.

Emerson, Ralph Waldo. *Nature.* Boston: J. Munroe and Co., 1836.

>Emerson's statement of the principles of his New England transcendentalism. Provided philosophical basis for American romanticism and the nineteenth-century American landscape tradition. O'Keeffe has been viewed as carrying on some of the principles of transcendentalism.

"Exhibition at Downtown Gallery." *Arts,* May 1961.

>Positive review of some of O'Keeffe's work related to her air travel, i.e., the river paintings.

"Exhibition of New Paintings at Downtown Gallery." *Art Digest,* 29: 21, April 15, 1955.

>Favorable review of some of O'Keeffe's patio paintings.

"Eye of an Inventive Beholder." *New York Daily World,* June 13, 1966.

>Review of retrospective at Houston Museum. Show seen as "far more than a 'woman on paper.'" Work seen as "brave, bold, and boiled down to the essentials."

Feldman, Frances I. "American Painting During the Great Depression, 1929–39." Ph.D. dissertation, New York University, 1963.

>Study of American scene painting. Discussion of artists such as Grant Wood, Thomas Hart Benton, and John Steuart Curry.

Female Imagery?" *Ms. Magazine,* May 1975, pp. 63–65, 80–83.

>Documentation of discussion concerning the question, "Is women's art different than men's?" by Johnnie Johnson, printmaker; Celia Mariott, art historian; Joy Poe, painter and sculptor; and Royanne Rosenberg, filmmaker.

"Finally a Woman on Paper." *Longview Texas Journal,* June 12, 1966.

>   Review of retrospective exhibition at Houston Art Museum. Brief overview of career given.

Fine, Elsa. *Women and Art: A History of Women Painters and Sculptors from the Renaissance to the Twentieth Century.* Montclair, N.J.: Allanheld and Schram, 1978.

>   Survey of work of women artists, European and American.

"First Book Devoted to Art of Georgia O'Keeffe Published by Studio Books," *Publishers Weekly,* October 4, 1976, pp. 57–58.

>   Description of the process of putting together the Viking Studio book (on her work) by O'Keeffe.

Fisher, William Murrell. "The Georgia O'Keeffe Drawings and Paintings at 291." *Camera Work,* nos. 49–50, June 1917, p. 5.

>   Eloquent praise of O'Keeffe's work as approximating the language of music. Discussion of inner law of harmony in O'Keeffe's work.

"Fisk University Dedicates Alfred Stieglitz Collection." *The Crisis,* March 1950.

>   Description of dedication of Stieglitz collection given to Fisk after Stieglitz's death.

Flexner, Eleanor. *Century of Struggle.* Cambridge, Mass.: Belknap Press, 1966.

>   Study of the role and struggle of women and women artists in the twentieth century; rise of the women's rights movement.

Flint, Ralph. "Exhibitions in New York." *ARTnews,* January 24, 1931; January 2, 1932; January 14, 1933.

>   Reviews of O'Keeffe's yearly exhibitions in the early thirties.

Flint, Ralph. "Lily Lady Goes West." *Town and Country,* January 1943, pp. 34, 64–67.

>   Describes O'Keeffe's personality and work as being constant as well as her frank and simple approach to people and life that didn't seem to change. According to Flint she had a relentless devotion to the world of nature.

Flint, Ralph. "O'Keeffe Show a Revelation of Varied Flowers." *ARTnews,* January 14, 1933.

>   Praise of O'Keeffe's flower paintings using terms of growth and analysis—ripe, full, mature, etc. Work seen as visionary.

Forman, Nessa. "Georgia O'Keeffe and her Art: 'Paint What's in Your Head.'" *Philadelphia Museum Bulletin,* October 22, 1971.

Discusses O'Keeffe's ideals and personal response to her fame and her work.

"Forty-five Portraits show Noted New Yorkers." *New York Herald Tribune,* November 23, 1948.

Account of show of portraits at 460 Park Avenue. Photograph of O'Keeffe looking at a portrait of herself as a young girl by Eugene Speicher, while both were students at the Art Students League.

Fosca, Francois. "Femmes Peintres." *Formes and Couleurs 5,* Lausanne, 1943.

Describes various women painters from as far back in time as 100 B.C. up until the nineteenth century.

Foster, Joseph. *D. H. Lawrence in Taos.* Albuquerque: University of New Mexico Press, 1972.

Account of Lawrence's stay in Taos and the influence of the area on his work.

Frank, Waldo; Mumford, Lewis; Norman, Dorothy; Rosenfeld, Paul; and Rugg, Harold, ed. *America and Alfred Stieglitz: A Collective Portrait.* New York: Doubleday, Doran, and Co., 1934.

Contains essays by people such as W. C. Williams, Dorothy Brett, Sherwood Anderson, Paul Rosenfeld, etc. Put together as a commemorative volume for Stieglitz's birthday, dedicated to Stieglitz and the spirit of his galleries and photography.

Frank, Waldo. *Time Exposures.* New York: Boni & Liveright, 1926.

Essays by Frank, novelist, cultural critic, and friend of Stieglitz. Contains one section, entitled "Alfred Stieglitz the Prophet."

Frankenstein, Allen. "The Shapes of O'Keeffe's America." *This World,* April 17, 1966, pp. 23–24.

Discussion of the shapes O'Keeffe selects to represent America and the technique employed to interpret them.

Fraser, C. Gerald. "Georgia O'Keeffe Loses Stolen Paintings Lawsuit." *The New York Times,* July 16, 1978.

Report of O'Keeffe's losing case to regain possession of three small paintings legally purchased by Barry Snyder in 1976 which were stolen from her thirty years before.

Friedman, Martin. *The Precisionist View in American Art.* Minneapolis: Walker Art Center, 1960.

One of early definitive studies of the Precisionist movement in American art, including discussion of artists such as Sheeler, Demuth, and O'Keeffe.

Gabriel, Bertram. "New Mexico: The Mainstream and Local Currents," *ARTnews,* April 1982, pp. 120–125.

Description of current art scene in New Mexico and variety of approaches used by artists living there.

Gallup, Donald, ed. *The Flowers of Friendship.* New York: Alfred Knopf, 1953.

Collection of letters by artists and writers of the early twentieth century and commentary by Gallup. Includes figures such as Gertrude Stein, Alfred Stieglitz, Henry McBride, and Marsden Hartley.

Geldzahler, Henry. *American Painting in the Twentieth Century.* New York: Metropolitan Museum of Art, 1965.

Overview of changes in American painting in the twentieth century. Exploration of trends in abstraction. Good section on Early American moderns and O'Keeffe.

"Georgia O'Keeffe." *ARTnews,* March 1958, pp. 38, 57.

Brief description of O'Keeffe's watercolors shown at the Downtown Gallery.

"Georgia O'Keeffe." *Current Biography,* June 1941, pp. 62–63.

Brief biographical sketch and description of O'Keeffe's work until 1940.

"Georgia O'Keeffe." *Exhibition Catalogue.* Lincoln, Neb.: Nebraska Art Association, 1980.

Catalogue with color illustrations. Contains short essay by Jon Nelson with emphasis on critics' opinions and chronology.

"Georgia O'Keeffe: An American Original," Mary Lynn Kotz. Condensed from *ARTnews,* December 1977; *Readers Digest,* May 1979, pp. 169–175.

Overview of O'Keeffe's life and work with a number of color illustrations of her paintings.

"Georgia O'Keeffe—An American Place." *ARTnews,* January 2, 1932.

Review of O'Keeffe's show at An American Place, emphasizing the solemnity, starkness, and simplicity of the work.

Georgia O'Keeffe, A Portrait by Alfred Stieglitz. Introduction by O'Keeffe. New York: Viking Press, 1979.

Quality reproductions from the complex photographic portrait of O'Keeffe by Stieglitz over a period of thirty years. Done in conjunction with exhibit at the Metropolitan Museum of Art.

"Georgia O'Keeffe at the Whitney." *Arts Magazine,* November 1970.

O'Keeffe's work described as being tied up with the senses with a mystical and Oriental sensitivity.

"Georgia O'Keeffe Not Interested in Spelling Things Out." *Bloomington Courier and Tribune,* October 21, 1970.

Description of O'Keeffe and her work in conjunction with the opening of her 1970 retrospective. Comments on O'Keeffe's disinterest in extensive verbal interpretation of her work.

"Georgia O'Keeffe, Pintora de Huesos y Flores." *Atlántida,* July 1943, p. 42.

O'Keeffe is considered the most original American painter of the time.

"Georgia O'Keeffe Turns Dead Bones to Live Art." *Life,* February 14, 1938, p. 28.

Photographs and description of O'Keeffe's skull paintings.

"Georgia O'Keeffe Who 'Makes Death Beautiful.'" *Art Digest,* March 1, 1937, p. 13.

Response to O'Keeffe's skull paintings, interpreting them as symbols of death.

Gerdts, William. "Woman Artists of America 1707–1964." *Newark Museum Catalogue,* April 2–May 16, 1965.

Study of trends in American woman artists' work from 1707 to 1964. Discussion of miniature painting, still lifes, etc.

Getlein, Frank. "In Paint and Film They Saw a Precise Image of America." *Smithsonian,* Vol. 13, No. 8, November 1982, pp. 130–145.

Review of exhibit of precisionist painting and photography that appeared in San Francisco, St. Louis, Baltimore, Des Moines, and Cleveland. Includes discussion of O'Keeffe as a precisionist. Her *Shelton Hotel, No. 1,* 1926, pictured.

Getlein, Frank. "In the Light of Georgia O'Keeffe." *The New Republic,* November 7, 1960, pp. 27–28.

Discusses Georgia's treatment of two colors, her overall composition, and the relationship of the whole to objects from life. Emphasis on pelvis paintings.

Gibbs, Jo. "The Modern Honors First Woman—O'Keeffe." *Art Digest,* June 1, 1946.

> Account of O'Keeffe's retrospective at the Museum of Modern Art, New York.

Gilpin, Laura. "The Austerity of the Desert Pervades Her Home and Work." *House Beautiful,* April 1963.

> Photographic essay describing O'Keeffe's home and work.

Glueck, Grace. "It's Just What's in my Head." *The New York Times,* October 18, 1970.

> Review of retrospective. Contains comments by O'Keeffe on being successful in a man's world. "All the male artists I knew, of course, made it very plain that as a woman I couldn't hope to make it . . . I think it's pretty funny that women have always been treated like Negroes in this country and they don't know it . . ."

Glueck, Grace. Untitled. *The New York Times,* November 16, 1979, p. C18.

> Appeals Court in Trenton reversed ruling on Snyder case concerning works stolen from O'Keeffe. Snyder filed request for review of case by Supreme Court of New Jersey.

Glueck, Grace. "The Woman as Artist." *The New York Times Magazine,* September 25, 1977, pp. 48–68.

> Review of exhibition, "Women Artists: 1550–1950," seen as milestone on the long path to women's full liberation . . ." Discussion of various women artists and problems they have faced.

Goodrich, L. "Exhibition Preview: Retrospective for Georgia O'Keeffe." *Arts in America,* September 1970.

> Preview by Goodrich who curated this last major retrospective of O'Keeffe's work.

Goodrich, Lloyd. *Georgia O'Keeffe: Drawings.* New York: Atlantis Editions, 1968.

> Compilation and description of O'Keeffe's early drawings.

Goodrich, Lloyd. *Pioneers of Modern Art in America.* New York: Whitney Museum of American Art, 1946.

> Study of experiments in abstraction and European influences on American art in the first half of the twentieth century. Includes section on the Early American moderns.

Goodrich, Lloyd and Bry, Doris. *Georgia O'Keeffe.* New York: Whitney Museum of American Art, 1970.

A major catalogue written in conjunction with O'Keeffe's retrospective exhibition in 1970–71 at the Whitney, which traveled to San Francisco and Chicago. Volume contains brief biographical description of O'Keeffe's paintings as well as discussion of O'Keeffe's work and its relationship to nature. Well-illustrated with color and black-and-white illustrations.

Goosen, E. C. *The Art of the Real: U.S.A. 1948–1968*. New York: The Museum of Modern Art, 1968.

Discussion of O'Keeffe and her ability to depict commonly seen objects in a new and fascinating light that was important for twentieth-century changes in spatial and perceptual concerns.

Goosen, E. C. "O'Keeffe." *Vogue*, March 1, 1967, pp. 174–179, 221–224.

Contains pictures, comments about O'Keeffe as an existentialist and as a woman painter, and a discussion of O'Keeffe's influence on later artists.

Gottschalk, Louis. *Understanding History*. New York: Alfred Knopf, 1950.

Study of methods of studying history such as "critical–analytical," "substantive–historical," and "social–cultural."

Gray, Paul. "Teaching a Century to See." *Time*, February 28, 1983, pp. 68–70.

Review of two current books on Stieglitz, one by Sue Davidson Lowe and the other a collection of his writings and photographs by the National Gallery of Art. Gives some background on O'Keeffe and Stieglitz.

Green, Jonathan, ed. *Camera Work: A Critical Anthology*. New York: Alfred Knopf, 1950.

Description and samples of the periodical *Camera Work* and its impact on the growth of modern art and photography from 1903 to 1917.

Greenberg, Clement. "Art." *The Nation*, June 15, 1946.

Greenberg criticizes O'Keeffe's work as being of little value. He claims it was only her timing, being at the right place, and knowing the right people that made her successful.

Greenough, S. E. "From the American Earth: Alfred Stieglitz Photographs of Apples." *Arts*, Spring 1981.

Discussion of Stieglitz's use of elemental earth forms inherent in the apples, and how these photographs related to the rest of Stieglitz's work.

Greenough, Sarah, and Hamilton, Juan. *Alfred Stieglitz, Photographs and Writings*. Washington, D.C.: National Gallery of Art, Callaway Editions, 1983.

Quality reproductions of photographs from throughout Stieglitz's career and collection of his writings with essay and notes by Sarah Greenough. Done in conjunction with exhibit at National Gallery. Includes photographs of O'Keeffe. O'Keeffe also had input into the putting together of the book.

Gruen, John. "Georgia on Our Mind." *New York Magazine,* October 19, 1970.

According to Gruen, O'Keeffe's style and technique is like no other. She transforms her subject into pure abstract, dream-like dimensions.

Grundberg, Andy. "Stieglitz Felt the Pull of Two Cultures." *Sunday New York Times,* Arts and Leisure Section, February 13, 1983, pp. 35–36.

Review of exhibition of Stieglitz's photographs at the Washington National Gallery of Art. Show organized with cooperation of O'Keeffe. Discussion of European and American influences. O'Keeffe's portrait seen as "tour-de-force." Importance of Stieglitz's contribution to photography seen, as he "forged the union between the machine and the human spirit."

Guimond, James. *The Art of William Carlos Williams.* Chicago: University of Illinois Press, 1968.

Critical study of the life and work of the poet William Carlos Williams. Some discussion of his relationship to other artists of his time.

Gussow, Alan. *A Sense of Place: The Artist and The American Land.* New York: Friends of the Earth, 1971.

Discusses the strong connection between man and nature and the artist's need to create his own landscape. Contains color plates and biographies.

Haftmann, Werner. *Painting in the Twentieth Century.* American ed. New York: Praeger, Inc., 1965.

Survey of twentieth-century painting, both European and American, including interaction of European and American influences.

Hagen, Charles. "Stieglitz: A Memoir/Biography." *Artforum,* April 1983, pp. 73–74.

Review of book by Stieglitz's grandniece and discussion of exhibit of Stieglitz's photographs at the Washington National Gallery.

Halasz, Piri. "The Moody Work of a Lonely Painter is Now Reassessed." *Smithsonian,* March 1980, pp. 123–128.

Description of the Hartley exhibition at the Whitney Museum as well as of Hartley's life and his relationship to the Stieglitz circle.

Hapgood, Hutchins. *A Victorian in the Modern World.* New York: Harcourt, Brace and Co., 1939.

> Study of Stieglitz and his associates in the early part of the century.

"Happy Birthday, Georgia O'Keeffe." *Vogue,* 167, November 1977, p. 144.

> Short piece in celebration of O'Keeffe's ninetieth birthday.

Harris, Ann Sutherland and Nochlin, Linda. *Women Artists: 1550–1950.* Los Angeles County Museum of Art. New York: Alfred Knopf, 1977.

> Illustrated catalogue accompanying exhibition of women artists. Biographical sketches of women in show, including O'Keeffe.

Hartley, Marsden. "A Second Outline in Portraiture." *Exhibition Catalogue,* New York: An American Place, January 4–February 27, 1936, pp. 2–3.

> Hartley's discussion of O'Keeffe's personal history, as well as the elements of mysticism and infinity he saw throughout her work.

Hartley, Marsden. "Some Women Artists in Modern Painting." *Adventures in the Arts.* New York: Boni & Liveright, 1921.

> Discussion of O'Keeffe as a woman artist in a highly religious, fervent language that characterized Hartley's writing at this time.

Haskell, Barbara. *Arthur Dove.* San Francisco: San Francisco Museum of Art, 1974.

> Monograph on life and work of Dove, as well as his relationship to other members of the Stieglitz circle.

Hauser, Arnold. *The Social History of Art,* Vol. 4. New York: Vintage Books, 1969.

> Study of changes in twentieth-century art in the context of the larger culture, i.e., impact of "The Film Age."

Hedrick, Basil; Kelly, J. Charles; and Riley, Carroll, ed. *The Classic Southwest.* Carbondale: Southern Illinois University Press, 1973.

> Study of traditional images and artwork in the American southwest.

Heller, Nancy and William, Julia. "Georgia O'Keeffe: The American Southwest." *American Artist* 40, January 1976, pp. 76–81, 107.

> Description of O'Keeffe's life and work. Some quotations by O'Keeffe about her work.

Hess, Thomas B. "Inside Nature." *ARTnews,* February 1958.

> O'Keeffe seen as uncovering some of the secrets of nature.

Hess, Thomas and Baker, Elizabeth, ed. *Art and Sexual Politics*. New York: Newsweek, Inc., 1972.

> Essays involving exploration of women artists' struggle for recognition in relationship to "sexual politics." Contains Linda Nochlin's essay, "Why Have There Been No Great Woman Artists?"

Hess, Thomas and Nochlin, Linda, ed. *Women as Sex Object*. New York: Newsweek, Inc., 1972.

> Historical overview of portrayal of women in art history, i.e., as virgin, vampire, prostitute, nature goddess, etc.

Hinkle, Rita. "The Critics of Georgia O'Keeffe." M.A. thesis, Bowling Green State University, 1975.

> Discussion of critics' theories about O'Keeffe's work, including such critics as McBride and Goodrich. Author refutes some of critics' ideas and views O'Keeffe's work in light of theories of creativity advanced by Herbert Read and poet Lu Chi.

History of an American, Alfred Stieglitz: 291 and After. Introduction by Henry Clifford and Carl Zigrosser. Philadelphia: Philadelphia Museum of Art, 1944.

> Catalogue of show concerning Stieglitz's work. Includes work shown at 291.

Hoffman, Frederick. *The Twenties*, 5th ed. London: Collier-Macmillan Ltd., 1962; The Free Press, 1970.

> Emphasis is upon postwar cultural history and American writing during the twenties. Discussion of major thematic lines. Impact of magazines such as *Vanity Fair* on the arts is seen.

Hoffman, Katherine. "*The Collection of Alfred Stieglitz* by Weston Naef." *Art Journal,* Summer 1979, pp. 293–295.

> Book review of Naef's study of Stieglitz's collection.

Hoffman, Katherine. "Cross by the Sea: A Reconsideration." *Currier Gallery Quarterly,* Manchester, N.H.: Currier Gallery, Fall 1981, pp. 2–11.

> Study of O'Keeffe's *Cross by the Sea* and the cross iconography.

Hoffman, Katherine. *Georgia O'Keeffe*. Columbia, S.C.: University of South Carolina Press, 1980.

> Catalogue for exhibit of O'Keeffe and members of the Stieglitz circle.

Hoffman, Katherine. "Georgia O'Keeffe and the Feminine Experience." *Helicon Nine,* Spring 1982, pp. 6–15.

Study of critics' responses to a feminine imagery in O'Keeffe's work, particularly in relation to the flower paintings.

Hoffman, Katherine. *"Georgia O'Keeffe* by Georgia O'Keeffe." *Art Journal,* Spring 1977, pp. 264–266.

Review of O'Keeffe's book.

Hoffman, Katherine. "A Study of the Art of Georgia O'Keeffe from 1916–74." Ph.D. dissertation, New York University, 1976.

Study of the paintings of O'Keeffe, critics' responses, and the milieu in which she instinctively first started to work.

Hollis, Janette. "Two American Women in Art—O'Keeffe and Cassatt." *The Delphian Quarterly,* April 1945.

Comparison and description of the contributors of two leading American women artists, O'Keeffe and Cassatt.

Homer, William. *Alfred Stieglitz and the American Avant-Garde.* Boston: New York Graphic Society, 1977.

Good in-depth study of Stieglitz as photographer, and gallery owner, and his impact on American art and artists of his time.

Homer, William Innes, ed. *Avant-Garde Painting and Sculpture in America, 1910–1925.* Wilmington: Delaware Art Museum, 1975.

Exhibition catalogue. Includes texts by William I. Homer and others, biographies of artists and art personalities; references; general chronology; list of modern art exhibitions in New York, 1910–1925.

Howard, Leon. *Literature and the American Tradition.* New York: Doubleday and Co., 1960.

Survey of trends in American literature and the relationship to the other arts and society at large.

Hughes, Robert. "Loner in the Desert." *Time,* October 12, 1970, pp. 64–67.

Describes O'Keeffe's images, without depicting the nude, as being filled with complex statements about female sexuality.

Hunter, Sam. *Modern American Painting and Sculpture.* New York: Harry N. Abrams Inc., 1972.

Study of twentieth-century American painting and sculpture. Sees O'Keeffe's work as being part of a larger tradition of biomorphic abstraction.

Hunter, Vernon. "A Note on Georgia O'Keeffe." *Contemporary Arts of the South and Southwest*. November–December 1932.

Description of O'Keeffe's early work and years in the southwest.

Index of Twentieth Century Artists, 1933–1937. New York: Arno Press, 1970.

Lists artists alphabetically, providing both brief and detailed biographical information. Short biographical sketch of O'Keeffe included.

Janeway, Elizabeth. "Images of Women." *Arts in Society–Women and the Arts* 11, (Spring–Summer 1974): 9–18.

Views of women in the arts and literature and their struggle for recognition.

Janis, Sidney. *Abstract and Surrealist Art in America*. New York: Reynal & Hitchcock, 1944.

Includes discussion of O'Keeffe's creation of new realities which transcend everyday representation and of O'Keeffe's portraying the "secret life" of an object.

Janos, Leo. "Georgia O'Keeffe at Eighty-four." *Atlantic,* December 1971, pp. 114–117.

Interview with O'Keeffe. Overview of life and work.

Jessup, Josephine. *The Faith of our Feminists*. New York: Richard Smith Publishers, 1950.

Explains how feminism appears in modern fiction in the works of Edith Wharton, Ellen Glasgow, and Willa Cather. Feminism is discussed as an expression of woman's desire to be herself.

Jewell, Edward Alden. *Americans*. New York: Alfred Knopf, 1930.

Anecdotal account of the American scene in art as distinct from European art. O'Keeffe and several artists of the Stieglitz circle are among those included.

Jewell, Edward Alden. "Georgia O'Keeffe Exhibits Her Art." *The New York Times,* December 28, 1937.

For Jewell, some of the best work of O'Keeffe's career is to be found in this 1937 exhibit of New Mexican landscapes.

Jewell, Edward Alden. "Georgia O'Keeffe Gives an Art Show." *The New York Times,* January 7, 1936.

Review of O'Keeffe's most recent New Mexican paintings. A variety of interpretations are given from a "mystic apotheosis of transfiguration" to "a bundle of perverse incongruities."

Jewell, Edward Alden. "Georgia O'Keeffe in an Art Review." *The New York Times,* February 2, 1934.

> Discussion of motif of *Two Blue Lines* carried out in later work. Emphasis on such works as *Jack-in-the-Pulpit No. 7,* in terms of design and musical rhythm.

Jewell, Edward Alden. "O'Keeffe: Thirty Years." *The New York Times,* May 11, 1946, p. 6x.

> Favorable review of O'Keeffe's 1946 retrospective exhibition.

Johnson, Alexandra. "An Influence on Oneself." *Christian Science Monitor,* November 15, 1977, p. 24.

> Written shortly after O'Keeffe turned ninety. Brief overview of O'Keeffe's development and influences on her work.

Jones, Howard Mumford, and Ludwig, Richard M. *Guide to American Literature and its Background Since 1890.* Cambridge, Mass.: Harvard University Press, 1972.

> An in-depth look at the changes in American literature from 1890 to 1972. Discussion of topics such as the genteel tradition, literature of childhood, literature of entertainment, forces of realism and naturalism, and novels of political and social reform.

Kalonyme, Louis. "The Arts in New York." *Arts and Decoration,* 24 (April 1926): 46–47.

> Includes mention of impact of O'Keeffe's flower paintings.

Kalonyme, Louis. "Georgia O'Keeffe: A Woman in Painting." *Creative Art,* January 1928, pp. 35–40.

> Discusses Georgia O'Keeffe as a successful female painter in a traditionally male-dominated field. Gives lavish praise of O'Keeffe's expression of a feminine imagery, i.e., "the rhapsodic literature born of Georgia O'Keeffe's paintings of flowers and fruits, of hills and trees and skyscrapers, pivots inevitably upon the fact that she is a woman . . . "

Kalonyme, Louis. "Sealing the Peak of the Art Season." *Arts and Decoration,* 26 (March 1927): 57.

> O'Keeffe's work seen as a peak in the New York art scene.

Kandinsky, Wassily. *Concerning the Spiritual in Art,* 1912. Documents in Art series. New York: George Wittenborn, 1947.

> Kandinsky's expressionist philosophy of art. Discussions of inner necessity and correspondences of visual arts and music. This book influenced both O'Keeffe and Stieglitz.

Katz, Leo and Lane, James. *Georgia O'Keeffe: A Portfolio of Twelve Paintings*. New York: Knight Publishing, Inc., 1972.

> Description of twelve O'Keeffe paintings that Lane and Katz particularly admired. Emphasis on flower paintings.

Kay, Jane Holtz. "Georgia O'Keeffe's City Vision." *The Christian Science Monitor,* January 26, 1977, p. 24.

> Discussion of O'Keeffe's images of the city as compared to her flower paintings and other painters of urbanism and industrialism.

Kermode, Frank. *Continuities*. New York: Random House, 1968.

> Collection of literary reviews and criticism from 1962 to 1967, as well as a discussion about various aspects of modernism.

Kirkland, Winifred and Frances. *Girls Who Became Artists*. Freeport, N.Y.: Books for Libraries Press, Inc., 1934.

> A sugar-coated, fairytale-like group of essays about women artists. Brief biographical material most substantive aspect of essays.

Klein, Jerome. *New York Post,* February 20, 1937.

> Discussion of "psychological attitudes" of life-death polarities in juxtaposition of flowers and bones in recent paintings.

Klein, Jerome. "O'Keeffe Works Highly Spirited." *New York Post,* January 11, 1936.

> Review of show at An American Place. Discusses the combination of intense femininity and independent spirit present in O'Keeffe's work, as well as the polarity of life and death seen in her paintings. Work seen as "forceful reminders that women are no longer to be kept in the background in the field of artistic creation."

Kootz, Samuel Mervin. *Modern American Painters*. Norwood, Mass.: Brewer & Warren, Inc., 1930.

> Conservative response to experiments in modernism. Saw O'Keeffe's flowers as "an uneasy selection of phallic symbols" where O'Keeffe "was being a woman and only secondarily an artist." In general Kootz viewed intellectual experience as more important than intuitive experience.

Kootz, Samuel Mervin. *New Frontiers in American Painting*. New York: Hastings House, Publishers, 1943.

> Discusses naturalism, realism, romanticism, abstract and non-objective painting, and expressionism that were present in American art. Does not mention O'Keeffe or Stieglitz but briefly discusses Hartley and Marin.

Kotz, Mary Lynn. "A Day with Georgia O'Keeffe." *ARTnews,* December 1977, pp. 36–45.

> Interview with O'Keeffe shortly after she turned ninety. Overview of life and work, as well as description of most recent work. Excellent color photographs.

Kramer, Hilton. "The American Precisionists." *Arts,* March 1961.

> Discussion of precisionist style and O'Keeffe's relationship to the precisionists.

Kramer, Hilton. "Georgia O'Keeffe." *New York Times Book Review,* December 12, 1976.

> Review of O'Keeffe's book published by Viking Press.

Kramer, Hilton. "Photography as High Art." *New York Times Book Review,* December 19, 1982, pp. 1, 25.

> Review of *Alfred Stieglitz: Photographs and Writings* by Sarah Greenough and Juan Hamilton. Kramer also comments on impact of Stieglitz on the twentieth-century art world.

Kramer, Hilton. "A Poet's Taste in Painting." *The New York Times,* December 24, 1978, p. 23.

> Review of exhibition, "William Carlos Williams and the American Scene, 1920–1940," at the Whitney Museum. Discussion of Williams' relationship to visual artists of the time. Importance of broader cultural scene stressed. "Our painters, sculptors and photographers did not function in a cultural void."

Kuh, Katherine. *The Artists Voice.* New York: Rinehart and Co., 1962.

> Seventeen artists comment about their own art during interviews with the author. O'Keeffe is among those included.

Kuh, Katherine. *"Georgia O'Keeffe* by Georgia O'Keeffe." *Saturday Review,* January 22, 1977.

> Review of O'Keeffe's book, which is seen as a "new kind of autobiography in which personal confessions, famous names and psychological investigations are strictly taboo; all that counts are irresistable stimuli."

LaFollete, Suzanne. *Art in America.* New York: W. W. Norton Co., 1929.

> Survey of American art until 1929. Feels O'Keeffe's buildings are stronger than flower paintings. Discusses O'Keeffe's refinement and control of her medium; a control that is a rarity among American artists.

"Lake George Window." *Arts,* October 1955.

> Description of O'Keeffe's painting *Lake George Window.*

Lane, James W. *The Work of Georgia O'Keeffe: A Portfolio of Twelve Paintings.* New York: Knight Publishers, 1937.

> Portfolio of O'Keeffe's paintings in the twenties and thirties with introductory essay.

Larkin, Oliver. *Art and Life in America.* New York: W. W. Norton Co., 1949.

> Early survey of American art and its relationship to society at large. Interesting section on the twenties.

Lask, Thomas. "Publishing O'Keeffe." *The New York Times,* June 25, 1976.

> Favorable review of O'Keeffe's book and description of process of putting it together.

Laurie, J. R. "Georgia O'Keeffe: Visionary in God's Wilderness." *Christianity Today,* 20 (January 16, 1976): 18–19.

> Discussion of mystical and visionary qualities in O'Keeffe's work.

Lawrence, D. H. *Mornings in Mexico.* Introduction by Ross Parmenter. Layton, Ut.: Peregrine Smith Books, 1983.

> Eight essays written while Lawrence was in Mexico and the Southwest in the mid-twenties.

Lawrence, D. H. *The Portable D. H. Lawrence.* New York: Viking Press, 1947.

> Collection of Lawrence's work, primarily his short stories.

Lawrence, D. H. "Taos." *The Dial,* March 1923, pp. 251–254.

> Lawrence's description of his visit to New Mexico and the impact the area had on him.

Lawrence, Ruth. *Five Painters.* Minneapolis: University Gallery, Minnesota University, 1937.

> Description of O'Keeffe included. Her work seen as symbolic of new inner truths. Seen as creating a new color, white, in her white flowers, which "gives us that miracle, the fresh, fragrant innocent melody which is youth. . . "

Levy, Mark. "Twenty American Artists—Sculpture at the San Francisco Museum of Modern Art." *Images and Issues,* November–December 1982, p. 48.

> Review of sculpture show in which O'Keeffe's large-scale sculpture, *Abstraction* came as a complete surprise.

Lewis, R. W. B. *The Poetry of Hart Crane*. Princeton: Princeton University Press, 1967.

Critical study of Hart Crane's poetry, including *The Bridge*.

Lieberman, William. *Art of the Twenties*. New York: Museum of Modern Art, 1979.

Illustrated catalogue of European and American art of the twenties. O'Keeffe is included.

Lifson, Ben. "O'Keeffe's Stieglitz, Stieglitz's O'Keeffe." *Village Voice,* December 11, 1978.

Discussion of reciprocal influences of Stieglitz and O'Keeffe on each other.

Lipman, Matthew. *What Happens in Art*. New York: Appleton-Century-Crofts. 1967.

Discusses the function of critics, and ways of looking at works of art.

Lippard, Lucy. *From the Center: Feminist Essays on Women's Art*. New York: E. P. Dutton, 1976.

Series of essays dealing with feminist issues and "female iconography."

Lisle, Laurie. *Portrait of an Artist: A Biography of Georgia O'Keeffe*. New York: Seaview Books, 1980.

The only major biography written about O'Keeffe. Contains dense details. Does not, however, discuss much of the artwork.

Looney, Ralph. "Georgia O'Keeffe." *The Atlantic,* April 1965, pp. 106–110.

Overview of O'Keeffe's life and work.

Lowe, Sue Davidson. *Stieglitz: A Memoir/Biography*. New York: Farrar, Straus & Giroux, 1982.

Detailed memoir of Stieglitz, his life, his work, and those close to him by Stieglitz's grandniece. Contains many touching personal details, including impressions of O'Keeffe.

Lubasch, Arnold. "Federal Agents, Hunt for Suspect in Georgia O'Keeffe Fraud Case." *The New York Times,* April 29, 1981, p. 4.

Description of search for James Stieglitz, grandnephew of O'Keeffe, and grandson of a brother of Alfred Stieglitz, who was reported to have illegally arranged for the sale of lithographs from O'Keeffe's paintings.

Luhan, Mabel Dodge. "Georgia O'Keeffe in Taos." *Creative Art,* Volume VII, no. 6. June 1931, pp. 407–410.

Account of O'Keeffe's first years in the Taos area by her friend Mabel Dodge Luhan, who first invited her to the Taos area.

Luhan, Mabel Dodge. *Intimate Memories. Vol. III: Movers and Shakers.* New York: Harcourt Brace and Co., 1936.

> Volume III of Luhan's rambling memories, concentrating on her years in New York and those who came to her salons.

Lyonel Feininger-Marsden Hartley. New York: Museum of Modern Art, 1966.

> Catalogue with descriptive essays. Section on Hartley has some reference to other members of the Stieglitz circle.

M. Carey Awards to Hannah Arendt and Georgia O'Keeffe. Exhibition Catalogue. Bryn Mawr, Penn.: Bryn Mawr College, October 1971.

> Honorary award presented to O'Keeffe and Arendt. Documentation of citation. Illustrations of O'Keeffe's work in exhibition at that time.

McBride, Henry. "Curious Responses to Work of Miss O'Keeffe on Others." *New York Herald,* February 4, 1923.

> Review of O'Keeffe's early work.

McBride, Henry. "Georgia O'Keeffe's Exhibition." *New York Sun,* January 14, 1933.

> Review of some of O'Keeffe's skull paintings.

McBride, Henry. "O'Keeffe at the Museum." *New York Sun,* May 18, 1946.

> Review of O'Keeffe's retrospective at the Museum of Modern Art.

McBride, Henry. "Paintings by Georgia O'Keeffe." *New York Sun,* January 11, 1936.

> Exploration of O'Keeffe's "symbols" of the southwest, which for McBride offered a mysterious beauty related to death.

McCausland, Elizabeth. "Georgia O'Keeffe in a Retrospective Exhibition." *Springfield Republic,* May 26, 1946, p. 6c.

> Review of O'Keeffe retrospective show held at the Museum of Modern Art. Discussion of feminine viewpoint as applied to O'Keeffe as "maybe irrelevant."

McCoubrey, John. *The American Tradition in Painting.* New York: George Braziller, 1963.

> Survey of American painting and its American qualities.

McCracken, Harold. *Portrait of the Old West.* New York: McGraw–Hill Book Co., 1952.

> Survey of painters portraying the American Old West.

McCullough, David. "The Great Bridge and the American Imagination." *The New York Times Magazine,* pp. 28–40.

> Article concerning the building of the Brooklyn Bridge and its subsequent inspiration for artists and writers. Includes painting by O'Keeffe.

MacDowell Colony Newsletter, Vol. 2, No. 2, Fall 1972.

> Description of ceremony awarding O'Keeffe a medal at the MacDowell Colony, in absentia. Introductory remarks by Lloyd Goodrich.

McGee, Barbara. "Documenting Georgia O'Keeffe." *Women Artists Newsletter,* December 1977.

> Discusses film on O'Keeffe by Perry Miller Adato—"an inspiring and beautiful film."

McMurran, Kristin. "A $13 Million Lawsuit Over Georgia O'Keeffe Highlights a Portrait of the Artist's Young Man." New York: Artist's file, Whitney Museum of American Art, pp. 18–21.

> Description of O'Keeffe's and Hamilton's life in New Mexico and of Doris Bry's $13 million suit against Hamilton.

McShine, Kynaston, ed. *The Natural Paradise, Painting in America 1800–1950.* New York: Museum of Modern Art.

> Catalogue of exhibition tracing the evolution of landscape painting in America from 1800 to 1950.

Malcolm, Janet. "Photographs, Artists and Lovers." *New Yorker,* March 12, 1979.

> Article concerning Stieglitz's photographs of O'Keeffe and the relationship of O'Keeffe and Stieglitz.

Maritain, Jacques. *Creative Intuition in Art on Poetry.* New York: Pantheon Books, 1953.

> Explores the relationship of art to poetry and the importance of "poetic intuition" for both.

Marling, William. *William Carlos Williams and the Painters, 1909–1923.* Ohio: University of Ohio Press, 1982.

> Focuses on Williams' alliances with various painters and movements from 1909 to 1923.

Marsden Hartley. Exhibition Catalogue. Austin, Tex.: University Galleries of the University of Southern California and the Museum of the University of Texas.

> Catalogue of Hartley exhibition. Includes critical and biographical material on Hartley.

Martin, Bob. "Exhibit Brings New Look." *Tampa Times,* November 19, 1970, p. 14.

> Describes O'Keeffe as portraying nature in a very personal and piercing manner; dealing with nature in such a pure way as to produce a universal meaning.

Mathey, Francois. *Six Femmes Peintres: Berthe Marisot, Eva Gonzales, Serphine Louis, Suzanne Valadon, Maria Blanchard, Marie Laurencin.* Paris: Éditions du chêne, 1951.

> Describes traditional roles of women and gives short biographies about each woman.

Matthias, Blanche. "Stieglitz Showing Seven Americans." *Chicago Evening Post, Magazine of the Art World,* March 2, 1926.

> Friend of O'Keeffe writes about O'Keeffe's early work shown by Stieglitz.

May, Henry F. *The End of American Innocence.* New York: Alfred Knopf, 1959.

> Study of the "innocent rebellion" in the early twentieth century in American intellectual and social life as reaction to traditional mores and values of the nineteenth century.

Mellquist, Jerome. *The Emergence of an American Art.* Port Washington, N.Y.: Kennikat Press, 1969.

> Study of trends in American art that are distinct from European art. Emphasis on twentieth-century art.

Michener, Charles. "The Year's Books," *The New Republic,* December 16, 1978, pp. 21–24.

> Discussion of the year's books on photography. Includes review of *Georgia O'Keeffe, a Portrait by Alfred Stieglitz.* Book is seen as "a breathtaking visual document of one of the most extraordinary love affairs in modern art."

Milliken, William. "White Flower by Georgia O'Keeffe." *Museum Bulletin.* Cleveland: Cleveland Museum of Art. April 1937, pp. 51–53.

> Discussion of *White Flower* painting, purchased by Cleveland Museum in 1930. Reference to mystical qualities in work. Contains quotations by O'Keeffe about painting.

Moffatt, Frederick. *Arthur Wesley Dow.* Washington, D.C.: Smithsonian Institution Press, 1977.

> Monograph on the life and work of Dow, O'Keeffe's teacher at Columbia Teachers College.

Momaday, N. Scott. "Forms of the Earth at Abiquiu." *Albuquerque Journal,* November 13, 1977, Section C. p. 1.

Poem dedicated to O'Keeffe. Feature also contains photographs of O'Keeffe.

"Money is not Enough." *The New York Times,* February 5, 1945, p. 86.

Discusses the requirements for purchasing an O'Keeffe painting from Stieglitz. Not only did one need money but also intellectual qualifications as well.

Moore, Ethel, ed. Letters from thirty-one artists to the Albright-Knox Art Gallery. *Albright-Knox Gallery Notes* 31–32, no. 2:28. Buffalo: Buffalo Fine Arts Academy, Spring 1970.

O'Keeffe is included among the artists' writing.

Moss, Irene. "Georgia O'Keeffe and 'These people.'" *Feminist Art Journal* 11, No. 2:14, Spring 1973.

Discussion of impact of O'Keeffe as a woman artist.

Mumford, Lewis. "Autobiographies in Paint." *New Yorker,* January 18, 1936, pp. 29–30.

Discussion of O'Keeffe's skull paintings and relationship to surrealists. Comments on "consummate craftsmanship" and "mysterious force" of work.

Mumford, Lewis. *The Brown Decades.* New York: Macmillan Co., 1931.

Study of arts in America with emphasis on years 1865–1895. Includes discussion of O'Keeffe's new "symbolic language" that "conveys directly and chastely in paint, experiences for which language conveys only obscenities."

Mumford, Lewis. *Exhibition Catalogue.* New York: Intimate Gallery. January–February 1928, p. 3.

Review of O'Keeffe's new paintings at Stieglitz's gallery that year.

Mumford, Lewis. *New Yorker,* February 10, 1934.

Discusses the symbols and beautiful language present in O'Keeffe's work. Emphasis on recent flower paintings.

Mumford, Lewis. "O'Keeffe and Matisse." *The New Republic,* March 2, 1927.

Discussion of O'Keeffe and Matisse and of O'Keeffe's discovery of a new language of melodies and rhythms.

Mumford, Lewis. "Reflections—Prologue to our Time." *New Yorker,* March 10, 1975, pp. 42–63.

Response to rise of influence of machines and technology, as leading to dehumanization in American culture.

Munro, Eleanor. *Originals: American Women Artists*. New York: Simon & Schuster, 1979.

Traces historical origins of women artists' work. Interviewed some forty major American women artists. Major chapter on O'Keeffe, who is seen as a successful matriarch for women artists.

Munsterberg, Hugo. *A History of Women Artists*. New York: Clarkson N. Potter, 1975.

Broad survey of women artists dealing with a variety of art forms—crafts, graphics, painting, sculpture, photography—from prehistoric times to the present.

The Museum (Winter–Spring 1961): 25.

Describes how O'Keeffe enlarges and abstracts her forms into beautiful vibrant images. Views flower paintings as new approaches to still-life painting.

"Museum Acquires Georgia O'Keeffe Painting." *Boston Museum of Fine Arts Preview*, December 1980, Acquisitions section.

Description of acquisition of O'Keeffe's *White Rose and Larkspur #2*, 1927 by the Boston Museum of Fine Arts.

"My World is Different." *Newsweek*, October 10, 1960.

Discussion of O'Keeffe's works as reflective of her inner feelings, and as a personal response to her beloved New Mexican environment.

Naef, Weston. *The Collection of Alfred Stieglitz*. New York: Metropolitan Museum of Art and Viking Press, 1978.

Study of the photographs Stieglitz collected and his relationship with the photographers.

Neilson, Frances and Winthrop. *Seven Women: Great Painters*. Radnor, PA.: Chilton Book Co., 1969.

In-depth description of seven women artists including Berthe Morisot, Mary Cassatt, Marie Laurencin, Georgia O'Keeffe, Elisabeth Vigée-Lebrun, Angelica Kaufmann, and Cecilia Beaux.

"New Landscapes of the Southwest at Downtown Gallery." *ARTnews*, May 1955, p. 46.

Review of O'Keeffe's recent paintings of the Southwest.

"New York: Night." *Art in America*. (col.) 45: (cover) Summer 1957.

O'Keeffe's work appeared on cover of issue devoted to New York and its impact on artists.

Nochlin, Linda. "Some Women Realists: Part I." *Arts Magazine,* Vol. 48, February 1974, pp. 45–49.

O'Keeffe's work described under category of evocative realism. "It was of course, a woman artist, Georgia O'Keeffe, who first severed the minutely depicted object—shell, flower, skull, pelvis—from its moorings in a justifying space or setting, and freed it to exist, vast, magnified as a surface manifestation of something other (and somehow deeper, both literally and figuratively) than its physical reality on the canvas."

Nordness, Lee, ed. *Art: U.S.A.: Now.* New York: Viking Press, 1963.

Discussion of the contemporary art world, of a new aesthetic involving "new conceptions of space, light, movement and infinity."

Norman, Dorothy. *Alfred Stieglitz: An American Seer.* New York: Random House, 1973.

Study of Stieglitz as photographer, gallery owner, supporter of modern art, and close friend by Norman, who helped run Stieglitz's later galleries and whom Stieglitz photographed. Contains quotations from conversations with Stieglitz from 1927 to 1946. Contains numerous photographic illustrations by Stieglitz, Norman, and other Stieglitz contemporaries.

Norman, Dorothy. *Selected Writings of John Marin.* New York: Pellegrini & Cudahy, 1949.

Collection of Marin's writings and commentary by a close associate of Stieglitz and his circle.

"The Object as Subject." *Exhibition Catalogue.* New York: Wildenstein Gallery, April 4–May 3, 1975.

Essay and illustrated catalogue of changes in approaches to still life painting throughout art history. O'Keeffe's rock paintings are cited.

O'Brien, Frances. "Americans We Like: Georgia O'Keeffe." *The Nation,* October 12, 1927.

Account of impact of early work of O'Keeffe.

O'Keeffe's Art." *New York Sun,* April 1, 1937.

Critical review of an exhibition of O'Keeffe's flowers and landscapes at the Gallery of the American Women's Association, 355 West 57th Street.

O'Keeffe, Georgia. "About Myself." *Exhibition Catalogue.* An American Place, January 22–March 17, 1939, pp. 2–3.

Comments on pelvis and skull paintings.

O'Keeffe, Georgia. "About Painting Bones." *Georgia O'Keeffe: Painting–1943*. New York: An American Place, 1944.

> Catalogue and statement about O'Keeffe's bone paintings.

O'Keeffe, Georgia. *Alfred Stieglitz Presents Fifty-one Recent Pictures, Oils, Watercolors, Pastels, Drawings by Georgia O'Keeffe American*. New York: The Anderson Galleries, 1924.

> Catalogue of yearly O'Keeffe exhibit at Stieglitz's Anderson Gallery. Contains statement by O'Keeffe.

O'Keeffe, Georgia. *Alfred Stieglitz Presents One Hundred Pictures, Oils, Watercolors, Pastels, Drawings by Georgia O'Keeffe American*. New York: The Anderson Galleries, 1923.

> Catalogue of O'Keeffe's work and statement by O'Keeffe.

O'Keeffe, Georgia. "Can a Photograph Have the Significance of Art: Statement." *Manuscripts*, December 1922, p. 21.

> Comment on the importance and impact of photography as an artform.

O'Keeffe, Georgia. In *Exhibition Catalogue*, Anderson Galleries, January–February 1923, p. 1.

> Comments on schooling in academic tradition and decision to rebel against such. "School and things that painters have taught me even keep me from painting as I want to."

O'Keeffe, Georgia. In *Exhibition Catalogue*. An American Place, February 3–March 17, 1940.

> Having spent some months in Hawaii. She gives her reaction to a new place and explains how one cannot help but take along part of one's own world.

O'Keeffe, Georgia. *Equal Rights,* June 1942, p. 41.

> Statement on equal rights, stating the importance of women being recognized as equal in labor practices.

O'Keeffe, Georgia. *Georgia O'Keeffe*. New York: Viking Press, 1976.

> Large, beautifully illustrated book with accompanying text by O'Keeffe. Some works never before seen. The only major book published by O'Keeffe about her life and work.

O'Keeffe, Georgia. *Georgia O'Keeffe: Catalogue of the Fourteenth Annual Exhibition of Paintings with Some Recent O'Keeffe Letters*. New York: An American Place, 1938.

> Catalogue of O'Keeffe's work with quotations from her letters.

O'Keeffe, Georgia. *Some Memories of Drawings.* New York: Atlantis Editions, 1974.

> O'Keeffe recalls and describes her early drawings.

O'Keeffe, Georgia. "Stieglitz: His Pictures Collected Him." *New York Times Magazine,* December 11, 1949, p. 14.

> O'Keeffe's commentary concerning Stieglitz's photographs and how they were reflections of his very essence.

"O'Keeffe Glass Design Shown in Paris Display." *Sante Fe New Mexican,* July 22, 1951.

> Description of O'Keeffe's flower design in Steuben glass shown with twenty-six other contemporary artists' designs.

"O'Keeffe in Review." *The Art Digest,* February 15, 1943, p. 14.

> Review of O'Keeffe's skull and early pelvis paintings.

"O'Keeffe is Stirring." *New York World Telegram,* February 3, 1934.

> Discussion of "soaring feeling" in relation to O'Keeffe's work, and "exquisite" craftsmanship.

"O'Keeffe's Pineapple." *The Art Digest,* February 15, 1940, p. 23.

> Description of O'Keeffe's trip to Hawaii to do her first painting for a commercial firm—Dole.

"O'Keeffe's Woman Feeling." *Newsweek,* May 27, 1946, pp. 92, 94.

> Review in conjunction with retrospective exhibition in Chicago. Some discussion of feminine imagery in work.

Olson, Roberta. "*Georgia O'Keeffe* by Georgia O'Keeffe." *Soho Weekly,* December 16, 1976.

> Positive review of O'Keeffe's book.

"One White Flower." *Artist, Jr.,* Vol. 5, No. 6, April 1964.

> In a magazine for children, O'Keeffe's ability to eliminate details, "to find a new way to see," is described in connection to a flower painting.

Paige, D. D. *The Letters of Ezra Pound.* New York: Harcourt Brace and Co., 1950.

> Collection of, and commentary about Pound's work and philosophy.

"A Painting by Georgia O'Keeffe—Cross by the Sea." *Currier Gallery of Art Bulletin.* Manchester, N.H.: Currier Gallery, January 1960.

> Discussion of the painting *Cross by the Sea,* acquired by the Currier in 1960.

Paintings by Nineteen Living Americans. New York: Museum of Modern Art, 1929.

> Catalogue of exhibit of nineteen artists, living at the time, including O'Keeffe.

"The Paintings of Georgia O'Keeffe in Taos." *Atelier,* June 1931.

> Description of O'Keeffe's early New Mexico paintings.

Parker, Rozsika and Pollock, Griselda. *Old Mistresses: Women, Art and Ideology.* New York: Pantheon Books, 1982.

> Study of major women artists, "old mistresses" instead of "old masters," and their impact throughout art history.

Pemberton, Murdock. "The Art Galleries." *New Yorker,* February 20, 1926.

> Review of O'Keeffe's flower paintings on exhibit.

"People." *Time Magazine,* August 30, 1982, p. 42.

> In People section, a photograph and brief description of O'Keeffe's large-scale sculpture, completed at ninety-four and shown at the San Francisco Museum of Modern Art in the summer of 1982.

Pepper, Stephen. *The Basis of Criticism in the Arts.* Cambridge, Mass.: Harvard University Press, 1949.

> Discussion of types of criticism—mechanistic, contextualistic, organistic and formal—and their application to looking at a work of art.

Peterson, Karen and Wilson, J. J. *Women Artists: Recognition and Reappraisal.* New York: Colophon Books, 1976.

> Study of contributions of women artists from the early Middle Ages to the twentieth century. Contains section on O'Keeffe.

Phelps, Timothy. "Georgia O'Keeffe's Relative Accused of Fraud Involving Her Paintings." *The New York Times,* April 28, 1981.

> Report of O'Keeffe paintings illegally copied and printed as lithographs by a relative of Alfred Stieglitz, James Stieglitz.

Phillips, Duncan. *A Collection in the Making.* Cambridge, Mass.: Riverside Press, 1926.

> Phillips' feelings about the general public's lack of knowledge of art as well as the rationale and process of putting together his collection. His collection now includes several O'Keeffe's and works by other members of the Stieglitz circle.

"Pineapple for Papaya." *Time,* February 12, 1940.

> Account of O'Keeffe's trip to Hawaii and doing work for the Dole Pineapple company.

"Pioneers of American Abstraction: Andrew Crispo Gallery: Exhibit." *Artform,* January 1974.

> Review of exhibit of early twentieth-century abstractionists, including O'Keeffe.

Pisano, Ronald G. *The Students of William Merritt Chase.* Huntington, N.Y.: Heckscher Museum, 1973.

> Catalogue for exhibit of works of Chase's students. O'Keeffe studied with Chase at the Art Students League.

Plagens, Peter. "The Critics: Hartmann, Huneker, De Casseres." *Art in America,* July–August 1973, pp. 66–71.

> Role of critics in relation to rise of the Early American moderns.

Plagens, Peter. "A Georgia O'Keeffe Retrospective in Texas." *Artforum,* May 1966, pp. 27–31.

> Discussion of O'Keeffe's spaces, how they are pierced by cars, etc. Raises questions of O'Keeffe's relationship to a technological age. Good color reproductions.

Pollitzer, Anita. "That's Georgia." *The Saturday Review of Literature,* November 4, 1950, pp. 41–43.

> Friends of O'Keeffe talk about O'Keeffe's deep love and devotion to painting.

Pollock, Duncan. "Artists of Taos and Sante Fe: From Zane Grey to the Tide of Modernism." *ARTnews,* January 1974, pp. 13–21.

> Description of O'Keeffe's ability to capture the universal qualities of the nature of the New Mexican countryside. Article in conjunction with exhibit at Denver Art Museum of artists who painted southwest. Color photograph of O'Keeffe on cover of issue.

Pollock, Duncan. "New Mexico: An Earthbound Iconography." *Art in America,* July–August 1973, pp. 98–101.

> Description of works of contemporary artists who have been attracted to the New Mexican terrain.

Pound, Ezra. *Selected Poems of Ezra Pound.* New York: New Directions, 1957.

> Anthology of Pound's work.

Radcliffe News, Summer 1973.

> Description and photographs of O'Keeffe being awarded honorary degree.

Radycki, J. Diane. "The Life of Lady Art Students; Changing Art Education at the Turn of the Century." *Art Journal,* Spring 1982, pp. 9–13.

> Study of educational situations for women artists at the turn of the century. Emphasis on Paula Becker and Käthe Kollwitz.

Raynor, V. "Figure at Downtown Gallery." *Arts,* September 1962.

> Review of O'Keeffe show.

Read, Helen Appleton. "The Feminine Viewpoint in Contemporary Art." *Vogue,* June 15, 1928.

> Discussion of a feminine imagery in O'Keeffe's work.

Read, Helen Appleton. "Georgia O'Keeffe—Woman Artist Whose Art is Sincerely Feminine." *Brooklyn Eagle,* 1924, p. 4.

> Discusses the feminine qualities present in O'Keeffe's work, in a more objective manner than some of the critics associated with the Stieglitz circle.

Read, Herbert. *The Philosophy of Modern Art.* Cleveland: World Publishing Co., 1952.

> Discussion of the rise of modern art. Importance of experience and intuition in relationship to the artwork.

Reich, Sheldon. "John Marin and the Piercing Light of Taos." *ARTnews,* January 1974, pp. 16–17.

> Influence of the land and light on the work of Marin.

Rich, Daniel Catton, ed. *The Flow of Art: Essays and Criticisms of Henry McBride.* New York: Atheneum, 1975.

> Anthology of, and commentary about the writings of critic McBride.

Rich, Daniel Catton. *Georgia O'Keeffe.* Worcester, Mass.: Worcester Museum of Art, 1960.

> An in-depth look at O'Keeffe's work, discussing her approach as being close to Chinese and Japanese tradition, rather than European. Also, discussion of her rejection of critics' comments on the influence of photog-

raphy and surrealism. Catalogue done in conjunction with major exhibition of O'Keeffe's work at the Worcester Art Museum, organized by Rich.

Rich, Daniel Catton. *Georgia O'Keeffe*. Chicago: Art Institute of Chicago, 1943.

Catalogue done in conjunction with retrospective organized by Rich at the Art Institute. Comments on O'Keeffe's lyrical abstraction and her ability to condense and eliminate. In-depth discussion of some of the works, including *Cross by the Sea, Black Cross, New Mexico,* and *Summer Days.*

Rich, Daniel Catton. "The New O'Keeffes." *Magazine of Art,* March 1944, pp. 110–111.

Discusses O'Keeffe's love of nature as seen through her work. Also refers to her reduction of her subject to the essentials and her love for hard materials such as stones, shells, and bones.

Richardson, Herbert. *"Nun, Witch, Playmate—the Americanization of Sex."* New York: Harper & Row, 1971.

Exploration of various roles women have played or been in American culture—nun, witch, playmate, etc.

Risatti, Howard. "Music and the Development of Abstraction in America: The Decade Surrounding the Armory Show." *The Art Journal,* Fall 1979, pp. 8–13.

Discussion of the influence of artists abroad, such as Whistler and Kandinsky, on American artists of the early part of the twentieth century, and the relationship between music and visual abstraction.

Ritchie, Andrew Carnoff. *Charles Demuth*. New York: Museum of Modern Art, 1950.

In-depth account of Charles Demuth's life and art and his relationship with other artists of his time.

Robinson, Vivian. "Artist's Journey to the Top Began at West Texas." *Amarillo Globe Times,* August 17, 1965.

Account of O'Keeffe's days as head of the art department at West Texas State Normal School, Canyon, Texas, where she taught for almost two years.

Robinson, Vivian. "Famed Artist Remembers Amarillo as Brown Town." *Amarillo Globe Times,* August 26, 1965.

O'Keeffe's recollections of days spent in Amarillo as supervisor of art in the public schools, and its effect on her work.

Rose, Barbara. *American Art Since 1900: A Critical History*. New York: Praeger, Inc., 1967.

Study of trends in American art since 1900. Discussion of Early American moderns included.

Rose, Barbara. *American Painting: The 20th Century*. New York: Rizzoli, 1980.

Survey of twentieth-century American painting. Good section on O'Keeffe and Early American moderns. O'Keeffe seen as being "constantly in touch with life's deepest secrets."

Rose, Barbara. "Georgia O'Keeffe: The Paintings of the Sixties." *Artforum,* November 1970, pp. 42–46.

Discussion of mystical and minimal qualities of the sixties paintings. Emphasis on "patio" paintings and "cloud" series.

Rose, Barbara. "O'Keeffe's Trail." *New York Review of Books,* March 31, 1977, pp. 29–33.

Review of O'Keeffe's 1976 book. Also discussion of influence of Dow, and O'Keeffe's relationship to an American transcendental tradition.

Rose, Barbara. *Readings in American Art Since 1900: A Documentary Survey*. New York: Praeger, Inc., 1968.

Excerpts from various artists and critics' writings since 1900 (i.e., Craven, Hopper, Burchfield, Johns, etc.).

Rose, Barbara. "Visiting Georgia O'Keeffe." *New York Magazine,* November 9, 1970, pp. 60–61.

Interview with O'Keeffe. Discussion of influence of environment on O'Keeffe.

Rosenfeld, Paul. "After the O'Keeffe Show." *The Nation,* April 8, 1931, pp. 388–389.

Impact of O'Keeffe's paintings of the late twenties and early thirties.

Rosenfeld, Paul. "American Painting." *The Dial,* December 1921, pp. 649–670.

Discussion of trends in American painting. Praise of O'Keeffe and Stieglitz circle. Evidence of Stieglitz's influence.

Rosenfeld, Paul. *By Way of Art*. New York: Coward-McCann, Inc. 1928.

Romantic and humanist view of art. Stresses the importance of the primacy of the heart versus the intellect.

Rosenfeld, Paul. "The Paintings of Georgia O'Keeffe." *Vanity Fair,* October 1922, pp. 56, 112, 114.

O'Keeffe's work seen as bringing together the cycles of birth, death, etc. in a life lived passionately.

Rosenfeld, Paul. *Port of New York*. New York: Harcourt Brace and Co., 1924; University of Illinois Press, 1961.

> Anthology of essays relating to the arts in the early twentieth century. Includes one on O'Keeffe. ". . . the paintings of Georgia O'Keeffe are made out of the pangs and glories of earth lived largely."

Rubenstein, Charlotte Streifer. *American Women Artists*. New York: Avon Books, 1982.

> Survey of contributions of American women artists from Early Indian times to 1982. Substantial section on O'Keeffe's life and work.

Rubinstein, Meridel. "The Circles and the Symmetry: The Reciprocal Influence of Georgia O'Keeffe and Alfred Stieglitz." M.A. thesis, University of New Mexico, 1977.

> Study of the reciprocal influences of O'Keeffe's and Stieglitz's lives and work.

Rugg, Harold. *Culture and Education in America*. New York: Harcourt, Brace & Co., 1931.

> Rugg, a civil engineer and professor of education at Columbia Teachers College, comments on the state of culture and education in America. Importance of Stieglitz as artist and teacher is noted.

Russell, John. "The Natural Image," *The New York Times,* November 19, 1982.

> Brief review of exhibition at the York Gallery showing approaches to plant forms by painters and photographers in the Early American modern period.

Sabine, Lillian. "Record Price for a Living Artist." *Sunday Eagle Magazine* (Brooklyn, New York), May 27, 1928.

> Account of French collector paying $25,000 for O'Keeffe calla lily paintings.

Sagar, Keith, ed. *D. H. Lawrence and New Mexico*. Layton, Ut.: Peregrine Smith Books, 1983.

> Lawrence's major writings in the American Southwest. "I think New Mexico . . . was the greatest experience I ever had."

Saint-Gaudens, Homer. *The American Artist and His Times*. New York: Dodd, Mead and Co., 1941.

> A brief overview of the American artist near the turn of the century. Impact of Armory Show. Saint-Gaudens had met Stieglitz but not O'Keeffe. A comment about Stieglitz, "He stands guard over his wife . . . I have never known whether it was fostered by love, general irascibility or a yearning for publicity. I think it is the latter."

Sante Fe New Mexico Sun, July 22, 1951, p. 1.

> Discusses the symbolism in Georgia O'Keeffe's work and her relationship to other midwestern artists such as Benton, Curry, and Wood.

Schwartz, Constance. *Nevelson and O'Keeffe: Independents of the Twentieth Century.* New York: Nassau County Museum of Fine Art, 1983.

> Illustrated catalogue accompanying exhibition. Essay contains biographical and critical material.

Schwartz, Sanford. *The Art Presence.* New York: Horizon Press, 1983.

> Collection of essays by art critic Schwartz. Includes chapter on O'Keeffe in which he reviews her book.

Schwartz, Sanford. "O'Keeffe Writes a Book." *New Yorker,* August 28, 1978.

> Discusses O'Keeffe's book, her position in the art world, and her relationship to Stieglitz.

Schwartz, Sanford. "When New York Went to New Mexico." *Art in America,* July–August 1976.

> Description of impact of New Mexican environment on O'Keeffe's work.

Seiberling, Dorothy. "Horizons of a Pioneer." *Life,* March 1, 1968, pp. 40–53.

> A pictorial essay. Excellent photographs of O'Keeffe in her New Mexican home.

Seldis, Henry. "Georgia O'Keeffe at 78: Tough Minded Romantic." *Los Angeles Times West Magazine,* January 22, 1967.

> Nature seen as O'Keeffe's "unfailing companion." Importance of New Mexican terrain for O'Keeffe. Color photographs included with article.

Seligmann, Herbert. *Alfred Stieglitz Talking.* New Haven: Yale University Library, 1966.

> Record of Seligmann's years in Stieglitz's galleries as audience, friend, and unpaid secretary. Lively, anecdotal accounts of conversations and events in the galleries.

Seligmann, Herbert. *D. H. Lawrence, An American Interpretation.* New York: T. Seltzer, 1930.

> Praise and critical review of Lawrence's work. Lawrence's emphasis on a liberation of the instinctual life seen as particularly important.

Seligmann, Herbert. "Georgia O'Keeffe, American." *Manuscript,* no. 5, March 1923, p. 10.

> O'Keeffe seen as a "musician of color" where sound and vision are united. Her intensity is viewed as most certainly that of a woman.

Seligmann, Herbert. "A Woman in Flower." *Exhibition Catalogue,* New York: An American Place, January 1, 1933, p. 1.

> Discussion of passion and intensity of O'Keeffe's flower paintings.

Shapiro, Meyer. "Rebellion in Art." In Aaron, Daniel, ed. *America in Crisis.* Hamden, Conn.: Archon Books, 1971.

> Discussion of the Armory Show as a point of acceleration for American art and the changes that resulted from the show.

"Skeletons in the Plain." *The Sun,* January 2, 1932.

> Discusses O'Keeffe's female following and the way women more often than men, picked up on the sexual overtones in O'Keeffe's work.

Smith, Miles. "Modern Painter Analyzed." *Fayetteville Observer,* October 29, 1970, p. 106.

> Discusses O'Keeffe as an early modernist and as one who anticipated some of the "black paintings" of later abstractionists.

Smith, R. "Georgia O'Keeffe." *Art in America,* March 1977, pp. 53–55.

> Book review of O'Keeffe's book.

Soby, James Thrall. "Alfred Stieglitz." *Saturday Review of Literature,* September 28, 1946, pp. 22–23.

> Commemoration of life and work of Stieglitz following his death.

Soby, James Thrall. "To The Ladies." *Saturday Review of Literature,* July 6, 1946, pp. 14–15.

> Statement about O'Keeffe and her relationship to nature, as well as the majestic intensity of her work.

Sochen, June. *The New Women, Feminism in Greenwich Village, 1910–1920.* New York: Quadrangle Books, 1972.

> Study of contribution of early Village feminists such as Crystal Eastman, Henrietta Rodman, Ida Rauh, Neith Boyce, and Susan Glaspell.

Spender, Stephen, ed. *D. H. Lawrence—Novelist, Poet, Prophet.* New York: Harper & Row, 1973.

> Anthology of critical essays concerning Lawrence and his work.

Spirit of an American Place. Philadelphia: Philadelphia Museum of Art, 1980.

> Illustrated catalogue of photographs by Stieglitz in conjunction with exhibit at museum. Brief essay by Martha Chahroudi and citations from Dorothy Norman, Lewis Mumford and other critics.

Stebbins, Theodore E., and Troyen, Carol. *The Lane Collection: Twentieth Century Paintings in the American Tradition.* Boston: Museum of Fine Arts, 1983.

> Fully illustrated catalogue with approximately 120 color illustrations of Lane collection which includes good representative paintings by O'Keeffe and other members of the Stieglitz circle. Particularly large number of Dove paintings. Accompanying essay discusses the collection and trends in American twentieth-century art.

Stevens, Wallace. *The Palm at the End of the Mind.* New York: Vintage Books, 1972.

> Anthology of Stevens' poems.

The Stieglitz Circle: Demuth, Dove, Hartley, Marin, O'Keeffe, Weber. Foreward by Peter Selz. Claremont, Calif., Pomona College. 1958.

> Exhibition catalogue includes statements by artists.

Strand, Paul. "Georgia O'Keeffe." *Playboy,* July 1924.

> Profile of O'Keeffe written by photographer and friend of O'Keeffe and Stieglitz.

Tashjian, Dickran. *William Carlos Williams and the American Scene, 1920–1940.* New York: Whitney Museum of American Art in association with the University of California Press, 1978.

> Illustrated catalogue in conjunction with exhibit at Whitney Museum. Covers interrelationship of Williams and visual artists from 1920 to 1940.

Taylor, Carol. "Miss O'Keeffe, Noted Artist is a Feminist." *New York World Telegram,* March 31, 1945, p. 29.

> Interview with O'Keeffe. "She revealed herself as something of a feminist, but of the kind that discusses the subject over tea cups, not from a soap box."

Taylor, Joshua. *America as Art.* National Collection of Fine Arts, Smithsonian Institution. Washington, D.C.: Smithsonian Institution Press.

> Concentration on work and aspects of art less well known in America. Analytical look at eight moments in which art and the identity of America were alike. Chapters include; "America as Symbol," "The American Cousin," "Virtue of American Nature," "The Frontier and the Native

American." Each section develops chronologically from the eighteenth century to the twentieth century. Many artists and many media are covered. Paintings by O'Keeffe listed and discussed.

Taylor, Robert. "Georgia O'Keeffe: Her Art and Her Lifestyle," *Boston Globe,* December 13, 1977, pp. E17, E24.

Description of PBS documentary on O'Keeffe, on occasion of her ninetieth birthday, and overview of her life.

Taylor, Robert. "Shedding New Light on American Originals." *Boston Globe,* April 17, 1983, pp. A4–5.

Review of exhibit of Lane collection at the Boston Fine Arts Museum which included several O'Keeffes. "The Lane Collection . . . challenged accepted opinion about a generation of American painters too seldom recognized for its high accomplishments."

Taylor, William. *Cavalier and Yankee.* New York: George Braziller, 1961.

Discussion of literature and myth as a reflection and explanation of the intellectual and social climate of a particular time.

"Thefts, Wills and Moral Rights." *ARTnews,* Summer 1978, pp. 40–41.

Discussion of various court cases in the arts including O'Keeffe's suit against Barry Snyder, who owned three works stolen from O'Keeffe thirty years prior to suit.

"Three Paintings in Search of an Owner." *ARTnews,* October 1980, pp. 13–14.

Suit against Barry Snyder by O'Keeffe, for receiving stolen paintings.

Tomkins, Calvin. "Georgia O'Keeffe—The Rose in the Eye Looked Pretty Fine." *New Yorker,* March 4, 1974, pp. 40–67.

In-depth profile of O'Keeffe giving biographical and critical details about her life and work.

Tomkins, Calvin. "Paul Strand." *New Yorker,* September 16, 1974, pp. 44–94.

In-depth profile of the photographer Paul Strand, whom both O'Keeffe and Stieglitz were friends with.

Trenton, Patricia. "Picturesque Images of Taos and Sante Fe." *American Art Review,* March–April 1974, pp. 96–111.

Contains information concerning the Taos art scene and quotes by O'Keeffe about her New Mexican surroundings.

Tryk, Sheila. "O'Keeffe." *New Mexico,* January–February 1973.

>   Discussion of O'Keeffe's work in relation to the New Mexican environment.

Tsujimoto, Karen. *Images of America: Precisionist Painting and Modern Photography.* Seattle: University of Washington Press, 1982.

>   Done in conjunction with exhibit at San Francisco Museum of Modern Art. Explores relationships between painters and photographers of this period.

Tyrell, Henry. "Esoteric Art at 291." *The Christian Science Monitor,* May 4, 1917.

>   Review of O'Keeffe's early work, emphasizing a female message. O'Keeffe seen to have "found expression in delicately veiled symbolism for 'what every woman knows . . .' Now perhaps for the first time, the style is the woman."

Vanity Fair. "Series of American Artists in Color." No. 1. C1920.

>   Discusses O'Keeffe's extraordinary gift for design and color that allowed her to be chosen as the only woman artist to be represented in this series.

Wallach, Amei. "Georgia O'Keeffe." *Newsday,* Sunday, October 30, 1977.

>   Interview with O'Keeffe in her home. Discusses life and work, and "wonderful emptiness" of the desert.

Wallach, Amei. "Under a Western Sky." *Horizon,* December 1977.

>   Discusses O'Keeffe's work in New Mexico shortly after she turned ninety.

Warner, Langdon. *The Enduring Art of Japan.* New York: Grove Press, Inc., 1958.

>   Historical survey of developments in Japanese art.

Watson, Ernest W. "Georgia O'Keeffe." *American Artist,* June 1943, pp. 7–11.

>   Interview with O'Keeffe. Description of skull and flower paintings and responses of critics, such as Mumford and McBride, to these paintings. Her career seen as "based on early renunciation of the canons of traditional European painting and her conversion to the flat compositional mode of Oriental painting . . ."

Wein, Roberta. "Women's Colleges and Domesticity, 1875–1918." *History of Education Quarterly* XIV (Spring 1974): 28–40.

>   Study of roles of women in the home and outside the home as a result of educational opportunities.

Wheeler, Monroe, ed. *Painters and Sculptors of Modern America.* New York: Thomas Y. Crowell Co., 1942.

> Collection of articles that originally appeared in the *Magazine of Art* from 1934 to 1942. Introduction by Wheeler.

Wight, Frederick. *Arthur Dove.* Berkley: University of California Press, 1958.

> Monograph on the life and work of Dove and his relationship to other members of the Stieglitz circle.

Wilder, Mitchell, ed. *Georgia O'Keeffe, an Exhibition of the Artist from 1915–1966.* Fort Worth, Tex.: Amon Carter Museum of Western Art, 1966.

> Illustrated catalogue accompanying 1966 exhibition. Includes excerpts from various critics' writings from 1915 to 1966.

Willard, Charlotte. "Georgia O'Keeffe." *Art in America,* October 1963, pp. 92–96.

> Interview with O'Keeffe. Biographical and critical details. Good photographs of O'Keeffe included in piece.

Willard, Charlotte. "Woman of American Art." *Look,* September 27, 1960, pp. 70–75.

> Photographic essay of major women artists in 1960, whose work "may yet equal the best of America's male artists." Includes O'Keeffe, Grace Hartigan, Louis Nevelson, Helen Frankenthaler, Claire Falkenstein, Joan Brown, and Lee Bontecou.

Williams, J. "Georgia O'Keeffe: the American Southwest." *American Artist,* 40 (January 1976) pp. 76–81.

> Description of the impact of the Southwest environment on O'Keeffe's work.

Williams, Oscar and Honig, Edwin. *The Mentor Book of Major American Poets.* New York: The New American Library, Inc., 1962.

> Anthology of American poetry.

Williams, William Carlos. *In the American Grain.* New York: Random House, 1925.

> Williams' view of history emphasizing a search for the new. His heroes included Columbus, Boone, Burr, Whitman, and Poe. Although somewhat poorly written as a scholarly study, it was praised by figures such as D. H. Lawrence, Hart Crane, Charles Sheeler, Alfred Stieglitz, and Martha Graham.

Williams, William Carlos. *Paterson.* New York: New Directions, 1948.

> Williams' long poem concerning life in Paterson, New Jersey.

Williams, William Carlos. *A Recognizable Image: William Carlos Williams on Art and Artists.* Bram Dijkstra, ed. New York: New Directions, 1978.

Essays, lectures and addresses by Williams on art and artists from about 1915 through the fifties. Includes section on Stieglitz.

Williams, William Carlos. *Selected Essays.* New York: Random House, 1954.

Essays concerning Williams' views of history, art, and poetry.

Williams, William Carlos. *Selected Poems of William Carlos Williams.* New York: New Directions, 1963.

Anthology of Williams' poetry throughout his career.

Wilson, Edmund. *The American Earthquake. A Documentary of the Twenties and Thirties.* Garden City, N.Y.: Doubleday/Anchor Books, 1958.

Addresses, essays, and lectures concerning American cultural life in the twenties and thirties.

Wilson, Edmund. *Axel's Castle.* New York: Charles Scribner's Sons, 1931.

Study of the imaginative literature of 1870–1930. Includes chapters on symbolism, T. S. Eliot, Gertrude Stein, and Paul Valéry.

Wilson, Edmund. *The Shores of Light.* New York: Farrar, Straus, and Young, Inc., 1952.

A literary chronicle of the twenties and thirties.

Wilson, Edmund. "Stieglitz Exhibition at the Anderson Galleries." *New Republic,* March 18, 1925.

Critic Wilson's review of latest work of Stieglitz's Anderson Gallery.

Winn, Marcia. "Georgia O'Keeffe, Outstanding Artist." *Chicago Sunday Tribune,* February 28, 1943.

O'Keeffe's ideas about what her works represent and what psychoanalysts believe.

Wolfe, Tom. "The Painted Word." *Harper's,* April 1975, pp. 57–82.

Traces the development of modern art theory and the role critics have had in "making the artist." Emphasis on abstract expressionism, pop, and minimal art.

"Woman From Sun Prairie." *Time,* February 8, 1943.

Discussion of O'Keeffe's work as symbols of the unconscious. Comparison of work with Emily Dickinson's poetry in its economy, purity, and lyric quality.

"Women Artists of America." *Illustrated Weekly of India,* August 4, 1963.

> O'Keeffe seen as a pioneer is a traditionally male dominated world, and as a founder of contemporary American art.

"Wonderful Emptiness." *Time,* October 24, 1960, pp. 74, 75, 77.

> Description of O'Keeffe's feelings about New Mexico and the influence of Arthur Dow.

York, Richard. *The Natural Image—Plant Forms in American Modernism.* New York: Richard York Gallery, 1982.

> Short, illustrated catalogue with essay comparing painters and photographers of the early modern era and their approaches to plant forms. Catalogue accompanied exhibition. Seven O'Keeffe works included.

Young, J. W. *Catalogue of Selected Paintings by Southern Californian Artists,* c1940.

> Contains painting by O'Keeffe's sister, Ida, *Black Lily of the Nile,* and brief description of Ida and the other O'Keeffes.

Young, Mahoriri Sharp. *Early American Moderns.* New York: Watson-Guptil Publications, 1974.

> Stieglitz's influence on the Early American moderns as well as discussions about the symbolism in O'Keeffe's work.

Zigrosser, Carl. "An American Collection." *The Philadelphia Museum Bulletin,* Philadelphia: The Philadelphia Museum of Art, May 1945.

> Description of the Stieglitz collection at the Philadelphia Museum.

Zito, Tom. "Georgia O'Keeffe." *Washington Post,* November 9, 1977, p. C3.

> Written on occasion of O'Keeffe's ninetieth birthday, where she "preferred to be at home alone rather than at a Washington Party." Contains comments from O'Keeffe such as "I grew out of the grass," and "you live out here and you become very aware of change—I don't know if it's my age but somehow the twenties seem to have been a very exciting time to live through."

Index